The Ethnic Encounter
in the Secondary School

The Ethnic Encounter in the Secondary School

Ethnocultural Reproduction and Resistance; Theory and Case Studies

Brian M. Bullivant

 The Falmer Press

(A member of the Taylor & Francis Group)
London New York and Philadelphia

USA   The Falmer Press, Taylor & Francis Inc., 242 Cherry Street, Philadelphia, PA 19106-1906

UK   The Falmer Press, Falmer House, Barcombe, Lewes, East Sussex, BN8 5DL

© B. M. Bullivant 1987

First published 1987

Library of Congress Cataloging in Publication Data

Bullivant, Brian Milton.
   The ethnic encounter in the secondary school.

   Bibligraphy: p.
   Includes index.
     1. Minority youth—Education—Australia—Case studies.
2. High schools—Australia—Case studies.   3. Discrimination in education—Australia—Case studies.   4. Academic achievement—Case studies.   I. Title.
LC3739.B84   1987   371.97′0994   87-13912
ISBN 1-85000-255-X
ISBN 1-85000-256-8 (pbk.)

Jacket design by Caroline Archer

Typeset in 10/12 Bembo by
Imago Publishing Ltd, Thame, Oxon

Printed in Great Britain by Taylor & Francis (Printers) Ltd, Basingstoke

To Jenny and Sue-Anne

In the conditions of modern life the rule is absolute, the race which does not value trained intelligence is doomed.

(A.N. Whitehead)

Contents

Acknowledgments

The research on which this book is based was carried out on behalf of, and funded by, the Human Rights Commission, Canberra during 1985–6, and with the valued support and assistance of the Dean and members of the Faculty of Education, Monash University, Melbourne. Preliminary planning started in September 1984 and lasted until the main fieldwork phase in the first half of 1985. Throughout this period I was greatly assisted by advice from a number of people. In particular, I wish to thank Dr P.J. Creed, Chief Planning Officer of the Victorian Education Department, Senior Research Officers Mark Wilson and Andrew Sturman at the Australian Council for Educational Research, and my colleagues, Maurice Balson, Gerald Burke, Paul Gardner, Peter Musgrave and Glenn Rowley in the Faculty of Education.

The project could not have been undertaken without the cooperation of the principal and staff of the pilot school briefly studied in December 1984, and of each of the seven schools in the sample. They cannot be identified by name, as a condition of the research was that their confidentiality should be preserved. My most grateful thanks are nonetheless due to all of them.

Fieldwork started at the beginning of March 1985, lasted until mid-April, and was followed by the preliminary analysis of data, which was completed by the end of August in the same year. I am grateful for the research assistance of Adele M.E. Jones during that period.

Throughout the whole of the last phase from mid-1985, I assumed sole responsibility for further analysis of data and writing up the final report (Bullivant, 1986c). In this process I was greatly helped by the constructive criticism of the Commissioners on the project's Steering Committee and Dr A. Vervoorn of the Human Rights Commission. I am particularly grateful to Emeritus Professor W.F. Connell, Fellow of the Faculty of Education, who read and commented constructively on the full final draft.

This book is an edited and in parts virtually rewritten version of the report to the Human Rights Commission which was submitted in 1986. All conclusions expressed in the book reflect my own interpretation of the data, and should not be attributed to either the Commission or the Faculty of Education, Monash University.

Thinking about the kinds of issues this study investigated is frequently clouded by emotional and ideological assumptions that find no support in fact. Consequently, I have endeavoured to maintain a stance of hard-nosed scepticism that may be unfashionable, but errs on the side of caution and looks for evidence. This critical approach has been influenced by conversations and subsequent written communication with Dr Thomas Sowell, Senior Fellow at the Hoover Institution, Stanford, California. As he has commented about his own research on discrimination and the successes of several major ethnic groups in the United States: 'Above all, we need to look at *evidence* as to what has and has not worked. We cannot simply "feel" that this or that should be done ... we cannot educate on the basis of assumptions, but must test even our most cherished beliefs against the facts of the past and the present.'

What follows is the result of developing research findings into a book in a way that reflects such admirable sentiments. It owes a great deal to the practical assistance and patience of my wife Jenny and daughter Sue-Anne. During the last two years both have been models of tolerance in themselves.

Introduction

Many secondary schools in Western societies cater for students from contrasting ethnic backgrounds. They relate to each other in various degrees of encounter that range from the amicable to the hostile. Amicable relations cannot be taken for granted and how they can be fostered remains problematic. The hostility towards the attempts of students from minority ethnic groups to work towards rewarding futures can take many forms: prejudice, racism, sexism, covert discrimination, physical violence and overt discrimination from both staff and other students. Examples of each are present in the two case studies portrayed in this book.

The features may be manifestations of inequalities in the wider society that are brought into the school, and theoretical models of cultural reproduction proposed by Bourdieu, Apple, Bowles and Gintis among others, provide one kind of explanation for them. However, it is inherently limited as the models tend to focus more on socio-economic differences in society and play down or ignore ethnic dimensions. An alternative model used in this study combines the socio-economic status (SES) and ethnic perspectives in a theory of *ethnocultural hegemony* along lines of social closure suggested by Max Weber.

The theory hypothesizes that inequalities among ethnic groups are reproduced through systemic elements of the school. Prejudice, discrimination and sexism on the part of its dominant Anglo members — staff and students — towards those from different ethnic backgrounds can be interpreted as forms of 'social closure' aimed to reduce their competitive capacity for scarce qualifications. One period when we might expect this to be intensified is during the *occupational socialization* that takes place in the last two or three years of students' school careers, when they are preparing to move out into the workforce or tertiary education.

Occupational socialization is not confined to the school, and prejudice and discrimination may reflect influences from its wider social and ecological context. From this macro-structural point of view, parental direction and encouragement, role models in relatives and peers who may already have jobs, the availability of official careers advice from governmental and semi-governmental bodies, together with a whole host of other, often informal influences from the mass media and the general economic climate also exert influences.

All this may suggest that cultural reproduction controlled by the dominant Anglo majority is inevitable. However, the case studies provide clear evidence to add to the steadily accumulating findings in all English-speaking societies that many students from ethnic backgrounds are able to resist the forces of social and cultural reproduction that affect their futures. The conventional picture of the inevitably disadvantaged ethnic child in school that educationists have tended to take for granted — often for ideological reasons — is misleading and, for many ethnic students, plainly wrong.

We must now ask ourselves how it is that many students from ethnic backgrounds manage to 'beat the system' and 'make it' successfully into the wider world of employment and future opportunities. In other words, how do they resist and achieve the degree of *usurpation* of the routes to success that one usually only associates with the strategies of social closure used by members of the dominant group?

This book presents the results of research into these universal issues. It portrays two case study high schools in Melbourne, Australia in which students at Years 11 and 12 are endeavouring to plan their career scenarios about future employment opportunities and undertake the kinds of academic preparation necessary to attain them. 'Inner City High School' is a detailed portrayal of an actual but almost stereotypical school in a deprived urban ecological context.

According to the conventional wisdom we might expect that systemic factors within the school and from the wider community would adversely affect students' occupational socialization. In particular, those from ethnic and lower socio-economic (SES) backgrounds might be discriminated against in comparison with their Anglo-Australian peers. But when all the evidence is examined this is not the case. Ethnic students are able to resist Anglo ethnocultural hegemony. It is the Anglo students who are more disadvantaged — an unexpected finding that poses a challenge to conventional wisdom.

Findings from the second case study strengthen the challenge. Suburbia High School is a constructed-type, composite case study based on the many similarities among six schools set in various suburban districts of Melbourne. To select each of these a conceptual model of the *ethclass* was used based on the seminal work of Milton Gordon (1964), which enabled us to highlight the interrelationships between SES and ethnicity. In each school factors summarized in the composite case study suggest that many students from ethnic backgrounds are successfully resisting Anglo-centric social and cultural reproduction — another nail in the coffin of conventional wisdom.

These findings were not only based on researchers' 'external' observations but were borne out by the opinions of students themselves. These were obtained verbatim during intensive group interviewing in each of the schools, and many of the comments are reproduced in full throughout this book. They force us to re-evaluate our understanding of the way prejudice and discrimination operate in ethnoculturally pluralist Western societies, and help to destroy much of the mystification and myths that surround this area.

What is the real picture? If our findings are accurate — and there is no reason to suggest otherwise — we need to alter radically our understanding of ethnic students' situations. There is no doubt that some are disadvantaged, but it is equally true that many more than we imagine are successful, despite the socio-economic and ethnocultural strategies of social closure used by Anglos to contain their aspirations.

In the last chapter of the book we suggest that the ways in which ethnic students are getting ahead constitute a form of serial usurpation which has its intrinsic strengths, but also exploits the weaknesses of many Anglo students. The latter can be summed up by the concept of a 'self-deprivation syndrome', which is a blend of inhibiting social, cultural and psychological factors. They are in marked contrast to the 'self-motivation syndrome' that characterizes ethnic students. We suggest that the self-deprivation syndrome may also be one key to understanding the causes of prejudice on the part of Anglos against students from ethnic backgrounds. This is something that is not confined to Australian conditions, but has wider applicability. This book thus transcends parochial concerns and hopefully will contribute towards a better understanding of ethnic encounters in pluralist Western societies.

1   The School Arena for Ethnic Encounters

School provides one arena where ethnic encounters take place. They can occur in several ways: between students of different sexes from the same ethnic group; between students of both sexes from different ethnic groups; and between students and staff from different ethnic groups and even the same ethnic group. There is virtually an infinite variety of such encounters as they ebb and flow in daily and weekly rhythms, are responsive to the many social, political and economic forces and shifting allegiances in the wider community, are compounded by social class factors, and assume greater or lesser importance according to the age and grade levels of the students concerned.

One of the important periods during a student's school career when we might expect ethnic encounters, prejudice and discrimination to be tense is the last two years when he or she is actively making career plans and getting ready to move out into the workforce or further education. This is the period of occupational socialization. Although this has its foundation in previous years, when general socialization is occurring, it reaches a climax at the senior level.

Theoretically this could be when competitive tensions between students are most severe. Pressures intensify from all sides: staff, parents, friends in the workforce, mass media advertizing and injunctions to get out into a job and 'make something of oneself', university and college entrance requirements or quotas, and the ever present threat of the tests and examinations that under a meritocratic system ultimately determine how successful students will be.

Again, it is during this critical period of schooling that we might expect to find some students being favoured over others, if the theories of social and cultural reproduction suggested by Bourdieu, Apple and others are valid. Whether this does occur or whether forms of student resistance overcome systemic forces of social reproduction should remain open questions until the evidence is examined. It is also likely that interethnic prejudice will be involved in these forces. To take this into account later a theory of ethnocultural hegemony is developed based on the ideas of social closure from the work of Max Weber.

This book uses these kinds of theoretical ideas to analyze and understand the complexity of the ethnic encounters in two case study schools. They happen to be in Melbourne, Australia, but many of their features will find echoes in other pluralist Western societies. Ethnic encounters are universal and recognize no geographical boundaries.

The Cultural Context

A society's culture provides the overarching matrix of ideas and meanings which program all social processes. Ethnic encounters and the web of relationships and pressures in which they occur are no exception, and to understand their full significance some consideration of the concept of culture is needed. Definitions of this concept abound and range from the early but outmoded version of Tylor (1871) to the one proposed here based on and synthesizing the views of a number of cultural anthropologists (e.g., Kroeber and Kluckhohn, 1952; Dobbert, 1976; Goodenough, 1964; Geertz, 1973; Keesing, 1976). In our view, culture is a generalized complex of interdependent, valued traditional and current public knowledge and conceptions, embodied in behaviours and artifacts, and transmitted to present and new members through systems of signs and symbols, which a society has evolved historically and progressively modifies and augments to give meaning to and cope with its definitions of present and future existential problems.

The usefulness of such a definition lies primarily in its emphasis on culture in instrumental terms as a form of 'blueprint' or program for a society's survival in relation to the environments in which it is located (see fuller discussion in Bullivant, 1981a, 1984). Each member of society must also be equipped with a share of its common stock of knowledge and conceptions as a form of personal survival device to operate effectively within the society and to contribute to its collective survival. One of the key processes which ensures that this occurs is termed enculturation — cultural transmission — which is itself arranged in ways laid down in the cultural program.

The cultural stock also contains elements that have an intrinsic expressive rather than instrumental importance. That is, they encapsulate important values, and give quality to human existence through such activities as recreation, religion, arts, crafts and similar aesthetic pursuits. Expressive aspects of culture 'say something about' human existence; instrumental aspects 'do something towards' human existence.

This distinction assumes considerable importance in relation to the kind of schooling and curriculum selected for children from ethnocultural backgrounds. They have to be given their share of the common culture of the plural society in which they live, but also need access to elements of their ethnic cultures. Reconciling these twin needs without being discriminatory is difficult. Although this study focuses primarily on the phase of occupational socialization, it should be kept in mind that it is as affected by the dictates of the cultural blueprint as the all-encompassing enculturation process itself.

Occupational Socialization

Within that process the more specific phase of socialization occurs, one that has long been of interest to sociologists of education (e.g., Durkheim, 1956; Waller, 1932) and even social anthropologists. Among the last group, Mayer (1970:xiii) defined socialization 'as the inculcation of the skills and attitudes necessary for playing given social roles.' A related concept is 'anticipatory socialization' (Merton and Kitt, 1950). This is 'the learning of the rights, obligations, expectations, and outlook of a social role preparatory to assuming it. As a person learns the proper beliefs, values, and norms of a status or group to which he aspires, he is learning how to act in his new role' (Theodorson and Theodorson, 1970:397).

When it is used to focus on the period of adolescence within the total birth-to-death time span of enculturation, the concept of anticipatory socialization has obvious relevance for understanding how young people learn their statuses and roles in the workforce. However, because it usually refers to a wider frame of reference and can also be used to describe how children learn to become members of society generally, we have chosen to adopt the term 'occupational socialization' for our purposes. It is taken to be a specific process during middle and late adolescence when young persons construct possible *occupational scenarios* about their futures in the workforce, in the sense of putting together a 'synopsis of a projected course of action or events' (*Webster's New Collegiate Dictionary*, p. 1032). To do this, they draw upon any experiences of work that they may have already had, together with perceptions of their own social competence, and incorporate into the scenarios inputs from external systems and structures, such as school, home and family, friendship networks and institutions in the community.

Perspectives on Occupational Socialization

From the structural-functional or systemic point of view, the study of socialization commonly, but not exclusively, focuses on the institutions, agencies and activities external to the individual that transform him or her into an adult member of the society, able to carry out the role behaviours incumbent in such a status. The agency of the school and its curriculum looms large as one of the key institutions involved in this task. These are taken for granted as 'givens', somehow external to and influencing or constraining students' development.

The young person is seen as a more-or-less passive learner of already decided beliefs, values, norms, skills and so on that exist in society's institutions, or is being inculcated with them. In either case, the individual does not have much say in his/her occupational socialization. Such a view 'tends to be one of a passive actor being socialized into a consensual institutional framework rather than one which allows the actor to participate in his own conceptual construction of the world and his own fate in the project' (Sharp and Green, 1975:5).

Another perspective is based on taking a symbolic interactionist and phenomenological view of social interaction and behaviour. In this approach, as typified by the work of Berger and Luckmann (1971), Mead (1938, 1964), Blumer (1971) and Schutz (1964), individuals construct their social realities and views of the world, using information feedback from the environments and numerous sociocultural contexts and processes with which they interact. Berger and Luckmann (1971:150–8) suggest that this process takes place in two stages, primary socialization and secondary socialization, of which the latter is most relevant here.

Secondary socialization is defined (p.158) as 'the acquisition of role-specific knowledge, the roles being directly or indirectly rooted in the division of labour.' It is in this secondary stage that the developing child begins to construct plans about its future status and role in the work-force, without having to accept one view of objective reality imposed by significant others, as occurs in the more passive stage of primary socialization.

The process sees the child interpreting the systemic and structural influences from its various sociocultural contexts, and developing a personal plan or 'tacit theory' of the world (Kay, 1970). One of the important contexts within which this process occurs is provided by the school and its classrooms. Other contexts are the home and kin group, the community and local neighbourhood, and the peer group. The result of the process is a synthesis which combines systemic and structural influences with the child's own interpretations. As Edgar (1974:12) states, 'both interpretive feedback from significant others and the child's own self-view intervene and modify the effects of structural factors ... and such basic personal resources as sex, intelligence and early childhood achievements.' It is this dual characteristic that is fundamental to our view of occupational socialization.

Features of the Process of Constructing Occupational Scenarios

(i) *Difficulties in the Process*

The process is not achieved quickly or easily. Several theorists have commented on both its complexity and even apparent lack of rationality. As Poole (1983:25) has stated 'the processes by which young people, especially young women and girls, make their first job choice and indeed obtain their first job is by no means clear.... Some of the evidence suggests that individuals themselves are the major source of decision-making ... but the process is complex and can even be random or accidental.'

Ford and Box (1967) and Psathas (1962) among others have also queried the assumption that job choice is a rational process. Psathas suggested that potential performers of future roles have incomplete knowledge about both the number and types of occupations available and about the appropriate means of getting into the workforce. Roberts (1968) has commented that school leavers' limited knowledge about future occupations might help to explain why young people's ambitions adapt so readily to the occupations that they actually happen to enter. This has an important bearing on the common distinction that is made between occupational aspirations and occupational expectations discussed below.

Timing decisions about future occupations is also an important consideration for young people. Findings from the pilot study school described in Chapter 4 indicated that students were not in a position nor mature enough to make firm decisions about their occupational scenarios at Year 10, but were more able to do so at Year 11. By Year 12 more decisions were able to be made, but the crucial year appeared to be Year 11, and the two senior years were targeted for our research.

(ii) *Occupational Aspirations versus Expectations*

A basic distinction is commonly made between children's career aspirations and their career expectations. As Kuvlesky and Bealer (1966:274) pointed out these are two completely different and separate aspects of the occupational choice process. To these theorists aspirations are 'essentially motivational', that is, referring 'to a person's orientation towards a goal area' (Timperley, 1974:67). Expectations, on the other hand, refer to 'the individual's estimation of his probable attainment in reference to a particular goal area' (Kuvlesky and Bealer, 1966:274).

A broadly similar dichotomy was suggested by Han (1969). He argued that there is a conceptual distinction between career wishes and career expectations. The former respond to a person's awareness of the values that society places on certain occupations. The latter are more realistic appraisals of what is achievable given the structural and social restrictions placed on attaining them. An extension of this line of argument is Edgar's (1974, 1975) use of the concept of the 'social competence' possessed by adolescents. This consists of the skills and competencies necessary for effective action in social situations, together with the knowledge or sense of one's own ability or power, which enables an individual to see him or her self as being competent to exercise the skills and knowledge and thus take advantage of future opportunities.

(iii)   Influences of Sex and Gender

An individual's sex has an important bearing on occupational choices, and numerous studies have commented on this aspect and built it into research designs. A major American study by Harway and Astin (1977) showed how sex discrimination operates in careers counselling. As Edgar (1974:28) has pointed out:

> Sex is by definition a resource which limits both early socialization experience and potential life situations.... Nothing can be done about one's sex, but how one is expected to behave as a result and the status accorded to the same actions when carried out by male or female are subject to challenge and reinterpretation.

There seems little doubt that the prevailing female gender role may not be entirely innate but is institutionalized through schooling and the curriculum. This is despite the prevailing ideologies of equality of opportunity for girls pervading much educational thinking in Western societies. As Wolpe (1974:140) has commented, by the time girls get to the stage of qualifying for examinations,

> Their aspirations about their future employment and the realization of these aspirations for the vast majority of girls does not go beyond the scope of what are regarded as 'suitable' feminine jobs. And to this extent the curricula that girls pursue is [sic] appropriate both to their occupational roles in the labour market as well as their roles as wives and mothers.

A variation on this theme is caused by students' ethnic backgrounds. Anderson and Vervoorn (1983:Ch.7) and Sturman (1985) have cited numerous Australian research studies that show how the occupational aspirations and expectations of migrant girls differ from those of boys from similar ethnic backgrounds. Saha (1981:471) has commented on his own research findings:

> As might be expected, males appear to have higher career ambitions than females. Being male exercises particularly strong effects on career orientations (both preferred and expected orientations) for the

European and Mediterranean leavers. On the other hand, the consistent negative effects between SEX and STUDY suggests that females are more likely to have further study plans than males. This pattern is particularly true for the Australian and U.K. leavers.

(iv) 'Moral Positioning'

A final distinction can be made between two basic orientations that young people take towards future occupations. Research by Dickinson and Erben (1984) into the occupational socialization of hairdressers, secretaries and caterers in London training colleges providing for these trades showed that young people readily adopt what the authors term 'moral positioning'. This 'refers to a stance that minimizes the economic/instrumental aspects of an occupation, instead emphasizing moral cues and social skills.' The authors argued that 'the adoption of such a stance is a distortion of the real situation, where economic and instrumental considerations are of great importance' (1984:49). A similar distinction is made in the case studies described below.

Factors Affecting Occupational Socialization

There are numerous factors that affect students' occupational socialization. We can make a distinction between those that are provided by the school system, i.e., systemic factors, and those that are available in the community outside the school, i.e., external factors. Both these interact in complex ways, and in turn play a major part in determining patterns of ethnic encounters in school.

This institution's key role in the process is underscored by Timperley's (1974:91) comment that 'the importance of the education process as a socialization agent cannot be over-emphasized.' Timperley also referred to research by Liversedge (1962:33) in a comparative study of the aspirations of schoolchildren in grammar and secondary schools in Britain. This research concluded: 'Whilst previous experience may be of great importance in shaping the school–child's expectations of the future, the most potent force operating is undoubtedly the experience through which the child passes during his involvement in that part of the educational system to which he has been assigned' (Timperley, 1974:91).

Systemic Factors

(i) *The Curriculum.* Central to understanding the operation of schooling and cultural reproduction is the curriculum. In conventional thinking this is often equated with the list of subjects available for students, and their variety has an obvious bearing on their ability to construct future career or further education scenarios. However, the curriculum is somewhat broader than a list of subjects, and a more comprehensive model will provide the basis for most of our subsequent analysis.

The curriculum can be thought of as the set of knowledge, ideas and experiences resulting from ideologically influenced and value-laden processes of selection from a social group's public stock of current knowledge, ideas and experiences (i.e., its culture), their organization into sub-sets (syllabuses and units), transmission to clients (students, pupils) in teaching-learning interface settings, and periodic evaluation, which provides feedback into previous processes. A schematic diagram of the curriculum and its processes is shown in Figure 1.

Figure 1. A Model of the Curriculum

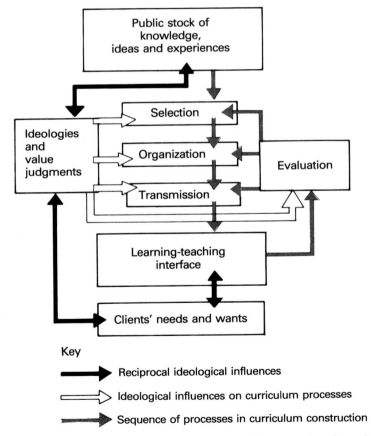

The inclusion of experiences draws attention to the fact that the curriculum contains more than knowledge and ideas. Equally, it needs to be stressed that all the processes are not necessarily confined to what takes place within the school campus. Important learning occurs on school excursions and visits. These are not extra-curricular activities as is often assumed. Rather they are extra-campus and have an important contribution to make to the total learning experiences open to children. For example, one of those available for senior students is work experience programs of various sorts, that operate within the community where the school is located. Such programs have to be taken into account in the curriculum model.

(ii) Related Features. Three related features of the model need to be stressed. Firstly, the curriculum should partly be, but quite often is not, a response to clients, i.e., students' and parents', wants. More often it reflects teachers' and other educationists' idiosyncratic interpretations of these needs and wants, and can therefore be subject to their unconscious and even deliberate bias. This can occur especially if some teachers and educationists place some of their clients into a category which is considered to be undeserving of a full share of the knowledge, ideas and experiences that constitute the curriculum.

Secondly, all four processes of the curriculum — selection, organization, transmission and evaluation — are subject to the influences of value judgments and ideologies that are not only held by teachers and educationists themselves within a school, but also emanate from the wider social forces and systems external to the school (see Bullivant, 1981a, 1981b; Lawton, 1975). Examples of the latter are subject associations and official government organizations such as the Australian Commonwealth Schools Commission, Britain's former Schools Council and the Department of Health, Education and Welfare in the United States.

We need not point out the implications of this feature of the curriculum for human rights and ethnic encounters. Value judgments and ideologies based on racist and ethnocentric assumptions, which devalue the rights of children from ethnocultural minorities, could lead to the selection, organization, transmission and evaluation processes being obviously biased against them. This can result in teachers favouring the life chances of children that come from socio-economic or ethnocultural backgrounds that are similar to their own.

Thirdly, the curriculum must preserve the balance between the instrumental knowledge and conceptions that are selected and the expressive knowledge and conceptions. This distinction follows from the way we discussed the concept of culture above. However, the problem of preserving balance between the two is exacerbated by several features of modern Western societies: rapidly and exponentially increasing stocks of knowledge due to the knowledge explosion, the cybernetic or computer revolution, obsolescence of knowledge as industries and social conditions change, recurrent trendiness and faddism — a feature of much expressive culture —

inevitable changes in environmental challenges to which the survival blueprint of culture must respond, and in turn young people must be equipped to master.

This third feature also provides opportunities for educators to exercise bias towards some children and favour others. For example, a curriculum that is unduly weighted with selection of the expressive aspects from the cultural stock, and stresses life styles may not provide young people with sufficient instrumental survival knowledge to compete for life chances when they leave school.

Instrumental knowledge itself is composed of many parts, some with less value for survival than others. Equipping children with a surfeit, say, of ethnic community languages, history and music in an attempt to improve their cultural awareness, may be of far less survival value in the final analysis than mathematics, skills in using computers, and accountancy. This is not to say that ethnic community languages and heritages have no intrinsic value, however, they may have less pragmatic value for a person's survival in a society dominated by English.

Fourthly, the evaluation and assessment that are part of the curriculum also provide ways of controlling the futures of students. Many professional careers are gained by passing 'hurdles' in competition for places at universities or colleges of further education, such as the Higher School Certificate (HSC) in Australia, the A-level and O-level examinations in Britain, or their equivalents in other countries. School staff are thus in a position to monitor how fast or easily students are allowed to climb the 'ladder' to university admission and prestigious careers. A corollary concerns the subjects which have a recognized status and survival value for successfully negotiating this ladder. Some are prerequisites for examinations and may have to be provided in the curriculum, despite the inherent attractiveness of subjects with less survival value.

For example, in a school catering for children from ethnocultural backgrounds an ethnic language, even if on the list of examinable subjects, may have high expressive value but may not be useful for obtaining a job or gaining university selection. Only high achievement in high-status subjects, such as sciences, mathematics, biology, accountancy, economics will achieve such goals. Channelling children from these into other, lower-status subjects may do them a disservice in the survival race. In a very practical way children's career choices and life chances thus can be assisted or impeded both by what has been made available to them in the curriculum, and by how they are allowed to negotiate the ladder towards high academic results.

(iii)   Careers Guidance versus Careers Education.   Part of the process of occupational socialization is formalized in the curriculum by various forms of careers advice. In a study of church schools in Britain, Law and Watts (1977:1) focused on 'careers education', which they pointed out 'is a relatively new addition to educational jargon ... sometimes used as a new

synonym for "careers work" and "careers guidance" — terms which have been in use for some time, even though the activities they describe have always tended to be rather peripheral concerns in most schools.'

Careers education is more comprehensive than merely providing students with 'diagnostic advisory services' that will enable them to make better decisions about their futures, in terms of further education or employment. 'Instead it sees the school's central task as being that of helping students to develop the skills, and to acquire the concepts and information that will help them to make such decisions for themselves' (*ibid.*).

This kind of approach enables students to construct scenarios about their futures in a way that is much more educational than merely diagnostic or advisory, as it extends into the curriculum of the school. Moreover, it is a process that moves beyond the careers interview room, in which information and advice constitute the main source, into every classroom. Providing advice to students about their futures — probably the most basic form of 'careers work' — is supplemented by counselling and broad education. In the former, 'the interviewer [focuses] his skill not on helping the student to *make wise decisions* (with the assumption that he knows what these should be), but on helping him to *make decisions wisely* (Katz, 1969)' (Law and Watts, 1977:1).

Factors in the External Context of Occupational Socialization

Children do not exist in a vacuum, and the influences on them from outside the school play a major part in helping or hampering them in the task of constructing future occupational scenarios. In effect, school and students are influenced by a context, which embodies the many factors in their environment. Indeed there may be grounds for thinking that external influences on students' academic achievement and, by extension, career scenarios, may be greater than the internal influences of the school.

An analysis by Knight (1974) proposed that the differences in social, racial, ethnic and class backgrounds that students bring to school are maintained or magnified as a result of their interaction with its organizational structures. The future life chances of the children are greatly affected as a result. Many are 'locked out' of successful participation in academic work and extra-curricular activities, and this produces an ascribed status which 'directs the student to a severely restricted choice of future work options.'

(i) External Factors. The kinds of external factors mentioned by research workers are numerous. Typical of early studies reported in the 1960s is the comment of Keil, Riddell and Green (1966:123):

... evidence from a wide variety of research suggested that family, neighbourhood, peer groups, education received, influences from the mass media, the extent of formal vocational guidance all need to be considered, and that experience from these sources, as well as the nature of the work undertaken, are relevant to the development of any particular reaction towards working life.

More generally, Sofer (1970) indicated that making decisions about occupations will be affected by such factors as the amount of information available through the media and official sources, the opinions and influences of key persons to whom the individual is exposed, and the broad employment prospects and state of the labour market. A time element is involved with this last aspect. Students' occupational aspirations and expectations will be different at a time of full employment from what they would be when unemployment and economic instability are major characteristics of the labour market.

(ii)   Influences from the Home and Peer Group. The influence of the home context is especially important. As Miller and Form (1951) pointed out, planning for occupational futures involves a 'preparatory work period' which 'contains two essential elements: socialization within the home, and socialization within the school.' Within the home context attitudes towards work are formed, aspirations developed and patterns of adjustment to realities of the work situation anticipated. Members of the family also provide primary role models who bring information about the world of work. In White's (1977:1) opinion: 'Parents are usually the most potent socializing force working on the individual in the early stages of childhood. ... Powerful influences are brought to bear on the learning child by teachers, adult friends and neighbours, and by peers and others.' Musgrave (1967) has suggested that 'pre-work socialization' works in a way that narrows the range of possible roles available for the developing individual, through the experiences he or she has with three key agents of socialization. These are the family, the school and the peer group.

(iii)   Social Class. Closely associated with it are the influences of social status and class. As Timperley (1974:89) has pointed out: 'There is a good deal of evidence available to show that the influence of the family, and related social class, can be far reaching in its effect on the operation of the occupational choice process.' Many early studies have demonstrated the relationship between the occupation of the father and the job choice of the son (e.g., Rosenberg, 1957; Kelsall, 1954; Bendix, Lipset and Malm, 1954). Empirical evidence has demonstrated the link between socio-economic status and level of occupational aspiration (e.g., Sewell, Haller and Strauss, 1957; Liversedge, 1962).

The combination of home and socio-economic background influences occupational choice in various ways. For example, secondary modern school leavers during the 1950s and 1960s in Britain placed most importance on parental influence in their career choice (Chown, 1958; Jahoda, 1952). The

Crowther Report in Britain (Central Advisory Council for Education, 1959) highlighted the way in which the economic and cultural factors associated with working-class backgrounds exerted pressure on young persons to leave school.

In the light of findings from our case studies, an observation by Wilson and Wyn (1983) is of considerable importance. They suggested that growing up in a lower-working-class area provides students with views of themselves that are not very different from each other, despite the range of ethnic backgrounds that may be present in the area. In other words class background and relationships may be more important than ethnic background when it comes to making a living.

Most of the above research has used father's occupation and educational qualifications as major variables. According to some researchers it is also important to take into consideration parental occupational status, instead of the more usual paternal occupational status, in conjunction with 'occupational situs'. The latter owes its origin to the work of such theorists as Morris and Murphy (1961), Samuel and Lewin-Epstein (1979). It consists of information concerning where a job is performed and what it consists of in operational terms.

There has been comparatively less research into the effects of the mother's occupation and educational qualifications on the job choices of young persons, especially of daughters. However, feminist ideological developments in the 1970s and 1980s have drawn attention to maternal influences. For example, research by Poole and associates (Poole, 1984:26) into the life possibilities of adolescents in Sydney showed that in making decisions about their lives 'within the family, adolescents valued the opinions of their mother and father above those of themselves and other family members or friends. Females considered their mothers' opinions to be more important. Boys were more influenced by the father.'

Price and Pyne (1976) suggested that in ethnic families the mother's influence on children is more important than the father's, because she plays the major part in determining their linguistic and cultural development. When such aspects are being researched, the mother's birthplace should be taken into account. In the case of fathers from migrant backgrounds, it also seems desirable to take into account that their socio-economic status in their countries of origin might be a better predictor of their children's academic achievements and occupational aspirations.

(iv) Ethnicity. A final major external factor in pluralist societies is the ethnicity of the pupils and their parents. For our purposes, ethnicity is taken to be a double-sided variable. It can be self-ascribed, as when members from an ethnic background choose to identify with it, whether or not they possess any ethnocultural diacritica (distinguishing characteristics) that enable ethnic affiliation to be established by an external observer. Ethnicity can be other-ascribed, as when an external observer attributes the social and

ethnocultural characteristics he sees in persons to the fact — correct or not — that they belong to an ethnic group.

Some consideration needs to be given to the kinds of ethnocultural diacritica that people adhere to. It is commonly but erroneously held that ethnicity is solely related to cultural differences, but as the following definition by Schermerhorn (1970:12) makes clear it is a far more complex phenomenon. An ethnic group is a

> ... collectivity within a larger society having real or putative common ancestry, memories of a shared historical past, and a cultural focus on one or more symbolic elements defined as the epitome of their peoplehood. Examples of such symbolic elements are: kinship patterns, physical contiguity (as in localism or sectionalism), religious affiliation, language or other dialectical forms, tribal affiliation, nationality, phenotypical features, or any combination of these. A necessary accompaniment is some consciousness of kind among members of the group.

The factor of common ancestry and consciousness of kind is recognized by most scholars as an important feature of an ethnic group, and enables it to be distinguished from more global, permanent associations such as major religious faiths. An influential example of this view is that of Shibutani and Kwan (1965:47). Members of an ethnic group 'conceive themselves as being alike, by virtue of their common ancestry, real or fictitious, and ... are so regarded by others.' 'Phenotypical features' (race) are qualitatively different from other diacritica as they are immutable and cannot be altered at will. They are possibly the most powerful boundary markers used for both the inclusion and exclusion of members of ethnic groups and, as comments from students given below indicate, they generate most intense feelings of prejudice.

A further feature is the variation that can exist in the aggregates of people that claim ethnic background. Their size can vary from that of a more or less homogeneous group to much more scattered entities and even individuals, termed 'ethnic categories' by the theorist M.G. Smith (1982:2–6). These are dispersed ethnics, and although they may not be readily distinguishable by an outsider they nevertheless retain feelings of self-ascribed ethnicity.

This makes it difficult to identify children from ethnic backgrounds for research purposes. Lacking any certain way for children to state their ethnic self-identification, Victorian state schools (like many other education authorities) have adopted a criterion of ethnicity which relies on the birthplace of one or both parents as its main distinguishing feature. Thus, for purposes of the Ethnic Education Survey or census, which the Victorian Education Department requires every year, schools classify as an 'ethnic' any child born overseas in a non-English-speaking country, or, if born in Australia, has one or both parents who were born in a non-English-speaking country. Using these criteria of ethnicity, details of the languages commonly spoken in the home are also collected.

The Relationship between Ethnic Background and Education

In the past three decades studies into the relationships between the ethnicity or migrancy of children and their academic performance or occupational aspirations in schools have proliferated in Britain, the United States, Canada and Australia. The growing wealth of data in these countries has revealed the seeming paradox that some young people from ethnic backgrounds aspire to higher educational and career scenarios than indigenous Anglos. Many achieve them in the face of all odds, such as lack of fluency with English, lower socio-economic status, prejudice and discrimination.

For example, in Australia individual studies such as those by Taft (1975), Connell *et al.* (1975), Rosier (1978) and Martin and Meade (1979) showed that large numbers of children from non-English-speaking groups maintained high aspirations and stayed on in senior forms at school although they did not have matching academic ability in terms measured by the school. Sturman (1985:69) has summarized Taft's (1975) findings that the vocational aspirations of some immigrants are higher than those of Anglo-Australians. Male immigrants from non-English-speaking backgrounds tended to aspire to higher levels than did Australian males. Females of these groups tended to have similar levels of aspirations. Southern European immigrants of both sexes seemed to have the highest aspirations of those from non-English-speaking backgrounds and higher than other groups from English-speaking backgrounds and Australians. These findings have been confirmed by other research studies (e.g., Poole, 1981; Meade, 1983).

A study by Marjoribanks (1980) adopted the concept of ethclass, in a way analogous to the one we propose to use, and his findings also showed the same pattern of differential occupational aspirations. Children from Greek and Italian families and their parents had the highest aspirations. These were followed by the lower aspirations of Anglo-Australian, middle socio-economic status (SES) families. Lower still were the aspirations of Anglo-Australian lower-SES families, with the aspirations of migrants from Britain below these again.

Smolicz and Wiseman (1971:8–9) referred to the phenomenon of high aspirations as 'migrant drive'. They suggested that it is a 'type of social mobility orientation in newly arrived families without property and influence in the country of settlement but with a great desire to make good for these deficiencies in the second generation through their children's excellence in academic and professional pursuits.' This phenomenon is not universal, however, and what the concept of migrant drive does not explain is why some ethnic groups, e.g., Maltese, Turks, and Latin Americans in Australia, do not appear to display the same drive.

It is not necessarily confined to newly arrived migrants. The persistence of 'migrant drive' in well-established and settled members of larger ethnic groups, such as Jews and Chinese in Australia, and Jews, Japanese and Chinese in the United States, suggests that it may be partly an ethnocultural characteristic. This produces a drive or push towards high achievement, but only after economic security has been achieved. As Sowell (1986:61) has pointed out in the American context: 'Education was one of the things the next generation acquired with its affluence; [it was] not the cause of it.'

It should also be borne in mind that other factors besides culture-specific drive and values placed on education and work may have a bearing on the differential aspirations of migrant groups. The economic climate of the times, governmental ideologies and policies concerning the degree and kinds of education to be given to ethnics, their socio-economic status, the history of ethnic family circumstances and immigration experiences, together with the general levels of inhibiting prejudice and discrimination from Anglos and other dominant ethnic groups are all important.

The Saliency of the Ethclass

From the above list one factor, socio-economic status, has been repeatedly stressed. In Sturman's (1985:81) opinion: '... the differences found between ethnic groups and Australians in connection with the relationship between socioeconomic status and educational attitudes may be real and of significant interest.' Other studies have mentioned the close correlation between social class and ethnicity. This suggests the importance of stressing these variables in combination rather than separately.

A concept which enables this is ethclass, originally introduced into sociological literature by Milton Gordon (1964:51) to refer to the 'subsociety created by the intersection of the vertical stratifications of ethnicity with the horizontal stratifications of social class.' Gordon also suggested that some consideration of a person's residence (urban or rural) and region of country lived in should be added to the ethclass as important causes that create the sub-societies in which people live. The concept of the ethclass is not only useful in drawing attention to these connections but also in our study provided a basis for obtaining a sample of schools and students to research.

Vernacular versus Observer Models of Occupational Socialization

Any attempt to present a comprehensive picture of occupational socialization and related prejudice and discrimination faces the classic anthropological problem of needing to describe what goes on in a research setting from two viewpoints: those of the external observer on the one hand, and the participant members on the other. In considering this problem, Mayer (1970: xvi–xvii) has drawn attention to 'two main targets of study in the field of socialization. One is largely oriented to vernacular models, the other largely to observer models.'

By 'socialization practices' are meant 'vernacular activities for which socialization (inculcation of role-playing skills or attitudes) is explicitly claimed by the actors as a deliberate aim.' Mayer suggests that 'systematic socializing practices — e.g. varieties of occupational training' are likely to be well developed in Western complex societies and are relatively easy to study through the observer having access to schools. The structure and organization of the curriculum and careers advice constitute part of such 'systematic socialization practices' and the teachers' descriptions of them can be thought of as a vernacular model accessible to description and analysis by the research worker.

The model which external persons use to describe the school is different from those used by its personnel. Mayer (1970:xviii) has drawn attention to this dimension:

> By 'processes' [of socialization] I mean all those social experiences that, one supposes, 'actually' advance people in their role-playing skills or attitudes, and the mechanisms whereby these socializing effects are 'actually' brought about. This, then, is an observer's model of 'what actually happens' in regard to socialization in the given field. It may coincide to a greater or lesser extent with actors' models — that is with people's vernacular accounts of their own vernacular socializing practices — but is not likely to coincide exactly. Some of the practices may seem to the observer to have no 'actual' effect, or to have effects different from those claimed.

In our analysis of occupational socialization, prejudice and discrimination in the two case study schools, a similar distinction will be drawn. We aim to describe vernacular socialization practices as claimed by actors in the schools (teachers, principal), and observers' views of the actual socialization processes as described by students, parents and others associated with the schools in external capacities.

A Block Recursive Focusing Model of Occupational Socialization

To assist analysis the many variables discussed above can be brought together in a block recursive focusing model along lines suggested by Blalock (1971). Its function is to show, or focus on, major variables involved in occupational socialization in schematic form, rather than for purposes of statistical analysis. Figure 2 illustrates the variables and their interrelationships.

Figure 2. A Block Recursive Focusing Model

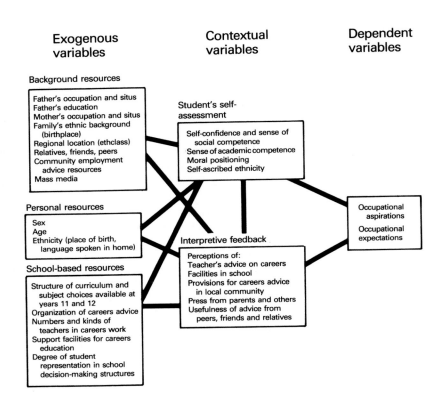

(i) *Exogenous Variables.* Three groups of variables constitute the uncaused, exogenous or independent category. The first group comprises a student's background resources. It is made up by family socio–economic status as measured by father's occupation, situs, and education, and by mother's occupation and situs, together with father's and mother's ethnicity as measured by place of birth. Also within this group are the family's regional location, relatives, friends and peers outside school, and community employment or advisory bodies, and mass media influences.

The second group of exogenous variables comprises a student's personal resources. These are sex, age, and ethnicity as measured by student's place of birth and parents' place of birth and language other than English spoken in the home.

The third group of exogenous variables comprises the 'givens' of school-based resources. These are the structure of and subjects available in the curriculum at Years 11 and 12, the teachers' assessments of students' performance and 'promotability', the provision of careers and related advice, number and experience of teachers engaged in careers 'work', and other organizational 'support' facilities, such as libraries, study rooms for the appropriate levels, and avenues for student representation in school policy.

(ii) Contextual or Intervening Variables. The exogenous variables are conceptualized as operating on dependent or caused variables through two groups of contextual or intervening variables. The first group comprises a student's self-assessment. This includes self-confidence, sense of academic competence, sense of social competence, moral positioning and self-ascribed ethnicity. The second group comprises a student's interpretive feedback. It consists of perceptions of teachers' assessment, advice on careers, facilities within the school, provisions within the wider community, press from parents, the availability and usefulness of advice from friends, peers and relatives.

(iii) Dependent Variables. Two variables or outcomes constitute this group for the purposes of the study. They are occupational aspirations and occupational expectations. Both are assumed to be causally influenced by the blocks of contextual and exogenous variables preceding them. The two blocks of contextual variables are considered not to be causally related, but are mutually reinforcing. They in turn are causally related to the three blocks of exogenous variables preceding them.

Prejudice and discrimination are assumed to influence all points of the occupational socialization process. However, we are particularly interested in the way they affect students in school as a result of the operation of social and cultural reproduction. This is taken up in the next chapter.

2 Social Reproduction and Resistance in Ethnic Encounters

The process of occupational socialization would be complex enough in the best of all possible societies. In the case of many pluralist societies, however, features arising from their multifaceted socio-economic and ethnocultural composition aggravate the complexity. Access to high-status jobs or tertiary education and their attendant political power, economic resources, and social rewards is unevenly distributed among members of the status–classes that comprise the society, among members of its constituent ethnic groups and also among their class-stratified segments, which often compete for resources on factional lines. Gender differences and the contrasts among ethnic groups in the ways these are regarded add further complications to the other pluralist features.

Such an inegalitarian situation provides an overarching context within which young people must construct future occupational scenarios and cope with prejudice. It is also a situation historically which reformers in the education systems of all English-speaking societies have tried to alleviate. They have attempted to formulate explanations of the causes of deprivation and thus suggest means to alleviate them, frequently using uncritical and ideologically motivated assumptions that have no basis in facts.

Three theories in particular are currently in vogue. *Social and cultural reproduction theory* is a major and persuasive attempt to show how socio-economic inequalities are reproduced through the curriculum. *Culture contact theory* suggests ways to assist students from ethnic backgrounds to resist inequalities by providing them with curricula and teaching-learning environments that stimulate learning about other cultures. This is based on the assumption that this kind of learning will lead to consequent reduction in prejudice and discrimination and better academic performance. Closely related to this, but more psychological in orientation, is *self-esteem theory*. In this the emphasis is placed on the importance of increasing minority students' self-esteem or self-confidence, on the assumption that this too will reduce prejudice and enhance their academic performance.

Social and Cultural Reproduction Theory

The major ideas of this explanation of socio-economic inequality in schooling have been generated among others by such theorists as Bourdieu (1973, 1974), Bourdieu and Passeron (1977, 1979), Bisseret (1979) in Europe, Young (1971), Bernstein (1971), and Willis (1977) in Britain, and Apple (1979, 1982a, 1982b, 1982c), Bowles and Gintis (1976) and Giroux (1981) in the United States. The main thrust of social and cultural reproduction theory developed by Bourdieu and his associates is that what they term the 'habitus' or culture of the dominant group or elite in society permeates all aspects of schooling and, by extension, the curriculum.

Habitus is defined as 'a system of durably acquired schemes of perception, thought and action, engendered by objective conditions but tending to persist even after a alteration of these conditions' (Bourdieu and passeron, 1979:156, fn. 2). It is not so much that the school explicitly transmits this dominant habitus. Rather it tends to permeate and influence every aspect of the school, and in particular what the school defines as success. A share of the dominant habitus by a child in such a school constitutes a form of cultural capital or 'currency' which is readily exchangeable for success or credentials. Children from non-dominant backgrounds will be disadvantaged because their homes provide them with a currency which is non-negotiable.

Bourdieu (1974: 32–3) has stated the essence of this relationship between family and class background, education and life chances:

> . . . each family transmits to its children, indirectly rather than directly, a certain *cultural capital* and a certain *ethos*. The latter is a system of implicit and deeply interiorized values which among other things, helps to define attitudes towards the cultural capital and educational institutions. The cultural heritage, which differs from both points of view according to social class, is the cause of the initial inequality of children when faced with examinations and tests, and hence of unequal achievement.

A much-quoted passage by Bernstein (1971:47) summarizes the essence of institutionalized social reproduction as it can apply to schools: 'How a society selects, classifies, distributes, transmits and evaluates the educational knowledge it considers to be public, reflects both the distribution of power and the principles of social control.' It will be obvious that this has a direct relationship to the model of the curriculum that was developed in our first chapter. An analogous view is Gramsci's (1971:350) contention that: 'Every relationship of "hegemony" is necessarily an educational relationship.'

Since Bourdieu's theories have become generally known, several empirical studies applying the ideas have followed. For example, Sharp and Green (1975) studied 'education and social control' in a British primary school. Noelle Bisseret (1979) studied the relationships between the characteristics of the schools attended and subsequent occupational histories of students from 'dominated classes' and women in France. She also analyzed their conversational discourse to establish how they reinterpreted their own life histories. Bisseret concluded from her research that 'at each stage in the educational curriculum, the degree of openness of the field of possibilities is a function of both the individual's social class origin and sex category ... to be a woman or a worker is to be dominated on the economic level and to lack the means of acquiring the necessary knowledge to exercise power in its various forms.' These findings give added support to our theoretical discussion of female occupational socialization above.

Extensions of the Theory into an Ethnic Dimension

Because Bourdieu and others have tended to focus primarily on social class differences, it is desirable to extend the basic theory into an ethnic dimension. This holds that a form of ethnocultural hegemony may be institutionalized through schooling and the curriculum to affect adversely the life chances of children from ethnocultural minorities in polyethnic societies.

The extension is necessary because ethnic groups are differentiated by a variety of diacritica, as we showed above, so that even Bourdieu's treatment of cultural reproduction does not take into account all the other non-cultural aspects of ethnic affiliation. Even the concept of ethnocultural hegemony may be an oversimplification as it implies that reproduction operates between discrete ethnic groups. However, it is an oversimplification to assume that ethnic groups are homogeneous; in fact evidence points to the operation of prejudice and discrimination within the same ethnic group, especially on social class and gender lines. Ethnic groups can also be as riven by 'political' factions as the wider society itself. Although we cannot develop this in detail here, it is likely that a broader model of *syncretic multifaceted pluralism* is required to deal with such complexity (see Bullivant, 1984).

Generally though, in such a situation members of dominant ethnocultural groups strive for 'social closure' (Weber, 1968; Parkin, 1974). This entails gaining power and control over minorities through strategies of inclusion and exclusion which utilize such 'boundary markers' as cultural symbols, ethnicity, race, status-class, and even gender with consequent maximization of economic and social rewards for the dominant groups' own members. 'Solidaristic' methods of resistance through their own strategies of social closure can also be used by minorities to 'usurp' fairer shares of such rewards. As Parkin (1974:3) stated:

> By social closure Weber means the process by which social collectivities seek to maximize rewards by restricting access to rewards and opportunities to a limited circle of eligibles. This entails the singling out of certain identifiable social or physical attributes as the justificatory basis for exclusion. Weber suggests that virtually

any group attribute — race, language, social origin, descent — may be seized upon provided it can be used for 'the monopolization of specific, usually economic opportunities ... its purpose is always the closure of social and economic opportunities to *outsiders.*'

Boundary markers used for exclusion and inclusion vary historically and according to the social and economic situation; what may be grounds for exclusion in one generation may not be in another. They can also be used singly, as with racism, or in combination, as in linking status–class with ethnicity. The concept of ethclass was adopted in the first chapter to indicate this connection.

Processes of social closure are the key to understanding how and why prejudice and discrimination can be generated in society at large and, for the purposes of this study, in schools. In an extensive review of major theories of prejudice, Le Vine and Campbell (1972:29–42) came out strongly in favour of a 'realistic group–conflict theory'. This rejects exclusively psychological interpretations of prejudice and discrimination. Instead it 'assumes that group conflicts are rational in the sense that groups do have incompatible goals and are in competition for scarce resources.' A comparable view is put by Schermerhorn (1970:6): 'If research has confirmed anything in this area, it is that prejudice is a product of *situations*, historical situations, economic situations, political situations; it is not a little demon that emerges in people simply because they are depraved.' In a broadly similar vein, Banton (1983) has made 'rational choice theory' a cornerstone of his recent work.

Prejudice is one of the attitudinal results of aiming to exclude another group by social closure, while discrimination consists of the biased behaviour towards those who are excluded that puts the attitude into action. Both terms will be discussed in more detail in the last chapter. Suffice it to note here that it is essential to avoid the weaknesses of a purely psychologistic and reductionist interpretation of these phenomena, and to take a more realistic view of the social world.

Critiques of Social Reproduction and Related Theory

Despite the persuasiveness of the general ideas of social reproduction and comparable theories, they have generated a significant body of criticism, which suggests that the power of a society's dominant groups to control the life chances of children from minority groups is not absolute. They are clearly influenced by such control, but are also able to resist it to some extent. To maintain otherwise is to accept that individuals are merely atomistic units in an integrated society and have no option but to respond to its structures and systems. Such an 'oversocialized' concept of people has been effectively challenged by Wrong (1961) and Turner (1962).

Giroux (1981) has suggested that individuals can and do resist the forces of social reproduction, and are able to maintain some relative autonomy in controlling their lives. As the theoretical model in our first chapter suggested, individuals construct their own realities, utilizing 'givens' from society as a whole and from the social contexts in which they live. They are not completely dominated by external forces and 'normative' characteristics in society. This applies equally to schools. As the Australian Commonwealth Schools Commission (1981:104) has commented:

> The commonsense view of the world that each child brings to school is the product of a complex social background. It acts as a screen through which new information is filtered, but it is also the foundation on which is built each student's objective understanding of his or her life circumstances. It is this understanding which enables students to distinguish between personal and socially imposed conditions.

We need to keep in mind that this is not to opt for a completely phenomenological position. Were individuals solely responsible for constructing their own social realities, with the corollary that each individual is 'an island unto himself', then the paradox of how social order is achieved and maintained would present itself. Social and cultural consensus necessitates the imposition of some common structures, rules and order.

At a less philosophical level, some research studies have suggested empirically that social reproduction is not absolute. Lewis and Wanner (1979) studied the influence of private schooling on the process of students' attainment of status in the United States. They showed that it is by no means conclusive that it has a more significant effect than the public school system.

Bullivant (1983a) studied and education systems in Fiji, in order to establish whether the curriculum favoured one or other of the two main ethnic groups, Fijians or Indians. He found that some evidence existed for suggesting that Fijians are able to control 'cultural capital' through the exercise of political power over the education system in general, and university entrance quotas favouring Fijians in particular. However, other evidence pointed to the influence of external factors, such as the direction being taken by the Fijian economy in response to multinational pressures and tourism, and by the New Zealand education system which still controlled the examinations at the senior secondary levels.

Even programs in schools that appear to be designed to resist social reproduction may be concealed forms of it. For example, work experience programs that are a common feature of Years 10 and 11 may be a form of occupational socialization which indoctrinates students into compliantly accepting the demands of the workforce well before they have to enter employment. The high unemployment rates among youth in all English-speaking countries have disrupted the educational process of maintaining and reproducing the workforce. As Freeland (1980) has suggested, unemployment produces a 'counter-work' culture, which negates the lessons of schooling and the force of social reproduction, as under such circumstances the legitimation of work becomes problematic. Youth employment schemes promoted by governments are also a form of counter to social reproduction, as they do not allow its operation to proceed unchecked.

However, even unemployment may not fully inhibit the force of social reproduction according to Freeland (1980). This is because the government tends to place an emphasis on such palliatives as careers education, technical training, planned labour markets and work experience programs in schools. These are an attempt to make school leavers more attuned to the demands of industry, that is, reproducing their relative powerlessness over their own lives.

In more general terms, Eckstein and Noah (1985) have criticized a number of studies that employed reproduction theory (including Bullivant's), and the closely related dependency theory on both methodological and theoretical grounds. They suggested that the current popularity of both theories, despite manifest weaknesses, is due in part to frustration experienced by theorists that education has not solved the ills of the world in the post-Second World War period. They also commented on the relative paucity of empirical research to support the social reproduction case. However, it is one thing to criticize the empirical research studies that have been carried out, but another to condemn social reproduction theory and dependency theory out of hand: a question of throwing out the theoretical baby with what little empirical research 'water' it floats in.

Major social reproduction theorists are not unaware of the shortcomings of the theory, and it now seems clear that a re-examination of its major tenets is under way. For example, Carnoy (1983:31) has pointed out that 'schools contain elements of reproduction and democracy, just as the State as a whole in capitalist and state bureaucratic societies contains these elements.' As a result, although the tendency is for hierarchical power relationships to be reproduced, schools are places where 'tensions' between both 'forces of reproduction' and 'forces of contradiction' are played out.

The essence of the tension is 'between hierarchical work relations/ individual competition and developing participative, democratic values — values that include equality and human worth' (Carnoy, 1983:32), Apple (1982b:4–5) has suggested another dichotomy and tension between 'property rights', i.e., the needs of capital, and 'person rights'. These are rights that do not concern the economic system or the 'symbolic property' a person or class possesses, but are rights over the reciprocal norms of authority, such as freedom of expression, freedom of movement and equal treatment before the law. One way of ensuring person rights — thus weakening the force of social reproduction — is for access to participation in decision-making in education to be broadened.

Classroom Strategies for Resisting Cultural Reproduction

The two theories that have been suggested to help students resist social and cultural reproduction have virtually assumed the status of conventional wisdom. Partly this is due to the fact that the premises on which they are based have largely gone unchallenged or unexamined. This section aims to redress that situation.

The Major Ideas of Culture Contact Theory

One approach that has been suggested to minimize the force of social and cultural reproduction, especially in polyethnic classrooms, is based on a cluster of assumptions that comprise what has become known as the culture contact theory or hypothesis. Its essential premise is that if people understand the cultures of those from different ethnic (and by extension social class) groups they will develop tolerant attitudes towards them, and this will lead to reduced prejudice and discrimination.

When employed as a guiding philosophy in schools, there is the added assumption that gains in reduced prejudice will carry over into after-school activities and even reduce interethnic competition for scarce resources and conflict in the wider society. Culture contact and assumed reduction of prejudice and discrimination are also suggested as a way of improving the academic performance of children from minority groups in schools.

The attraction of this theory is evident in the number of official bodies in Western societies that have adopted versions of it in their attempts to improve the treatment of ethnic minorities in schools. Gibson (1976) examined approaches to multicultural education in the United States that incorporated all or some of the above assumptions, and suggested that there were four major types. 'Benevolent multiculturalism' is the type of program that is offered by the dominant majority ('us') to the subordinate minority ('them'). Such a program is from an 'Anglo' perspective and interpretation. 'Cultural understanding' is the kind of program that is proposed by subordinate minorities and mainstream educators to teach 'us' about 'them'. A more radical kind of program is 'cultural pluralism', which is also proposed by subordinate minorities. It rejects majority-enforced cultural assimilation, and aims for increased power for ethnic groups in schools, through radical changes to the entire curriculum and school organization for all in ways that reflect the way power is controlled in the wider society. The fourth variant is 'bicultural education', which is proposed by non-English mother tongue minorities to gain bicultural competencies. Gibson found that the most common program was 'benevolent multiculturalism', and that the most uncommon and even resisted by school administrators was 'cultural pluralism'.

Historically, several bodies in Britain have adopted culture contact thinking in various guises. During the late 1970s and early 1980s it did appear that the ideology of multiculturalism was sweeping all before it, as LEA after LEA adopted this policy. However, a reconsideration of the uniquely racial and racist problems in British society led to some revision of the approach and an anti-racist type of teaching has begun to be endorsed.

In the mid-1970s, however, culture contact theory influenced government thinking. This was quite evident in the following influential statement where it appears in its classic and seductive simplicity, albeit with an international flavour, published in the Government Green Paper (Cmnd 6869, 1977:41):

> Our society is a multicultural, multiracial one, and the curriculum should reflect a sympathetic understanding of the different cultures and races that now make up our society. We also live in a complex, interdependent world, and many of our problems in Britain require international solutions. The curriculum should therefore reflect our need to know about and understand other countries.

How educational measures within school are able to throw light on highly complex issues that are generated by economic and political forces outside school is not clarified. This issue is taken up below.

Critiques of Culture Contact Proposals

Criticisms of culture contact theory take several directions in research studies and in general are inconclusive and often contradictory. Indeed, if a majority of pupils already hold racist and prejudiced attitudes, unintended consequences can result if one attempts to change them, as research by Miller (1967) has demonstrated. He studied more than 1000 part-time male apprentices attending a London technical college who were given limited instruction aimed at reducing prejudice. Results showed that the experimental group of subjects increased their interethnic hostility in comparison with subjects in the control group which did not take the same instruction. Miller suggested that these results support McGuire's (1964) contention that limited instruction using a weak form of argument may produce reactions to the argument in the form of increased prejudice.

Miller also reviewed thirty previous experimental research studies written in the period 1927–65 on the use of educational methods to change interethnic attitudes. Not all of them used control groups. Of the studies that did not, three showed no attitude change while nine showed that favourable attitude change had occurred as a result of the educational experiences. Of the studies that used control groups, five showed that no attitude change occurred while thirteen showed favourable attitude change. On balance, the use of educational techniques to change students' attitudes seems warranted; however, it should be borne in mind that many of the subjects in the studies reported were undergraduates who were not deeply racist before the research studies started. This could be one explanation why no negative changes in attitudes were observed in the studies reviewed.

A very thorough piece of developmental research into problems and effects of teaching about race relations in secondary schools in Britain was carried out for the Social Science Research Council over several years in the early 1970s by Stenhouse and associates (Stenhouse, 1975a: 126-7, 130-41, 1975b, 1977). Three strategies for teaching about race relations were developed. Strategy A involved discussions about race relations stimulated by sets of photographs and other visual material, and guided by a neutral chairman. Strategy B used the same materials but in this case the chairman was non-neutral. Strategy C attempted to teach about race relations through drama.

Findings of the research were outlined in the Final Report to the Social Science Research Council (Stenhouse, 1977; see also summary in Bullivant, 1981a:59–61). There was no essential difference in outcomes between Strategies A and B. Both were moderately effective in combatting interethnic prejudice. Teaching through drama did not produce significant improvements and did not lead to overall deterioration in ethnic attitudes. Schools would be unwise to rely solely on this method if their aim is to maximize improvements of attitudes.

Direct teaching about race relations in the age range 14–16 tended to have positive rather than negative effects upon interethnic tolerance, compared with not teaching about race relations. Although the data were fragmentary and subject to a high degree of error, it would be wise to assume that most of the advantages of teaching about race relations would probably have 'washed out' after a year. In a minority of school situations teaching about race relations is likely to be counterproductive in terms of bettering interethnic relations.

On the surface, this project would seem to indicate the success of at least this form of culture contact learning probably, one might surmise, because it was directed specifically at the affective domain which is most involved in attitudinal development. However, the statistics presented a less positive picture. In Strategy A, 49.3 per cent of the experimental group became less racist but 40.9 per cent became more racist. In the control group, 41.4 per cent of pupils became less racist, while 53.91 per cent became more racist. The directions of change in the experimental and control groups for Strategy B were comparable.

A well-known, extensive survey of research studies that had deliberately set out to improve intergroup awareness and reduce prejudice, especially in schools, was carried out by Amir (1969, 1972, 1976). The survey was stimulated by a request from Israeli policy-makers, concerned about the poor interethnic relations between Oriental Jewish children (from North Africa and other Mediterranean countries) and Ashkenazi Jewish children (largely of European background). The survey showed that culture contact did little to reduce prejudice and improve minority group performance in the long run, and would only operate successfully under quite specific, controlled conditions. Some of these virtually preclude culture contact approaches to general classroom pedagogy being adopted in schools.

Horowitz (1980) also examined studies in Israel to test the success of culture contact and arrived at broadly similar conclusions. Some reduction of prejudice occurred under highly specific conditions, and was maintained in the short term, but was not carried over into other conditions. For example, Israeli soldiers from the two major ethnic groups, Oriental Jews and Ashkenazi Jews, were able to fight side by side without mutual feelings of prejudice, but once that situation was over feelings of prejudice reasserted themselves when the troops were off duty. Studies of the outcomes of the official policy of integrating children from these two ethnic groups in Israeli schools also revealed the same tendency. Horowitz concluded that in the face of such evidence much of the present adherence to a policy of integration in Israeli schools was motivated more by official ideological considerations than concern for pedagogical realities.

More recent work by Bochner (1982) cited by Fitch (1984:26) suggested a comparable picture:

> ... contrary to popular belief, inter-group contact does not necessarily reduce inter-group tension, prejudice and discriminatory behaviour. Yet one often hears politicians, church leaders and other public figures saying that if only people of diverse cultural backgrounds could be brought into contact with each other, they would develop a mutual appreciation of their points of view and grow to understand, respect and like each other. Unfortunately the available evidence does not support this view, indeed at times inter-group contact may increase suspicion, hostility and tension.

A study by Berry (1984) on the other hand supported the positive effects of culture contact between the two 'charter groups' of French and Canadians in Canada. However, Berry also pointed out that this may have been due to the fact that many of the positive reinforcing conditions suggested by the above theorists were also present (p. 366).

The variety of claims and counter-claims in the literature about the use of culture contact in schools cannot be dealt with here in more detail; enough has been cited to suggest that the theory is suspect at best and unfounded at worst. The current 'state of the art' could also be compounded as much by our ignorance of what is involved as anything else. After reviewing a number of theories of cognitive processes in attitude formation and proposing her own model, Laishley (1975:281) concluded:

> For all the proliferation of research on ethnic attitudes in children, adolescents and adults, we still have very little understanding of the

processes at work. The emphasis in research has been on content, which is easier to collect. However, if we are ever really to understand the phenomenon of ethnic prejudice, research will have to be undertaken into the processes underlying the attitudes, into the development of these through childhood and their maintenance from adolescence through adulthood. And this is by no means an easy task.

The Importance of Societal Influences on Prejudice

Our own research and preference for the syncretic multifaceted model of pluralism discussed above lead us to support wholeheartedly the contention of Carithers (1970:41): 'There seems to be, however, a general agreement that racial contact *per se* will not bring about increased tolerance and acceptance.' This was based on a survey of the literature on desegregation and racial cleavage in the period 1954–70. The major conclusion pointed to the complexity of the variables involved in interethnic relations. As the American theorist Edith King (1984:35) has remarked:

> ... the historical, geographic, religious, social class, economic, political and linguistic aspects of ethnicity intertwine in dynamic relationships to define an individual's or group's heritage, roots and identity. In order to teach effectively for a multicultural society, it is important to recognize the complexity of the concept of ethnicity.

A further weakness of culture contact theory is that a great deal of classroom and school-based research has explicitly or implicitly adopted reductionist, psychologistic interpretations of interethnic prejudice and tensions. But when one examines sociological and anthropological views on the causes of racial prejudice and interethnic tensions, reasons for the inconclusiveness of many psychological, school-based research studies are easier to understand. For example, theorists have indicated that influences from the wider social system are closely implicated in the failure of schools to counter racism, prejudice and the failure of children from ethnic groups. In commenting on American experience, Gunnings (1972:284) stated:

> Head Start, Follow Through and Upward Bound, while they are feeble attempts to provide better education for the poor, will always face problems because they are organized around the philosophy that there is something wrong with the child. This clinical approach is inappropriate because it does not treat the cause of the problem — the system. The systematic approach means treating the societal system; it would be aimed at the attitudes, characteristics, and misconceptions of an unfair system.

La Mothe (1984) has suggested that even though a teacher may promote culture contact in the classroom, if the school is staffed by all-white teachers and principal, the structural message conveyed to black students implicitly devalues their status. Research by Landis, McGrew and Triandis (1975) used a model based on the concept of 'subjective culture' (see also discussion in Bullivant, 1973:Ch. 7). This is defined as 'the perception of the man-made part of the environment, with particular emphasis on the social environment' (*ibid.*, p. 118; also Triandis *et al.*, 1972). These researchers concluded (*ibid.*, p. 141) that 'race and sex may not be the most salient characteristics defining subjective cultural differences (and behaviour) in the classroom ... data indicate that the lack of similarity is related more to social class than it is to race or sex.'

Gilchrist and Wardle (1984) examined two strategies to increase awareness on the part of all children of racist messages in books, and to promote black children's and youths' own language skills. Many stereotyped views of ethnic groups were revealed. This suggested to the investigators that the mass media and television in particular are very powerful instruments of learning, 'there is little guarantee that new information, which counters the stereotypes, will always be recalled. Sympathetic and sensitive classroom work on different cultures, on its own, will not combat racism, if underlying myths and distortions are left unchallenged' (*ibid.*, p. 24).

A more radical interpretation based on Marxist and neo-Marxist analysis has been proposed by members of the Centre for Contemporary Cultural Studies in Birmingham, England (CCCS). In a publication strikingly titled *The Empire Strikes Back: Race and Racism in 70s Britain*, there is trenchant criticism of the politically ideological nature of much educational thinking about prejudice and racism. The Centre suggested (CCCS, 1982:194):

> The concepts of a multicultural, multiracial or multiethnic society ... assumed that equality could be achieved through cultural diversity and thus removed from the realm of politics. Race relations became totally absorbed with issues of black ethnicity at the expense of examining institutional racism. The educational philosophy of multiculturalism followed the sociologists of race relations in the reinterpretation of ethnic cultural forms for the classroom.

A comparable strategy of 'sanitizing' difficult issues relating to prejudice and racism has been shown by Bullivant (1981b, esp. Ch. 8) to operate in the Australian version of multicultural education. It has implications that hark back to our earlier model of social and cultural reproduction and social control. A comparable view of the approach was put by the Centre for Contemporary Cultural Studies (1982:194), which pointed to two aspects that can be identified. Firstly, by making it appear that racism is just a matter of individual ignorance, the sanitizing process can take the form of claims that prejudice and racial discrimination would be ended through education in schools that emphasizes cultural diversity. Secondly, the demands of black movements to have an awareness of black culture and history taught in British schools were 'turned by the state into a superficial gesture in an attempt to control the rising level of politicized black consciousness' (CCCS, 1982: 194). In a way similar to the strategy exposed by Bullivant's (1981b) analysis of the Australian government's attempt to sanitize rising ethnic groups' demands, in Britain 'the multicultural curriculum was from its inception part of state strategies of social control. Black culture and history were what the schools said they were' (CCCS, 1982:194).

Further discussion of this complex issue cannot be pursued here, but one of its striking features is the way even prominent academics and social theorists appear tacitly to acquiesce to such strategies of social control. Several motives have been suggested by Bullivant (1981b, 1983b), and also by Banton (n.d.) at a Conference on Teaching about Prejudice held in Britain in February 1983. Both views stress the seductive appeal of multicultural education, that could encourage such tacit acquiescence and blind educationists to the political realities of ethnocultural inequality.

However, this does not mean that the effort to minimize them should be abandoned, rather that it be tempered with a realistic view of what is involved. As Blanc (1984:38) has suggested:

> In a society in which there is a dominant culture and dominated cultures, cultural equality is a utopia. Yet utopia, as 'creative anticipation', ought to direct our day-to-day work. Cultural equality implies a new balance of power which will not happen if minorities do not fight for it. Social scientists are caught in a conflicting situation which they cannot escape, and must inevitably choose sides and perhaps even make a political [ideological] choice.

Countering Cultural Reproduction by Increasing Children's Self-Esteem

A closely related set of ideas and concepts that is possibly even more psychologically oriented than the culture contact hypothesis goes by the name of self-esteem or self-concept theory. Two of the seminal figures associated with it are the American theorists Coopersmith (e.g., 1959, 1967, 1974, 1975) and Rosenberg (1965, 1973 with Simmons). The 'Coopersmith Scale' or its variants has become one of the main instruments used in classroom research studies. It is also the basis of a thriving research 'industry' that has been developed in the fields of self-esteem theory, race relations and education, despite the fact, as Coopersmith himself notes (1975:145), that they 'are all under critical analysis and, to some extent, attack. The critical reactions come from within the professional fields of psychology and education as well as from legislators and the general public.'

Key Ideas in Self-Esteem Theory

At the risk of stating the obvious, it is first necessary to appreciate that self-esteem and self-concept are not synonymous. An individual's picture of himself or herself is the self-concept. Alternative names are self-image or self. The self-esteem is constituted by the positive or negative attitudes and feelings, i.e., evaluative sentiments, about the self. 'Thus the self-concept is the symbol or image which the person has formed out of his personal experiences while self-esteem is the person's evaluation of that image' (Coopersmith, 1975:148).

Self-concepts can range in scale and complexity from 'global', encompassing a broad range of attributes and several roles, to 'particularistic' and confined to a specific set of attributes associated with a limited role, such as athlete, son, daughter. Coopersmith (*ibid.*) comments:

> This question of general or specific self-concept and self-esteem is more significant than might appear to be true at first glance. Thus it may be that black children have an unclear image of themselves as effective learners in school and hold negative opinions of themselves as learners but are quite clear and positive about themselves regarding their capacities and effectiveness in the broader social world outside of school.

Weaknesses and Limitations of Self-Esteem Theory

(i) Inconclusive Correlation with Academic Performance. It is claimed that 'both self-concept and self-esteem are associated with academic performance' (*ibid.*, p. 150; also, e.g., Combs, 1952; Combs and Snygg, 1959; LaBenne and Greene, 1969; Purkey, 1970). Many other studies have claimed to support this association. However, it is far from being a strong one as Coopersmith (1975:150) himself admits. 'It is notable that while the correlations between self-esteem and achievement are statistically significant they tend to hover between .20 and .30 and are not particularly striking.'

In addition, the relationship between self-esteem and academic ability does not apply uniformly right across all levels of a self-esteem scale, but tends to be strongest at its lower end. 'Thus while self-esteem and self-concept have been consistently associated with academic performance the relationship appears much more clear in cases of lower esteem than where the student is relatively positive and confident of his worth' (*ibid.*).

It is also not possible to claim with absolute confidence that poor self-esteem *causes* poor academic performance, as 'the relationship appears to be circular rather than unidirectional' (*ibid.*, p. 152). Australian researchers Hattie and Hansford (1980) carried out an evaluation of the relationship between 'self and performance' by employing meta-analysis. They used a sample of 128 research studies derived from a total of 702 pieces of research into this relationship found by a computerized literature search. Their analysis established a data-base of 1136 effect sizes or correlations between variables. Their findings provided further support for Coopersmith's caution. Basing their opinion on one set of statistical measures, they commented (*ibid.*, p. 179) that 'it was not possible to reject a null hypothesis that the true relationship between measures of self and performance/achievement is zero.' After considering all other estimates, however, the authors were of the opinion that 'the average relationship between measures of self and performance/achievement is in the range of .21 to .26. However, it may be more meaningful to say the variance in common is between 4 to 7 percent' (*ibid.*). They also established from their data that 'the relationship between measure of self and performance/achievement is similar for males and females' (*ibid.*, p. 181).

There is also the possibility that the claimed relationship between one's academic performance and one's self-esteem, based on feelings of worth and other personality dimensions, may be due to another factor altogether. Argyle (1973:356–93) has employed 'self-image' and 'self-esteem' as the basic components of the 'me', which are gradually built up and internalized through social interactions. In effect this is a form of social comparison theory. However, Argyle suggests (*ibid.*, p. 360):

> ... if self-esteem is based on the reactions of others, we should note that people respond to one another socially in terms of *two* main dimensions — (1) status and power, and (2) warmth and friendliness. Self-attitudes could be assessed along the second dimension too — the extent to which individuals like themselves or see themselves as 'nice' or 'friendly' — as persons to whom others will normally react positively, but not necessarily regarding them as superior.

Argyle (1973:367) commented on Rosenberg's (1965) study of adolescents and pointed out that some of the results could be interpreted in terms of social comparison theory: 'Self-esteem was greater for those who did well at school, were leaders of clubs and were of higher social class.' This may throw some doubt on the idea in 'classical' self-esteem theory that an increase in self-esteem (component 2 in Argyle's model) will necessarily result from academic achievement (component 1). As Argyle (*ibid.*, p. 383) commented: 'Self-esteem can best be enhanced by receiving approving responses from others.'

Self-esteem theory may in fact be outdated. The Australian researcher Russell Docking (1980) employed Epstein's (1973) 'self-theory' to investigate 'the relationship between trait anxiety, educational self-theory and vocational interest' in a population of Australian high school students. Docking (1980:77) summarized the essence of Epstein's approach:

> Self-theory ... subsumes the idea of self-concept. Viewed as a set of

postulates one has about oneself that can be tested and falsified, self-theory is more dynamic than the more static self-concept. Educational self-theory refers to that set of postulates one holds about oneself in the educational setting.

(ii) Self-Esteem and Interracial/Interethnic Relations. The need to be cautious about the merits of self-esteem theory applies with even greater force when considerations of race and ethnicity are brought into self-esteem and related analysis. Grant (1973:401) has suggested that 'simply stated, research in the area of self-concept should more frequently consider race as an aspect of self-concept, as it has done with other factors. The importance of considering race as an aspect of self-concept has serious educational implications.'

Most research on these issues has been done in the United States (e.g., Kardiner and Ovesey, 1951; Pettigrew, 1964; Kvaracers *et al.*, 1965; Proshansky and Newton, 1968; Rosenberg and Simmons, 1973; Banks, 1984) and in Britain, although there the number is comparatively smaller (e.g., Hill, 1970, 1975; Bagley and Coard, 1975; Bagley, Mallick and Verma, 1975; Tomlinson, 1980; Stone, 1981). More recently, comparable research extending considerations to gender differences has been conducted in Australia (e.g., Edgar, 1974; Connell *et al.*, 1975; Poole *et al.*, 1976; Poole, 1977; Martin and Meade, 1979; Taylor, 1981; Jacka, 1982).

Coopersmith's own findings in the area of ethnic or race relations and educational achievement pointed to a number of surprising aspects. These throw strong doubt on claims by some educationists that enhancing the self-esteem of children from racial and ethnic backgrounds, by improving knowledge through intercultural contact or learning about their own heritage, will improve academic performance or vice versa. Part of this approach seems to imply that the self-esteem of children from racial and ethnic minorities is lower than that of 'white' or non-ethnic children. However, as Coopersmith (1975:155–6) commented on the basis of his own and others' research in America, 'there is increasingly empirical evidence that there is little, if any, difference between the self-esteem of children from different racial and ethnic groups.' It was also apparent that 'school grades appear to make less difference for the self-esteem of black children than for white children...black children do not value themselves less when they perform poorly in school' (*ibid.*, p. 162-3).

Rosenberg and Simmons (1973) looked at the evidence for the general lack of differences between the self-esteem of white and black children. They concluded that such socio-economic and social factors as family poverty and family breakup, the low prestige level of the black race generally, poor school performance and rejection of Negroes do not produce the kinds of negative consequences that are commonly assumed. An alternative explanation comes close to Argyle's social comparison theory discussed above. As Rosenberg and Simmons (1973:144) commented:

What does have an unequivocal impact on their self-esteem in these environments is what they believe their significant others think of them. The great proportion of the child's daily interpersonal interactions occur with parents, friends and teachers. If these significant others hold favourable opinions of him, respect him and like him then a firm foundation for a healthy self-esteem may be established.

Thus, assertions that the self-esteem of children from racial or ethnic backgrounds will be enhanced through programs of culture learning, and that this in turn will lead to or cause better academic performance and equality of opportunity, must be treated with considerable scepticism.

A study by Grant (1973) set out to examine the effect of relevant curriculum materials upon the self-concept, achievement and school attendance of black students at the third and sixth grades enrolled in ten randomly selected inner-city high schools in a large urban system in the United States. He found that materials which reflected the cultural values of black children had a significant effect on improving their academic performance, but no effect on their self-concepts. We might interpret this result to suggest that familiarity with their own cultural values in the materials would have assisted the children's learning and enhanced academic performance.

Research by Banks (1984) into the attitudes and self-concepts of black youths in predominantly white suburbs showed more surprising results. Although the sample of students was small (n = 98), it was clear that black students did not develop poor self-concepts (Banks, 1984:16):

> The findings suggest that Black children socialized within predominantly White suburban communities are likely to become highly attitudinally assimilated into White society and that this kind of assimilation may have complex effects on their racial attitudes towards Blacks and their levels of ethnocentrism. As attitudinal assimilation increased, these children became increasingly more positive toward their schools and neighborhoods and more positive toward Whites, but less positive toward Blacks.

A corollary or these findings was that the attitudinally assimilated blacks were also more 'internal', which in turn was positively related to academic achievement 'and to other success-related behavior' (*ibid.*). Banks also found that 'internality was negatively related to positive attitudes toward Blacks and to ethnocentrism.' He went on to comment: 'This latter finding raises a question about whether Black children can remain ethnic in their racial attitudes and attain high levels of internality — and thus academic achievement' (*ibid.*).

On the basis of her own research, which exposed many weaknesses in much of the self-concept theory and research in Britain, Stone (1981) launched a trenchant attack on classroom practices and the logic of the current form of compensatory education for young Afro-Caribbeans. This emphasizes a 'therapeutic' or 'mental health' approach on the part of teachers, who thereby cast themselves more in the role of social workers. The approach has attempted to assist the self-esteem of Afro-Caribbean and Asian pupils through a liberal curriculum and watered down 'multiracial education', on the assumption that their academic performance would be enhanced. In reality, as the second chapter of the book points out, such an approach is a major factor in increasing educational inequality.

It also led teachers into making ill-founded assumptions about curriculum development (Stone, 1981:236):

> These assumptions, shared by all teachers irrespective of teaching style, are based on the belief that black children have poor, negative self-concept and low self-esteem which need compensating and enhancing ... I would argue that to see black people and their children as passive beings, simply reacting to structural forces is a limited view which denies the facts of history and is supported neither by commonsense nor by rigorous sociological analysis.

In Stone's opinion (*ibid.*, p. 251) 'schools should be places for acquiring skills and knowledge and developing abilities associated with these skills and knowledge. The teacher's job should be to teach children these skills and knowledge and encourage the development of general abilities.'

General Conclusion

The sociological analysis on which Stone based much of her attack echoes what we have already said about the forces of social and cultural reproduction that operate through the curriculum to reduce the life chances of children from ethnic minority backgrounds. 'Mental health' or 'therapeutic' education is yet another example of failure to confront the *external* social and political causes of deprivation. Like culture contact theory, it is based on principles that are psychologistic and reductionist and ignores the fact that historical, structural and socio-economic forces outside school play a major part in reinforcing educational inequalities by influencing the 'cultural capital' or 'habitus' encoded in the curriculum.

It should not be so surprising that internal, systemic factors in school should be stressed rather than external factors. At least since the Second World War and post-war educational legislation in Britain and other Western countries, a liberal, social democratic ideology has pervaded much educational theorizing and attempts at curriculum reform. Multicultural, multiracial, contact theory and similar forms of education are but the latest in a long tradition of such ideologies of pluralist education. In essence, educational reform is seen as the solution to social and economic problems that are fundamentally only amenable to social, economic and political reform. Education is put forward as the solution to inequitable power relations.

A favourable climate within which such an ideology can flourish may have been provided by an overarching meta-ideology, tantamount to an ongoing debate with the ghost of Rousseau's *Emile*. Thoroughly utopian in its thrust, this meta-ideology maintains that the human condition is perfectible through education, as this is held to be the method for obtaining greater equality of opportunity. Much educational research has thus sought the panacea that will achieve this utopian condition (see discussion in Bullivant, 1983b). Reconstructionist philosophies (e.g., Brameld, 1977) have been proposed to bolster the claims of education to be able to ameliorate inequalities in the socio-political condition.

However, all has been to little or no avail. One of the most eminent protagonists of educational reform in Britain, A.H. Halsey, has been forced to conclude (1972:6) that 'the essential fact of twentieth century educational history is that egalitarian policies have failed.' In short, as Bernstein (1970) has put it: 'Education cannot compensate for society.' It is for these and similar reasons generated by our own research (e.g., Bullivant, 1981a, 1981b, 1984) that the theoretical model we have adopted for this study expressly rejects both culture contact and self-esteem theories. Our modification of social reproduction theory along neo-Weberian lines is preferred. Thus this study sets out to establish whether barriers to the occupational socialization of both Anglo-Australian and ethnic minority group students are present systemically in what each of the case study schools offers, and/or are present in what the students themselves bring to the task of forming their aspirations and expectations. This blend of structural, systemic and phenomenological theory informs the remaining chapters.

3   First Encounters of an Ethnic Kind

Our first opportunity to test the applicability of the theoretical models discussed above came during a series of visits to the pilot study school selected for the research. Here we had our first encounters of an ethnic kind, and obtained the first indications that cultural reproduction by Anglo-Australians could not be assumed.

The Pilot Study Approach

Rutter and associates (1979) in Britain advocated the use of a preliminary pilot study in one or more schools before setting up the design of their main research. It enabled them to test questionnaires and gain some 'feel' about the many issues involved in carrying out the major project. In effect, using a pilot study is one way of 'casing the field' advocated by Schatzman and Strauss (1973), and learning some of the strategies for negotiating with 'gatekeepers' and 'clients', i.e., subjects of research (Barnes, 1977; Burgess, 1984). The naturalistic approach to research we planned to use avoids constructing questionnaires and other instruments before going into a research site and strongly prefers a more exploratory approach. On the basis of this one can then construct questionnaires with more confidence that they will be adequate to the task for which they are designed.

(i)   The Pilot Study School

The high school selected is located in a high ethnicity and middle-to-low SES area of southeastern Melbourne. The area caters for light fabricating and assembly industries which attract migrant labour. Consequently the school has a very high percentage of students of recent migrant backgrounds and is noted for the care and thoroughness with which it copes with regular influxes of children from migrant hostels and language centres.

At the time of the school's Ethnic Education Survey in July 1984, it had a total population of about 870 students. Of these nearly 75 per cent were from a language background other than English. Some 460 students were born overseas, i.e., approximately 53 per cent of the total enrolment, or 63 per cent of those in the ethnic survey. In the group of students from Caucasian, non-English-speaking backgrounds, the predominant migrants were Greek (25 per cent), Italian (9 per cent) and Spanish (9 per cent). Students from Indo-Asian backgrounds were mainly Vietnamese (16 per cent) and ethnic Chinese (11 per cent). In all some thirty-seven languages or language backgrounds are represented in the school.

However, these figures of the major groups do not adequately convey a picture of the ethnic 'mix', as the percentages of children from other Indochinese backgrounds such as Cambodian, Lao and Khmer are too small to be included. On the basis of continental groupings, of the students from non-English-speaking backgrounds 39 per cent were from Asia, 53 per cent from Europe, and 8 per cent from South America. Most certainly, the 'visibility' of the Indo-Asian students was one of the most obvious features of the school, and had developed in less than ten years from a time when the majority of non-English-speaking students came from traditional Southern European and Latin American backgrounds.

(ii)   First Encounters of an Ethnic Kind

During visits to the school we held discussions with the Principal, English-as-a-Second-Language (ESL) teachers, Year 10 and Year 11 subject coordinators, the careers teacher and the student welfare coordinator. During morning recess it was also possible to chat with other staff and obtain more ideas about the kinds of students in the school, the problems teachers face with such a large migrant percentage and similar matters. Informal observations of students' activities during morning recess and lunchtime could also be made to obtain some picture of the ongoing 'life' of the school on which to base research strategies in other schools.

Discussions with groups of ethnic and Anglo students were also arranged. The first group of nine consisted of four boys and five girls from Anglo-Australian, Southern European (Greek and Italian) and South American backgrounds, all in Year 11 classes. The average age of the group was 16 years 8 months. The second group of seven students consisted of three boys and three girls from Vietnam and one boy from Turkey. Three of the Indo-Asian students had parents born in China or were of ethnic Chinese background. The average age of these students was noticeably higher than that of the other group and even then may have been understated, as it is apparently common for students from Vietnam to drop their ages in order to be eligible for immigration status.

It was obvious during the discussion that the Asian students were much more mature than those in the other group, and one outcome of this was a form of 'status authority hierarchy' which affected the spontaneity of female students' answers. One of the male Vietnamese students was just over 20 years of age and issued what appeared to be orders and comments in Vietnamese, especially during the filling out of the questionnaires. This served to indicate the possibility that during discussions with other groups of Asian students comments might be 'controlled' in a similar way, and would warrant Asian boys and girls being interviewed separately in subsequent schools.

Results of the Pilot Study

Discussions with the two groups of students showed that girls and boys from non-English-speaking (NES) backgrounds were far from inhibited in their comments. Most thought they would get jobs, although one or two girls from Southern European migrant homes conformed to the female stereotype: they did not need to get jobs as they 'could always get married.' One Greek girl's resigned comment to this effect — a good example of self-deprecation and awareness of the limits to her social competence — evoked an immediate and arrogant response from a Greek boy: 'that's right, and don't you forget it.'

However, all the girls in that group thought that it would be easier to find a job than boys. Jobs as checkout cashiers in the big supermarkets were more readily available for girls; boys do the heavier lifting, sorting and stacking tasks in the back of the stores. Girls able to speak one of the migrant languages common in the neighbourhood are an asset in the supermarkets; having feminine appeal was also thought to be an advantage.

On the other hand, boys in the same group considered that it was very hard to get jobs in the area, due to the currently poor economic situation. One boy commented that he had made forty phone calls and written fifteen letters for jobs, but had not been called for an interview. For both boys and girls there was a clear gap between aspirations and expectations, which tended to confirm previous research studies that have commented on the high aspirations of children from NES backgrounds. According to one of the ESL teachers in the school, girls' aspirations were greatly influenced by their self-confidence, which in turn was influenced by the maks they got in their subjects. For many children from ethnic backgrounds, poor English and communication skills posed major barriers to getting good jobs.

In contrast the Indo-Asian students were very reticent about their lives, and communication in English was obviously difficult. They needed nursing along by very diplomatic guidance in discussions. Like the NES students, their aspirations exceeded expectations, but in their case four of the seven

Indo-Asian students wanted to go to university or pursue careers that need tertiary training. Of greater significance was the fact that they were all taking science subjects. In contrast, all the students in the NES group were taking commerce subjects.

Comments on this pattern by one female member of staff revealed that Indo-Asians were 'channelled into science subjects' because they had poor English and in any case wanted to do subjects that would lead to careers in such occupations as medicine, engineering, science, computers. This, the same teacher considered, might even result in Asians getting into key occupations where they would control future developments in Australia. 'What is happening is that soon Australian society will be run by Asians in the computer industry and engineering, because they are opting to get into these areas. They are better motivated than Australian students, work harder and are more ambitious.' This announcement in the staffroom during morning tea evoked confirmatory nods from some other staff, even though it had subtle racist overtones.

Most certainly, according to the male careers teacher, Indo-Asian students were very future-oriented and keen to get academic qualifications, the best careers advice and work experience. They did not waste their time in class; the majority always took advantage of private study times and opportunities to gain more knowledge through subject teachers offering extra coaching and academic activity after school and during the lunch break. Instead of taking part in recreation activities during the morning break, Indo-Asian students were more likely to spend the time discussing their future careers. In 1982 the academic Dux of the school was an Indo-Asian.

Staff also pointed out somewhat resignedly that all this was in direct contrast to Anglo-Australian students, who made much less use of the careers advice facilities and had lower aspirations. Few of them visited the local Commonwealth Employment Service (CES) office, or looked for full-time employment in contrast to both Indo-Asians and other ethnic students.

Indo-Asian students generally had a much better understanding of work than non-ethnic students, because the large majority of them went out into industry and gained part-time work experience while studying for their Year 11 school leaving subjects or their Higher School Certificate (HSC). Although careers advice on both further education and jobs was offered to both Anglo-Australian and ethnic students jointly and not in separate groups, ethnic and Indo-Asian students were more likely to be the ones that actively sought out careers advice and counselling. Many facts about students' aspirations and views of the future echoed the previous research studies discussed in Chapter 1, with a consistency that strengthens their credibility.

Introduction to the Case Studies

(1)   Research Design

(i)   The Sample. Following the successful negotiations with the pilot school, a non-random (quota) sample of seven other schools for multi-site, case study research using naturalistic or neo-ethnographic methodology (Bullivant, 1978a and 1978b) was drawn from a population of schools selected from those used by Monash University's Faculty of Education for diploma students' teaching practice rounds. A first cut of thirty-six suburban and inner-city schools was selected to match the characteristics of the cells in a two-by-three matrix based on the concept of ethclass (Gordon, 1964), shown in Figure 3. In effect, each cell represents an ethclass catchment area for the schools in it, and students attending them were assumed to come from broadly similar backgrounds, even if some 'leakage' of students to neighbouring private or independent schools may have occurred (Ross, 1983).

Figure 3. Types of Suburban Ethclasses and Schools in Sample

Ethnicity

Quintiles	High >25%	Low <25%
1-2	Ethclass A Mountview High School	Ethclass B Northprospect High School
3	Ethclass C Southview High School	Ethclass D Foothills High School
4-5	Ethclass E1 Western Plains H.S. Ethclass E2 Southeastern H.S.	Empty Cell

Ethclasses:
A   High ethnicity/middle to high SES
B   Low ethnicity/middle to high SES
C   High ethnicity/middle SES
D   Low ethnicity/middle SES
E1 High ethnicity/middle to low SES – Western Suburbs
E2 High ethnicity/middle to low SES – Southeastern Suburbs

Each cell represents a combination of socio-economic status (SES) in quintile subdivisions, and high/low ethnicity as defined by the Education Department Annual School Census. In this children are counted as ethnics if they were either born overseas in a non-English-speaking country or have one parent who was born in such a country. A supplementary measure used by some schools is the language other than English spoken in the home.

The first cut of schools revealed that one of the cells (low SES and low ethnicity) was underrepresented while two clusters of schools were available to fill the low SES high ethnicity cell, which is the most common combination. They were a cluster in the western area of the metropolitan region and another in the southeastern area, both traditional destinations for immigrants' first settlement. This cell was subdivided into these two ethclasses and the low SES/low ethnicity cell left unrepresented. The first cut of schools was further sorted into groups of schools which would be as representative of the ethclass features of the remaining cells, and to include certain ethnic groups such as Turks, where it was suspected that gender discrimination might be extreme. Those schools that were not clearly differentiated according to the SES or ethnic criteria were discarded in this second cut, and a final population of twenty-three schools obtained.

All these schools were written to to ascertain whether they would be willing to take part in the research. Of the twelve that replied in the affirmative, six schools that provided the best fit for the five ethclasses were finally selected and the remainder put on a reserve list. Those selected were one city high school and five suburban schools, each showing distinctive ethclass characteristics that it was hoped would provide paradigmatic cases in which to test the applicability of the theoretical model and research aims. However, research at the first of the six sample schools showed that it was not as representative of a western metropolitan area high school as expected. Consequently another school from an outer western suburb was written to and agreed to take part in the research, making the final number of schools studied up to seven.

(ii) Form of Report. From the outset it had been planned to write up each of the schools in 'classic' case study style (Kenny and Grotelueschen, 1984.) However, this would have produced a very lengthy report, so two case studies were finally written up (Bullivant, 1986c). The first, Inner City High School, portrays the city school in detail as agreed on after prolonged negotiations with staff. The second, Suburbia High School, is a composite 'constructed type' (Becker, 1971). This kind of treatment is broadly similar to the more familiar ideal type proposed by Max Weber, but differs in the important aspect that it should be regarded as resulting from field research, rather than preceding it. In this case it is based on the many similarities among the structures, curriculum organization and systemic responses of the remaining six schools in the sample to the needs and aspirations of their students.

Each of the six schools from which Suburbia High School is constructed had its own individual variations, but there were many commonalities due to the still strongly centralized nature of the Victorian state education system. Much of what is portrayed about Suburbia High School is typical of many other schools in the state, even though it exactly matches none of them. In this sense it is broadly generalizable although this was not our aim. As Becker (1971:92) cautioned:

> ... if the constructed types of sociology are to have predictive power, they must be developed without primary regard to their generalizability. If they prove to be generalizable *in spite of* the fact that they are first of all designed to yield a shorthand description and analysis of the social actions, *etcetera*, permeating a particular historical configuration, in close relation with a broadly stated problem and its derivative hypothesis, so much the better, but such generalizability must not be the all-controlling aim of the endeavour.

The Ecological and Community Contexts of the Case Study Schools

Although there are numerous theoretical difficulties associated with the notions of human ecology (Theodorson and Theodorson, 1970:124–5) and community (Sjoberg, 1964; Martin, 1970), it seemed appropriate to locate each school in its ethclass context by a combination of ecological and community study approaches. The former focuses on the relationships between people and their environments. The latter is a 'method of studying human behavior that focuses upon the thorough analysis of an individual community. It is in fact the application of the case study method to the study of a community' (Theodorson and Theodorson, 1970:65).

In both the case studies that follow a summary of the school's ethclass context is provided to highlight some of the relationships between it and the wider community, and thus portray a broad picture of the ethnic and SES composition of the local areas from which students come. As will be apparent in each case study these features play a significant part in influencing their social constructions of reality, career scenarios and feelings of prejudice and discrimination.

Reading Case Studies

The case study style of presentation chosen for this book needs to be clarified at the outset, so that misconceptions are minimized and the impact of data enhanced. The overall methodology used for the research was multi-site case study, i.e., intensive studies of a number of cases. In each the researcher pursues the same research aims, uses the same methodology and research techniques to ensure a degree of comparability among cases, and endeavours to draw conclusions from comparing the cases, while avoiding the trap of claiming that results can be generalized beyond the cases investigated.

The case study approach was chosen because we considered that the time-frame and financial resources available for the study did not warrant a more elaborate quantitative research methodology. In addition much of the information we hoped to obtain was considered to be of the qualitative type that can best be found from a more naturalistic methodology.

(i)   Case Study Methodology and Techniques

Case study methodology involves research into individual sites. 'Typically they are intensive investigations of single cases which serve both to identify and describe basic phenomena, as well as provide the basis for subsequent theory development' (Kenny and Grotelueschen, 1984:37). Case study relies heavily on 'condensed fieldwork', so that limited time can be spent in the field. Thus the basic technique tends to be focused or semi-structured interviewing either singly or in groups (House, 1980).

Our research also made use of 'dialectical questioning' (Bullivant, 1978a). This is a technique where subjects are interviewed in small groups as informally as possible. Interview schedules are designed to set out the broad guidelines to be followed, while allowing scope for and in fact encouraging interviewees to diverge into side issues. Formal questions are thus kept to a minimum, and every effort is made to generate a 'dialectic' between members of the group by posing general questions, feigning ignorance and even claiming wrong knowledge about the subject being discussed. The intention is to reduce the formality of the setting to the point where respondents lose their inhibitions, and even get into arguments in an attempt to correct the interviewer or put their own points of view.

Use of tape recorders is common, as the aim of interviewing is to encourage individuals to express their ideas in free interaction settings rather than respond to a prestructured set of questions compiled before going into the field. In our case the pilot study enabled us to pretest and refine broad question outlines that were subsequently used for interviews with senior staff such as the school principal, vice principal, careers teacher, pupil welfare coordinator, senior level coordinators, ESL teachers and some ethnic teacher aides.

(ii)   Pitfalls and Advantages of Group Interviewing

The difficulties that beset research based on group discussions are well recognized: self-selected spokespersons, domination of the group by one or two articulate speakers, 'chorussing', inhibition on expressing views due to having to speak in an open forum, and the phenomenon of 'pluralistic ignorance'. This is 'a situation in which individual members of a group believe incorrectly that they are each alone or the only deviants in believing or not believing in particular values, while in reality many others, if not the majority, secretly feel exactly as they do' (Theodorson and Theodorson,

(1970:301). As a result persons are inhibited from expressing what they really think.

Despite these drawbacks, and the often temperamental behaviour of cassette tape recorders or other technical difficulties, the data obtained are often superior to those from single interviews and encourage one to persevere with the group discussion approach. In total our research generated voluminous field notes and transcripts from discussions with some 200 students and 60 staff in the seven schools. Much of the tape-recorded data are given verbatim in following chapters.

In several of the schools we also encountered difficulties due to inadequate or noisy classroom facilities in which to conduct discussions with students. On one notable occasion they had to take place in the school laundry, which was regularly used for ESL classes, and to the accompaniment of rumbling washing machines that ruined the tape recorded comments. At another school discussions in better surroundings were constantly interrupted by peremptory demands from a senior member of staff to see several of the students we were talking to — a classic example of the control an uncooperative 'gatekeeper' can exercise over researchers' access to their 'clients'.

Despite their negative effects, these difficulties had their positive side as they provided us with unsought data about the schools and their real concern to cater for students from ethnic and NES backgrounds. The most obvious impression about all but one of the schools was the lack of space and facilities to cope adequately with the problems of running ESL classes. In itself this may have indicated a form of systemic cultural reproduction related to the organization of the curriculum, but could also have reflected the generally rundown nature of some facilities due to the economic conditions under which many schools labour.

(iii)   Reporting Style

Reporting case study attempts to preserve the authenticity of the data and keep as close to the original as possible. Data are often transcribed in raw or 'journalistic' form so as to maintain the quality of subjects' responses and minimize distortions from the observer's interpretations. As time in the field is often limited primary data of this sort are supplemented by secondary documentary evidence such as, in our research, syllabuses, curriculum outlines, timetables, official records and so on. The journalistic style is also used to portray the context in which the case is situated. In multi-site studies this has the advantage of being able to establish by a form of journalistic 'suggestion' something of the contrasts among the cases being studied.

Although Kenny and Grotelueschen (1984: 38) claim that 'ambiguity in observation and reporting is tolerated' in case study research, every attempt must be made to keep as faithfully to the subjects' feelings and responses as possible. In research into such a sensitive area as prejudice, discrimination and racism this carries certain risks. In our case it was considered important to reproduce staff comments verbatim, especially in the way they habitually referred to ethnic groups, even if it appeared that we condoned the obvious stereotypes such references revealed.

For example, as our next chapter indicates, the school census counted all students from NES backgrounds as ethnics. However, staff also used students' language spoken in the home to distinguish between NES students, i.e., those from European and other traditional immigrant areas, from more recent arrivals such as Indo-Asians. Terms such as 'non-English-speaking', 'Anglos', 'Asian' and 'Indo-Asian' were used in common parlance and have been reproduced as such, even though they are blanket terms that conceal many differences among students. Constantly to draw attention to the inherent stereotyping would be to impose our own views on the data, whereas one aim of case study portrayal is to let the subjects speak for themselves. We hope that the risks and advantages of this are kept in mind in what follows.

4   Inner City High School: Systemic Responses to Needs and Aspirations

Inner City High School! The very name conjures up depressed urban living standards, passionate Victorian Football League loyalties, immigrant concentrations and socio-economic and cultural deprivation, and the type of conditions in a school that verge on a 'blackboard jungle'. Anybody not acquainted with Inner City High could be forgiven for having this mental picture — a case of giving an educational dog a bad name — but nothing could be further from the truth. As we shall see, this is one school that does not live up to such a stereotype.

Inner City High is situated in a geographical and social backwater on the edge of Melbourne's central business district. At first sight the school is unprepossessing. A main three-storey, red-brick, L-shaped teaching block built in 1969 occupies the majority of the small site. The building shows obvious signs of its age in the need for new paintwork, broken or damaged walls in places, and the 'worn' look that comes after prolonged and intensive use. There is a newer and more modern, large gymnasium adjacent to the main teaching block. This doubles as an assembly hall. Also on the site are four portable classrooms used for general teaching purposes including a music room. The remainder of the site is occupied by an asphalt quadrangle, a sports oval with soccer goalposts and a few basketball courts located behind the portables.

A short walk in one direction away from the school takes one into a lower-working-class city environment of tramlines and overhead cables, miscellaneous shops, small fabricating and assembly industries, automobile sales yards, petrol service stations, restaurants — many owned by members of Greek, Italian or Indo-Asian communities to judge from the names on the shopfronts — discount furniture and hardware stores. Interspersed among these are small, brick or timber single-fronted houses which look straight out onto busy and congested roads. Many were built in the period between the wars and now provide relatively cheap accommodation in the area, a fact that has attracted immigrant settlement. Some others have been bought up by 'trendies', eager to move into the inner-city region to reduce travelling costs, and have been converted into more stylish dwellings.

Taking another direction away from the school leads one into an inner suburban residential area of larger, more affluent and substantial houses. These are built in the solid style typical of the late Victorian and Edwardian period when this part of Melbourne catered for the well-off middle and upper classes. Some are brick and multi-storied and have been converted into flats. Others are constructed of timber and still retain the sprawling if rather seedy elegance typical of this style. The largest have been converted into small, private schools, nursing homes and similar service establishments.

The school is thus situated somewhat uneasily between two environments: professional middle class on one side, and busy, congested city and lower-working-class, multiethnic conditions on the other. The latter — constituting a lower SES high-ethnicity ethclass — are the most influential on the composition of the school's clientele.

The School Clientele and Their Needs: The Vernacular Model

(1) Clientele

The student population in 1985 totalled about 700 boys and girls in Grades 7 to 12, from twenty-seven countries of origin including Australia. The proportion of these from non-English-speaking (NES) ethnic backgrounds is extremely high. The school uses two criteria to establish this figure: the standard Ethnic Education Survey definition of ethnic, and whether a language other than English is spoken in the home. Staff consider that birthplace of parents and students as used by the Survey gives an uncertain indication of the language and cultural difficulties students face in the home environment, so the latter is preferred as a more useful indication of the degree of ethnic and cultural diversity in the backgrounds of students.

The non-English-speaking background (NESB) category is used for official purposes and other criteria to distinguish among its main ethnic components are rightly avoided. One could adopt cumbersome categories such as 'NES (Indo-Asian) background' or 'NES (European) background' and so on, however, the tendency we noted in this and other schools was for staff to refer specifically to 'Asians' or 'Indo-Asians', and use non-English-speaking (NES) as a blanket term for established former migrants (in itself an unsatisfactory term) such as Greeks, Italians, Yugoslavs and Turks, where these were not referred to by their nationalities. It seems preferable to follow suit to be as faithful to the implications of the way staff referred to groups, while recognizing that the term 'NES' strictly includes Indo-Asians and Asians in its original official usage.

Based on that criterion approximately 88 per cent of students came from NES backgrounds in 1985. This was a slight increase on the previous year. As Table 1 indicates, the percentages in some grades were even higher. Other figures are equally striking. For example, in 1985 every one of the twenty-five students in Grade 10M went home to a non-English-speaking environment. At least one class at Grades 7, 9 and 11 had a student composition in which all but one student came from a home where a language other than English is the main means of communication. One grade at Year 7, three grades at Year 9 and one grade at Year 10 had ten different language groups represented in the class.

Table 1. Percentages of Students from Homes Where English Is Not the Main Language Used

Grades	Percentage
Year Level 7	84.2
Year Level 8	85.0
Year Level 9	89.0
Year Level 10	90.8
Year Level 11	90.3
Year Level 12	88.6

Average for school = 88.2 per cent
Source: Education Department, Victoria (1984) Ethnic Education Survey.

The kinds of languages spoken in the home also provided an indication of the variety of all the NES backgrounds of students in the school. Table 2 gives the percentage totals of students and the languages spoken in their homes. It is clear that the majority came from Greek (35.2 per cent) and various Indo-Asian backgrounds (38.8 per cent). There were over twenty-six main languages used by parents or guardians in the homes, with an additional number of dialects. This kind of pattern 'emphasises the educational challenge arising from the diverse cultural and linguistic backgrounds' facing the school staff (Staff Information Sheet).

Table 2. Languages Spoken Most Frequently in the Home by Parents or Guardians, as a Percentage of all Homes

Principal language	1982	1983	1984	1985
Greek	42	41	37.8	35.2
Vietnamese	8	12	17.5	19.7
Chinese (various)	15	15	14.0	17.2
English	15	13	12.0	11.4
Yugoslavian (various)	5	4.8	5.5	4.5
Turkish	3.7	3.3	3.4	2.6
Khmer	1.6	1.8	2.0	1.9
Italian	2.7	1.5	1.3	1.6
Laotian	–	1.0	1.0	–

Other languages or dialects spoken:
Roumanian, Spanish, German, French, Tetum, Maltese, Polish, Hungarian, Pushto (Pakistani), Cypriot, Portuguese, Dutch.
Source: Education Department, Victoria (1984) Ethnic Education Survey.

There has been a marked change in student composition over the last ten years, and more especially the last five, which is revealed by the same table. The numbers of Greeks have steadily declined from 80 per cent ten years ago to 35.2 per cent in 1985. They have been replaced by Indo-Asians from various countries of origin, whose numbers have shown a steady increase during the same period from virtually nil to the current 38.8 per cent. In 1985 Inner City High School had one of the highest proportions of Indo-Asians in Victoria, and they have numerically supplanted Greeks as the major group in the school. As the discussion on apparent levels of prejudice and racism below indicates, this change has had several repercussions on the reactions of those students who were once in the numerical majority, but have been 'displaced' by the new arrivals. The implications of this for a general theory of ethnic 'serial usurpation' are discussed in the last chapter.

(2)   Students' Needs and Aspirations

The internal pattern of the student composition was in part also closely related to students' needs and aspirations. The proportion of students from Indo-Asian and NES backgrounds increased as one moved up through more senior grades in the school. The deputy principal's explanation of this was that some Anglo-Australian students and others from lower SES back-grounds tended to leave early if they got a job or wanted to go to one of the local technical schools for trade practice. Others from NES backgrounds were more professionally oriented and tended to stay on at school until Year 12.

There was a difference along lines of the major ethnic sub-groupings in this pattern of aspirations, which came out both implicitly and explicitly in staff comments. We were told that Indo-Asians, especially Vietnamese and Vietnamese Chinese, tend to stay on longest at school. According to one English-as-a-Second-Language (ESL) teacher Timorese Chinese are less tertiary oriented and they are followed by Yugoslavs, Greeks, Turks and Anglo-Australians in decreasing order.

The low socio-economic status of some students' backgrounds also influenced their aspirations. This applied particularly to Anglo-Australians, the majority of whom came from lower-working-class homes. Few of these students were upwardly socially mobile, in the opinion of one level coordinator, and their aspirations were not as high as those of Indo-Asians and some other NES groups.

The location of the school on the periphery of a middle-class, fairly affluent district was not reflected in the school population. The number of independent, 'public' schools which are located in that district and are accessible from the area of the school means that there was considerable 'leakage' of students who might otherwise come to Inner City High.

The high level of aspirations among the Vietnamese and ethnic Chinese students — a recurrent theme in discussions with staff at this school and others surveyed for this research study — was due to several reasons, according to the ESL Coordinator, herself a speaker and teacher of Chinese in the school. 'There is an old Confucian philosophy which says that it doesn't matter if you don't have a lot of money as long as you have a scholar in the family ... this is all important.' Scholarship has a lot to do with status among Indo-Asian families, and from the time they are small children boys and girls are impressed with the idea that when they grow up the family hopes that they will take and use all available opportunities, rather than waste them.

Modern technological developments have also attracted the avid interest of Indo-Asians. 'There's the whole science technology orientation that people coming from south-east Asia have a tendency to become terribly interested in. Also it's an area they consider they can achieve in, whereas in humanities areas they can't. So the tendency is for them all to go to sciences.'

However, it is not science per se that interests them, but rather the type of career that it can lead to. According to one ESL teacher:

> If you ask them from Year 9 on ... ask students, particularly from Vietnam, but also from some of the more highly educated Timorese families, what they want to be, they'll tell you that they want to be an engineer. That's, as far as I know, an almost across-the-board answer ... not a doctor or lawyer but an engineer. Some want to be chemical engineers, some want to be electrical engineers, some want to be civil engineers, but engineers is the answer. [I'm] not sure why that is ... whether it's just a word.

This was in marked contrast to even students from Greek background. They 'have a tendency to veer away from straight science courses ... to go into Humanities areas ... it's a marked difference.'

Students' Needs and Aspirations: The Observers' Model

The views of staff were broadly substantiated by the aspirations and needs of students with whom we discussed their career plans. However, there were some apparent anomalies, especially on the part of a small group of Indo-Asian boys. None of them opted for the mathematics/science stream and this was thought to be atypical of Indo-Asians in general. One or two students in each of the following groups showed individuality in career aspirations and expectations and aspired to non-traditional jobs, otherwise the students followed the norm stated by the teachers.

(1)   *Year 11 ESL Group of Indo-Asian Girls*

Four shy girls from Vietnam all over 17 years of age were interviewed and completed questionnaires. All wanted to do mathematics and sciences very strongly, for the reason that these subjects would help them get into Year 12 HSC Group 1. Two girls did not know whether sciences would give them the skills and knowledge useful for getting a job. All the girls mentioned that they chose sciences because they need help with English and sciences do not need much English. 'We will fail in other subjects where English is needed.'

The aspirations of the girls were a blend of traditional and non-traditional, coupled with considerable uncertainty about the jobs available in Australia. One girl wanted to be a research chemist at university; her father's occupation in country of origin was a driver, now he is unemployed. To her not passing HSC was a major barrier to this aspiration. She said that if she failed she would leave school and get a job, but did not specify what kind. Another girl aspired to be a nursing sister also at university; father's occupation now was not specified. The perceived barrier here was failing ESL and poor English, in which case she expected to go to a college or institute of further education. The third girl aspired to be a nurse in a hospital; the perceived barrier being poor English and lack of experience. Work in a laboratory was seen as an alternative. Her father's occupation in country of origin was a teacher and he is employed in the same capacity in Australia. The fourth girl wanted to become an engineer at the university; father's occupation in country of origin was not stated, but in Australia he is an office clerk. She saw the main barrier as not passing exams.

(2)   Year 11 ESL Group of Indo-Asian Boys

The five Indo-Asian boys were in marked contrast to the group of Indo-Asian girls. All were over 17 years of age. Three were doing mixed humanities and sciences, and two were doing commerce subjects. They chose these for a variety of reasons and the general pattern of responses to the questionnaire indicated a greater degree of uncertainty than was the case with the girls. Only two boys commented that their difficulty with English was a reason for choosing the subjects.

The boys had mixed opinions about whether the ease of studying the subjects was a strong reason for doing them. The usefulness of the subjects for getting a job was a very strong reason for two boys and a strong reason for another two. However, in contrast to the girls, the usefulness of subjects as guides to getting on with people in a future career was a fairly strong reason for two and a very strong reason for the others. This might indicate a stronger degree of 'moral positioning' on the part of the boys, who by-and-large did not see their futures in clear socio-economic terms and might have been constructing occupational scenarios which emphasize social aspects instead.

Some support for this was evident in their career choices. One boy wanted to be a post office or bank teller; father's job was not stated. Not passing exams was seen as the main barrier to that aspiration, and in that eventuality he had no alternative expectation. Joining the post office was chosen by two boys. One did not give father's occupation, the other's father is now unemployed. Not passing exams was cited by one boy as the likely barrier, and he expected to become a car mechanic. The other cited lack of ability as a barrier to the aspiration and did not know what he expected to do instead. Another boy did not have an aspiration and expected to do 'anything suitable.' His father was a car mechanic/driver in country of origin and is a mechanic now. The fifth boy aspired to 'study' (unspecified) and had no alternative expectation. His father was a bank manager in country of origin, but is a restaurant cook now.

(3)   Year 11 Boys from NES Backgrounds

Six boys from NES backgrounds were interviewed. Four were from Greek, one from Lebanese and the other from Italian backgrounds. Five were between 15 and 16 years of age; one was over 17 years. No mathematics and sciences for them — five were doing commerce subjects and one mixed commerce and humanities. Their reasons varied from seeing the subjects as easy to do through their usefulness to get into the HSC year or a future job.

Aspirations and expectations were also quite mixed, and to some extent could partly reflect the immaturity and even silliness of these particular boys. One aspired to be a police officer, but felt that he might lack interest in the job and that in any case there could be too many people going for it. His expectation was to join his father in a takeaway food business. Two boys had aspirations to go on to university or a college of advanced education. One thought that a barrier would be the difficulty of getting into higher education, the other feared getting behind in classwork. If they did not succeed one would 'start his own business', the other was not sure what he would do.

Of those that gave their fathers' present employment, two boys aspired to upwardly socially mobile occupations. One wanted to be a hairdresser — a source of continued mirth from his friends during the entire discussion — the other wanted to be an accountant. The barrier to the latter was considered to be poor results and the alternative expectation was to be a mechanic. The potential hairdresser expected to go back to school or take up an apprenticeship. Another boy wanted to join a Technical and Further Education College, but saw the unemployment situation as a barrier and expected to come back to school and do Year 12.

(4)   Year 12 STC Girls from Non-English-Speaking Backgrounds

We also interviewed five seemingly very self-assured girls from Greek, Italian and Yugoslav backgrounds and one somewhat overshadowed Australian boy all at Year 12 Schools' Year Twelve and Tertiary Entrance Certificate (STC). The ages of three of the girls and the boy were between 17 and 18 years, the other two were over 18. Two of the girls were doing humanities subjects; the remaining girls and the boy were doing mixed commerce and humanities including mathematics. All the girls thought that the fact that these subjects are interesting was a fairly or very strong reason for taking them. For the boy it was a fairly strong reason.

The majority of girls and the boy very strongly considered that the subjects would teach them to get on well with people, thus indicating strong moral positioning, though for two of the girls this reason was either fairly strong or not strong. Three girls were strongly motivated to do the subjects because they are needed to get to university, while two others and the boy thought that this was a fairly strong reason.

The career aspirations of these students showed a combination of traditional and non-traditional choices. The Australian boy aspired to be a male nurse in a bush nursing hospital, but expected to be a policeman if he failed to get into a college of nursing training. His father is a social welfare worker. Two of the girls would have liked to become primary teachers. Their fathers are milk-bar, takeaway food shop proprietor and pensioner. The barriers to these aspirations were thought to be failing the course, going overseas back to Greece and parents wanting the whole family to go back to the home country. Career expectations in these eventualities were to do a computer course or take up architectural drawing. One girl hoped to go to university or college; failing this if she did not pass her course she would like to do 'some area which appeals.' Her father is an engineering fitter and turner.

Another girl wanted to be a nurse but saw a barrier in being forced to work if there are economic problems. If this occurred she expected to go to Greece and use her excellent knowledge of the English language to get into English teaching, which is a lucrative and respected career in Greece. Her father is a mechanic who also takes part in first-aid training. The remaining girl would like to become an interpreter in a welfare centre or community language office, but saw having to go back to the parents' homeland as 'a big problem' and the main barrier to this aspiration. Her father is unemployed. She expected to do a part-time graphics course and design clothes.

Two Greek girls had mapped out interesting career plans at least in the short term. They were planning to go to Greece and teach English. To get a qualification to do this they planned to take the Cambridge Proficiency in English Certificate examination at La Trobe University in Melbourne.

The Curriculum: Vernacular Model

(1)   Selection and Organization of Content: General Provisions

The part of the curriculum for Years 10, 11 and 12, i.e., those levels most relevant for students' needs and occupational aspirations, consists of a selection of subjects shown in Figure 4. For the years up to and including

Year 10 the curriculum is organized on a traditional 'core-and-elective' basis. Staff feel that this structure is best suited to provide a broad general education, which should be covered by all students, even though this allows for a very small number of optional electives.

At the end of Year 10 students have to make a decision, with advice from the Year 11 coordinator, whether to specialize in mathematics/sciences or humanities/commercial subjects if they go on to Year 11. However, although the coordinator sees it as his job to 'get kids to think about their careers this is not easy ... a lot of kids have not given career choice serious thought.' The available choice between the two groups of subjects has had the effect of polarizing the student population at Years 11 and 12 into those choosing what they see as the more prestigious mathematics/sciences (two-thirds) and those doing humanities/commerce (one-third). The additional effect has been to reduce the scope of subjects, for example, there was no geography nor history offered at Year 11 in 1985.

According to senior staff, the structure of the subject offerings and operation of the curriculum at Years 11 and 12 are based to a very large extent on students' expressed needs and preferences, provided staff are available and willing to offer subjects. 'What we try to do is to meet the needs as students see them ... we don't make the students fit the blockings ... which is what happens in some schools.' Subject choices are made by each student at the end of the academic year in consultation with the careers teacher and the relevant level coordinators, who have final say in deciding which students are to be promoted or allowed to go on to the next year.

This system allows for subjects at Years 11 and 12 to be arranged in 'blocks' to maximize student choices. In theory a student can build up any combination of subjects by choosing one from each block. The structure of the blocks thus varies from year to year.

In 1985 at Year 12 there was a broad division between Group 1 and a few Group 2 HSC subjects approved by the Victorian Institute of Secondary Education (VISE) and the STC stream. The school saw a need to run both types of courses to cater for sixty-four students and forty-five students respectively. STC is more vocationally oriented and allows for a broader education than HSC Group 1. It attracts those students who are not so academically able but want to stay on at school. Other students who are academically able may well choose STC as a more realistic and practical course than HSC. Neither of these groups of students may want to go on to university, even though the STC qualification is recognized by some tertiary bodies for entry purposes.

The structure of the curriculum in upper levels reflects the increase in numbers and consequent demands of some students from NES and more particularly Indo-Asian backgrounds for mathematics/sciences at Years 11 and 12. In the late 1970s some staff were thinking about discontinuing all HSC Group 1 subjects, because of the poor academic performance and low socio-economic backgrounds of the students who made up the bulk of the

Figure 4. *Courses of Study for Years 10, 11 and 12*

Year 10, 1985

Mainstream	Group 1	Group 2	Group 3	Group 4
English/ESL Mathematics Social Science, Science Health PE	Greek	Cons. Ed.	Art	Art
	Begin. Typing	Typing	Textiles	Ceramics
Transition	Geog.	Drama	Graphics	Home Eco.
ESL/Humanities Mathematics Science Health PE	Typing	Begin. Typing	Home Eco.	Graphics
	Eng. I	Eng. I	Comput. St.	Comput. St.
	ESL	Eng. I	Autom. Prac.	Woodwork
		ESL	Sheet Met. Wk.	Filing and Machining

Year 11, 1985

English	Maths 1	Chemistry	Maths	Physics	Maths 1
English	Maths 2	Physics	Gen. Maths	Chemistry	Maths 2
English	Accounting	Economics	Biology	Advan. Typ.	Legal Studies
English	Accounting	English 2	Modern Greek	Graphics	Maths 2
ESL (1)	Outdoor Ed.	Art	English 2 English 2	Commerce	Health
ESL (2)		ESL (1)	ESL (2)	Commerce	

Year 12, 1985

Group 1						
	English	Pure Math	Applied Math	Physics	Chemistry	Biology
	English	Legal St.	Human Development	Art	Accounting	Greek
	ESL		Pure Math	English Literature	Australian History	

STC Group 2						
	English	Math	Graphics	Human Development	Integrated Studies	Creative Arts
	English	Commerc. Studies	PE	Commun. Language	Women's Studies	Business/ Legal

school population at the time. Other staff argued against this idea on the grounds that especially students from lower socio-economic backgrounds should be given a chance of going for the HSC Group 1 course if they wanted to. Then came the influx of Indo-Asian students and a reduction in the numbers of some students from other NES backgrounds. As a result of strong student demand it was decided to retain the Group 1 subjects and increase the provisions for mathematics and sciences based on students' choices, with the positive results that were evident in 1985.

(2) Evaluation and Assessment for Promotion to Year 12

STC is open to all students who have completed Year 11. Some students can transfer to STC from the HSC Group 1 in the first six weeks of the academic year if they become aware of their limitations. Unlike the HSC Group 1, STC does not prescribe courses of study but uses negotiation in class to decide the direction of the course, and can draw on about 200 subject titles listed with VISE. This kind of student participation is an essential component of the STC philosophy and structure. English is compulsory and students must gain a total of twelve units including three of English to complete Year 12.

In contrast entry to HSC Group 1 is not automatic. It tends to attract students who are more academically able and motivated to study. Group 1 subjects are limited to a set prescribed number of choices which are mainly, but not exclusively, oriented to entry into a tertiary institute. During the intensive program of deciding subject choices for Year 12 that takes place for Year 11 students in Term 3, teachers must advise students not to choose HSC Group 1 for Year 12 if they are at risk of wasting their time attempting a course in which they have no prospects. Despite this many students decide to do HSC Group 1, occasionally against the advice of staff but 'that's their prerogative', according to the deputy principal. This is particularly the case for students and parents from some Indo-Asian and NES backgrounds.

However, this situation poses a major dilemma for the school as students' choices for these subjects frequently appear unrealistic to staff. Students and their parents of ethnic backgrounds in particular insist on choosing mathematics and sciences against the advice of staff, because these subjects are associated with university entry into prestigious degree courses and subsequent professions. Mathematics is also increasingly required as a prerequisite for other courses and jobs, but many students are not able to cope with the subject yet cannot be persuaded against doing it.

The dilemma apparently arose because a directive from the Regional Director of Education has instructed that a child who wants to take mathematics and sciences must be allowed to do them, despite the unreality of his/her aspirations, provided there is a place in the school. Unless the child is being disruptive there is no way he or she can be excluded. No avenues of appeal against the directive exist for teachers and it is clear that they 'don't like it at all', in the words of one senior administrator. Even intensive counselling with parents can fail to persuade them that it would be in the best interests of the child to leave at Year 10. A few parents still insist on the child staying on in Years 11 and 12. All these factors contributed to the high retention rate in 1985 of 90 per cent from Year 7 to Year 12.

(3) Special Provisions for Students from NES and Indo-Asian Backgrounds

The high proportion of such students in the school is reflected in another feature of the curriculum. This is the highly organized ESL program at all levels, and in other subjects as much support as possible for English is provided. The latter is seen to be crucial as such students come into a school in which English is the dominant medium of instruction. All HSC students who have been in Australia less than five years and are thus eligible to do ESL English in the examination do so. In 1985 there were nineteen students in this category. This is an anomalous situation for others, as students who were born overseas but have been in Australia for six years do not qualify for this concession.

At Year 12 ESL is blocked so as to be parallel with English. Five regular periods of ESL instruction are thus available, and in addition ESL students can have five periods of support teaching more on a one-to-one basis. A broadly similar arrangement operates in Years 10 and 11. ESL students — in bigger numbers at these levels — are blocked with English and have five periods of ESL. This is also blocked as an elective so that a total of eight or ten periods of English can be used.

Those who are from Indo-Asian and NES backgrounds and are not doing ESL, but still need more work in English, can take mainstream English from Block 1 subjects and English II from Block 3 or 4. For some students this is compulsory while others choose to do the extra English work. 'They [Year 11 students] feel they would rather do ten periods of English a week than choose to do a sixth subject.'

The staff are aware that these arrangements have certain disadvantages but maintain that they are justified. For example, Year 11 students do not have any free periods for private study. Ten periods of ESL per week are seen as a necessary if restrictive measure.

> By forcing students to take 10 periods of English per week we do limit their subject choices, but we feel it's in their interests to do that. Now a maths./science student can still pick up his maths. 1, maths. 2, physics and chemistry, that is four subjects, and two lots of English. That's going against the principle of a broad general education but ... the needs of these students are more important than English [speaking] students, so they should be taking English 2.

ESL staff saw a direct connection between the need for ESL and students' career aspirations and success. Many of those from Indo-Asian and NES backgrounds who come into the school have had interrupted schooling and are conceptually behind their Australian peers. If they do not have ESL such students would be stuck in an ordinary school-learning situation.

> What we're doing is retaining them, keeping them at school and building up their communicative skills which then will allow them at least to go out and sit through an interview.... If it's the least we do, that's what we do. It's a great achievement that a school like this supports such a diverse ESL program.... In a way we do help.... We don't necessarily guide kids in a career choice ... but we give them some sense that they can achieve it.

This strict policy and the amount of ESL provision do not result in a drop-off in the numbers of students; in fact the proportion of students from Indo-Asian and NES backgrounds increases as one goes up the school. This is due to many wanting to stay on to obtain HSC Group 1 qualifications and the career opportunities these open up. This applies particularly to Indo-Asian students, very few of whom take STC. In addition, the reputation of the school and its concern to assist students from all NES backgrounds are so high that it has attracted students from other areas, even from suburbs at a considerable distance from the school.

Some indication of the success of these policies is not only reflected in its high retention rate already mentioned, but also in the examination results at HSC. In 1980 the HSC pass rate was 27 per cent of thirty-eight students, while in 1984 the pass rate was 60 per cent of eighty-eight students. In part, this improving rate of success could be attributed to the increasing percentage of highly motivated and bright Indo-Asian students doing HSC. They concentrate on mathematics and sciences, in which most have knowledge and concepts from previous education. Lack of facility with English may not be a major inhibiting factor in such subjects, even though the language of mathematics in itself is very difficult.

However, despite the provisions that are made for students from ethnic backgrounds, some extraneous difficulties work against their interests, being generated by family circumstances rather than by the school. For example, Greek families are content to stay in the local neighbourhood; only in the latter part of their lives have they begun to move out and away from its influence. In contrast, Indo-Asians see living in the local area as a transition stage and are prepared to shift out as soon as possible to higher-status outer suburbs. The reaction of ESL staff to this was unequivocal:

> We're upset about it from the school's point of view. We're a sort of second-stage language centre ... it is a bit of a transit camp for some kids ... people move from the flats so there is a fairly high turnover there and out to the eastern suburbs or whatever.... We know that

when the children leave here and go to B_____ High, for example, they don't get the support they really need.... We're disturbed to see students moving from the area because we know they'll be missing out when they get to the other areas. And we've got students who travel to us from a long way away, having dropped out of school in their own localities.

Parental involvement in their children's education was seen as a mixed blessing, especially at Year 12:

This year there are 19 doing ESL at Year 12, but there's no background of English in the home. Parents don't know how to help with informed discussions, talk, and just understanding the system. They tend to get on the back of year 12 kids all the time. 'Hard work, hard work' doesn't really help at that level. Parents think they're doing the right thing by putting on a lot of pressure, but in many cases it works against them.

Other parents see the need for their children to do ESL as evidence that they are academically dull. It has to be explained to them that the students are not coping with ordinary subjects because of lack of English.

The school gets a special ESL component to cope with the large numbers of recent immigrants from NES backgrounds. This component is less than what is needed, so the school has allocated twelve staff to this area by reducing other subjects. The demands on staff are very great, as Indo-Asians are arriving all the time and there is a big range of problems:

Some Timorese, new recent arrivals, have never been to school, even though they are sixteen or seventeen years of age. A lot of students have no schoolwork skills let alone language; they've never been used to sitting at a desk and working at schoolwork. It means with refugees you put them in a strange classroom environment for six to seven hours a day and expect them to work ... and carry on just like other students ... it's beyond them. We need to help them in social aspects as well as education aspects. Psychological problems and suspicion of authority are very common.

There was a feeling among staff that the school had to tackle these and other problems allegedly with little assistance from official bodies. Staff alleged that the number of external visits in the area of TESL or multicultural education had been minimal, and the school had had to cut back on ethnic teacher aides to maintain the financial allocations to other areas.

According to one senior staff member the school's portion of the Supplementary Grant Resource Program had fallen from $30,000 in 1983 to $12,500 in 1985. Apparently official policy in Victoria was to broaden the base for supplementary grants, by bringing more schools into the program, as well as by reducing the available financial resources. Over the last few years, allegedly the Victorian government had also been charging more of its administrative costs, such as consultants' salaries, against the program by taking these out of the supplementary grants that were strictly intended for the schools. When the program first started, administrative costs occupied about 1.5 per cent of the total budget it was alleged; in 1985 they were occupying close to 13 per cent.

The cutbacks in 1985 badly affected the ESL program and came as a serious shock to the teachers concerned. Formerly part of the grant was used to take students from Indo-Asian and other NES backgrounds on educational excursions to give them language practice and 'survival' knowledge. This was an integral part of the ESL program. But it had been reduced and students were being asked to pay despite the fact that some of them came from poor family circumstances. Parents were on welfare benefits and could not afford to help.

The worst cutback in 1985 had been to the translation service. Teachers commented that no funding whatsoever had been provided for this, even though allegedly the service had continued to be 'coordinated' at the bureaucratic level with considerable salary costs. Teachers felt that the amount involved could be used to supply all the schools in the area with translation assistance. 'This is not something the school can pick up. Certainly we can't use ethnic teacher aides for that ... this would take them out of a program dealing with children where they are needed in the classroom.'

In 1984 the staff ran a conference: 'Coping with Stress in the Multicultural School'. In light of the above, the reasons for the conference need no elaboration.

(4) Provisions for Girls

Inner City High was one of a group of schools to take part in a Participation and Equity Program, one section of which was concerned with equality of opportunity and the education of girls. At the beginning of 1985 one female member of staff conducted a brief survey of the career intentions at Years 9 and 10. Of the 112 participants in the survey the great majority chose traditional occupations as their first choice: hairdressing (22.3 per cent), primary teaching (14.3 per cent), nursing (10.7 per cent), child care (8.9 per cent). Other careers listed by a small number ranged from dressmaking, fashion design, beautician to secretarial studies, journalism and computing. One girl listed engineering as a first preference and one gave motor mechanic as a third preference.

The students were also asked to give reasons for their choices, and expressed a variety of personal views. The pattern of career choice is very limited. As the careers teacher commented:

... there are numerous other reasons for limited career choice. These range from low self-esteem, or conversely, unrealistic ideas as to their potential; lack of exposure to other career possibilities; lack of knowledge about job requirements; lack of role models; parental pressure regarding what is an appropriate career for a boy or a girl. It is so important that we attempt to devise strategies and broaden career options for both boys and girls.

This had not been for want of trying on the part of the careers teacher, and the picture she painted was far from encouraging for those educationists who are trying to get girls to aspire to a wider range of occupations.

I think that a lot of things we have tried to do to encourage girls into non-traditional lines of work don't succeed, and whatever you say to them about hairdressing and child-care etc. being dead-end jobs, leading nowhere, it doesn't seem to be very effective. Now I think for that sort of thing ... we must get to the parents.... They are the ones to be addressed and maybe that means advertising in the ethnic papers and things like that.... I think perhaps that's where the money should be going now.

I think that getting to the girls themselves is not the right kind of thing, because there has been a lot of that sort of semi-feminist stuff around for a good five or six years now, and I don't see it is effective. At the grass-roots level girls don't see it as being relevant to them, and I just think you have to keep on exposing them to as many different kinds of occupations as possible, and let them see that you can combine jobs with marriage and child-rearing as well. That is something very important because they often won't look at that ... they still see someone with a career as being that you couldn't combine it [with something else].

Despite these views one curricular response to the needs of girls consisted of a Year 12 STC elective course called Women's Studies. It catered mainly for girls but in 1985 included one boy. The aim of the course was to look at the role of women in society, through a sort of affirmative action framework to raise the awareness of girls. At the end of 1984 several staff ran a research project in the school to stress the notion of equality of opportunity, with particular emphasis on making boys aware of how girls can be belittled and discriminated against in class. An in-service curriculum day was also held in 1985 on the theme of equal opportunity.

Physical education staff also make special provision for girls in the area of sport and physical education. The gymnasium is reserved for girls on one afternoon a week when a special program is organized for their needs. A girls' rowing team had also been organized by PE staff, and girls had been able to field their own soccer and cricket teams, despite denigration from the boys. In 1984 the careers teacher also ran an after-school class in self-defence for girls in an attempt to heighten their self-confidence and counter the more extreme effects of boys' pushiness. This class ceased in the following year, but she had maintained contact with the group of girls and took them out to various organizations during scheduled 'Activities' periods at Year 10 level as one of several groups, in an attempt to expose them to various kinds of possible occupations.

> It has been really good fun and a place like Epworth [a local hospital] was wonderful, and it shows you a lot of things ... it is a limited number of kids that you can do that with. But I am glad that it is girls because in one way at least they are here.

Despite these provisions for girls, however, the general opinion was that they were metaphorically pushed out of sport by boys who attempted to take over facilities. There was considerable sexism in the school — boys versus girls — with Greek boys in particular being extremely 'macho'. Other aspects of this tendency are discussed below.

(5) Multicultural Education

(i) General Provisions. The multicultural and multiethnic composition of the school is reflected at least in principle in recommendations for multicultural education set out in the ESL Faculty's Guidelines. In addition to making provisions for ESL, it states that 'all teachers are teachers of language' and should be aware of its importance across the curriculum. Ways that teachers might use to foster an awareness of multiculturalism set out in the guidelines are to:

(i)   Acknowledge contributions of other cultures where appropriate, e.g., Archimedes (Greek), Abacus (Chinese).

(ii) Include multicultural activities where appropriate so students can draw on their own experiences and share them with others, e.g., the family, migration, food, events and festivals.

(iii) Where possible use the ethnic teacher aides as resources, e.g.:
— to translate lists of terms;
— to provide information about events, festivals;
— to assist in activities, e.g., making of Greek Easter eggs, lanterns for the Chinese Moon Festival.

The staff guidelines also encourage staff to use the correct spelling and order of Indo-Asian students' names and to make every effort to learn and pronounce them as correctly as possible.

Ethnic languages are also included in the curriculum. Chinese is taught in the school as a community language at Years 7 and 8 in a department organized by one teacher. Although not trained in curriculum materials development she is working in conjunction with another school to develop Chinese language materials. Their aim is to assist pupils coming into the school with poor English language skills. They produce exercises and vocabulary in Chinese on such events as the Chinese New Year and other festivals, together with translations in English. The teacher concerned is assisted in this project by an Ethnic Teacher Aide and the local Language Centres. Funding is supplied by a grant from the State Ministerial Advisory and Coordinating Committee on Multicultural Education.

In the Year 12 STC course there is a language block called Community Language, which 'sort of grew up out of necessity' to avoid forcing Greek students to do Chinese and vice versa. The teacher is able to teach Greek herself, but allows students taking this subject at a Saturday morning ethnic school to spend supervised time studying it during normal lessons. Chinese students studying Chinese in a Saturday morning school of modern languages are able to do the same.

All students work through a common component on the use of languages: skills for interpreters and skills in translating. These include going to see them in operation with social welfare workers, interpreters and others in the community. According to the teacher of Chinese: 'It's a very exciting course developing the use of language and building up the value of their home language in these situations.'

(ii) The Place of ESL in Multicultural Education. Members of the ESL Faculty considered that everything it does is with multicultural education in mind:

> We find it very hard to separate the two ... we are trying to develop a more school-encompassing multicultural program. In ESL we have a tendency to talk about where children come from, what kinds of festivals they have. They all share their experiences and ideas, and that happens in ESL. Probably doesn't happen outside the ESL Department ... in some subject areas ... very difficult for some teachers to introduce it ... difficult to get a grip of it and realise the importance of it.
>
> [We would like to see the support program] really take off in the school so that it functions concretely as opposed to being very tentatively on the outskirts at the moment. It's a matter of getting staff in subject areas confident enough to have somebody to help support them. We would like to see units of work being prepared for kids so that when they want to do units of work in sciences they would understand.

However, other staff are not so convinced. According to one senior administrator:

> I think that multiculturalism means many things to many people.

Now, what I would think it means is that you do as much as you possibly can to raise the self-esteem of children from ethnic backgrounds, and try to make students from other backgrounds tolerant of each others' ethnic backgrounds. You do that by things like publicising the Chinese New Year and making sure that everybody in this school is aware of the Chinese ... same with Greek festivals, Turkish and so on ... with flags around the school.

That's all in theory ... the amount of it is fairly slight ... I am conscious of not enough being done ... we get caught up in the day-to-day running of the school and teaching subjects ... we are certainly conscious of the need to do something about it. This did lead to an invitation to run a Chinese festival in Term 3 this year, but cutback in finances has led to plans being rethought. In my opinion, there needs to be more published guidelines about what other schools are doing.

In another teacher's opinion: 'It's a bit bitty, but perhaps that's all that can be done.'

Comments on the Curriculum: The Observers' Model

(1) The General Selection of the Curriculum

The availability of STC at Year 12 was a valuable provision for those students who did not want to take HSC Group 1, and the liberal entry qualifications — open to anybody who had completed Year 11 — made it doubly attractive. Prima facie it seemed quite undesirable that all students who wanted to should be admitted to Year 12 under a regional directive, as having obviously unsuited students in classes at this demanding level could put a strain on staff resources.

The students made several comments on the curriculum with particular reference to the suitability of subject choices and the STC course as a whole. Some of the boys from some NES backgrounds commented that unless one was very careful it was possible to make the wrong choice of subjects, so that after Year 11 career choices became very limited as there was little chance of changing the course. Difficulties with English were the major concern with the Indo-Asian students, but they did not comment either favourably or unfavourably on the ESL provisions in the school.

The major comments came from the group of STC girls. They obviously appreciated the availability of the course because it not only provided academic training but also included the work experience program that was regarded as very useful. It enabled them to see if they liked jobs and gave them a lead to what job to go for after leaving school. However, the STC was not accepted as a qualification to enter several tertiary courses and was not seen as the equivalent of HSC. Some universities demand eighteen units as an entry standard, but in 1984 some students only did fifteen units and found that they could not get into what they wanted. As one of the girls commented somewhat bitterly: 'A lot of people knock it down and say "sorry you want HSC". I don't see why people should get knocked down if they have the ability. It shouldn't be allowed — a lot of people go blank on the tests, you know, and get a shock.' All the girls agreed on what they saw as an anomaly in the STC system and felt that it hampered their chances of pursuing the types of tertiary education they wanted.

(2) The Multicultural Component

At the time of our visit one of the most obvious features was a huge red banner in Chinese and Vietnamese strung above the entrance to the main teaching block. It was the time of the Chinese New Year and it was being officially symbolized in this way. The banner would be taken down as soon as the festival finished and a different one featuring another ethnic festival would be erected when the time came. There was other evidence of 'public' recognition of the multiethnic and multicultural composition of the school such as signs in ethnic languages. The school library was well stocked and contained books, either written or recorded on audio-tape, and other materials in ethnic languages, which supported the ESL and limited community language programs.

The multicultural units in the general curriculum were almost entirely of the 'additive' type devoted to limited aspects of ethnic heritages included as topics in some syllabuses, rather than infusing the whole of the curriculum. They were mainly devoted to studying the life styles of major ethnic groups. An Aboriginal Studies course was provided at Year 8, but other topics such as those on Archimedes and the abacus referred to above were disappointingly superficial.

However, it had to be recognized that the official policy of the school was to cater for the needs of students from NES and Indo-Asian backgrounds, not necessarily through a special multicultural education program but in the general curriculum. Thus the Year 9 consumer education unit dealt with issues of relevance to such students. Year 10 social studies included units on the workforce, local government, employment and similar issues. The whole thrust of staff endeavour in the school was to give all students as much assistance as possible to achieve good life chances, within the limitations of the financial and other resources available.

The concentration on ESL was the most obvious feature of multicultural education and its need was supported by students' comments. Indo-Asian students in particular emphasized the need for English and anything that helped it. In the Chinese language department, while it was wedded to a bilingual philosophy, teachers used a program that seemed to be based more on a transitional rather than a maintenance approach to bilingualism, i.e., to make students functional in English as soon as possible while bridging across from Chinese. Indeed, one suspects that maintenance of other languages in the form of full community language programs was beyond the school's resources. It is also debatable whether such programs were needed as so many students came from homes where a language other than English was spoken, and one might have assumed that the ethnic language was maintained there. However, it appeared from staff comments that they could not make this assumption and felt that the provision of languages other than English was still warranted. According to one of the senior staff, if the school had the resources Vietnamese would have been included in the curriculum; at present it is not even on the HSC subject list. One benefit of having community languages for students to take at this level was amply demonstrated by the 1985 HSC results. These showed that twenty-one out of twenty-two students passed HSC Greek even though many failed in other subjects.

Comments that revealed students' perceptions of the multicultural nature of Australian society and related type of education in the school were very limited. The opinions of the one Anglo-Australian student and some students from NES backgrounds seemed to indicate that they saw having a second language as an advantage. The Anglo-Australian student in our sample admitted to feeling jealous about the advantages migrants and ethnics have: 'Y'know … if you've been … they've been brought up in two cultures kind of thing, they know two lifestyles, whereas I know only one.' However, some boys from NES backgrounds commented that although migrants have two languages, their own and English, they still had the task of learning how to comprehend in the latter.

From other comments it was apparent that some Australian customs obviously mystified Asian students and suggested that their schoolwork could well be augmented to include a degree of 'reculturation' (Bullivant, 1973) in order to learn some aspects of Australian culture. For example, the group of Indo-Asian boys felt that it was 'very strange' to leave home rather than live at home with parents and go to work from there. Not looking after elderly parents was also 'very strange' — as one said, with a wondering shake of the head.

Curriculum Organization for Careers Guidance: The Vernacular Model

The numbers of teachers to cope with the total student numbers and the ethnic complexity of the school were correspondingly large. In 1985 the staff totalled sixty-eight men and women and included at least eleven teachers who were themselves from NES backgrounds. Several other teachers were born overseas. There were also three ethnic teacher aides — Chinese, Vietnamese and Greek — funded partly by the Commonwealth Child Migrant Education Service, and by supplementary grants.

(1)   ESL Teachers

The ESL teachers constituted a Faculty, headed by the ESL coordinator. It was highly organized, and details of its work were duplicated in a booklet, which also contained a wealth of other information on desirable ways of helping and accommodating ESL students in normal classes and was made available to all staff. The Faculty provided courses and support from Years 7 to 12 for students of all non-English-speaking backgrounds who had not yet reached competence in the English language.

Two groups of these were especially identified and helped in the school. First-phase learners were those who had been at an Australian school for less than six years and who had not yet reached competence in English. Second-phase learners were students who had near competence in English. Generally those students had been at an Australian school for at least six years and in many cases were born in Australia.

The functions of the three ethnic teacher aides covered a number of areas which were peripheral to careers guidance. They supported teaching and were available to assist all staff and the regular teachers regardless of the faculty concerned. They assisted with such activities as meetings with students, pronunciation of students' names, vocabulary lists, development of units of work incorporating the culture of students into school programs, the preparation of visual materials and understanding the ethnic backgrounds of students. They also undertook interpreting and translating, worked in conjunction with the pupil welfare coordinator and could be invited to take part in school excursions or to assist with other special activities.

(2)   The Role of Level Coordinators

The staff of more direct relevance to occupational socialization were the level coordinators at Years 10, 11 and 12, the careers teacher and the student welfare coordinator. Among the many duties of the level coordinators were a number set out in the staff guidelines: giving advice on educational and vocational guidance for pupils, planning parent-teacher nights and interviews with parents and planning the courses and subjects taken by students particularly in the higher forms. In these tasks the level coordinators were expected to work in close liaison with the careers teacher.

Although the involvement of level coordinators in careers guidance and organization appeared to be substantial, some of their perceptions of their marginality in this role revealed reluctance about assisting with careers guidance in any formal way. Level coordinators tended to send students to the careers teacher and left most of the formal guidance to her. This policy was due to the regulations from the Victorian Education Department governing the legal responsibilities of teachers towards their students. If one gives incorrect advice to a student that involves him or her in a loss of employment opportunity, legislation allows for the student to sue the Education Department or the teacher in the courts for legal redress and compensation.

According to some teachers at Inner City High School, unless one had absolutely accurate details about such a matter as choosing a career it was safer to·leave this job to a specialist such as the careers teacher. As one coordinator put the position: 'I would try to guide a student as far as I could, especially on Careers Day, but leave most of it to her ... she has been chosen for her skills.' Another senior coordinator did not get involved in careers advice even informally. He left it to the careers teacher who was available most of the time and had interviews with about 60 per cent of Year 11 and all Year 12 students individually.

The same coordinator was also not in favour of making instruction in careers education a formal part of the curriculum. 'I think that's rather artificial. This is really a policy decision as to how much time you can take from students' total curriculum to give it to the careers area.' Although careers education was not a structured part of the curriculum the careers teacher was able to negotiate with other teachers so that she could take a unit on topics related with careers.

(3) The Careers Teacher

This is a full-time position, 'within VSTA (Victorian Secondary Teachers Association) guidelines', and at the time of the research was held by a female member of staff. 'Full-time' was something of a misnomer as her specified duties also included teaching one HSC English subject for five periods a week. The careers teacher's task specification written into the staff handbook consisted of the following responsibilities:

Counselling of students on such issues as their options after leaving school, job seeking, subject choices, etc.

Compiling and disseminating information re tertiary courses, apprenticeships, specific job requirements, etc.

Liaising with community groups, parent groups.

Liaising with staff re curriculum decisions and taking careers classes in individual subjects.

Organizing work experience. In this school this is available to students in Years 10, 11 and 12. Students are encouraged to take an active part in organizing this part of their curriculum.

Organizing careers information seminars.
Maintaining contact with school leavers.

Despite the extensive list of tasks the position entails, the careers teacher was not specially trained for it. She was appointed by consensus of her colleagues in the school, but had had no prior experience of careers education work. During her first term in the position she did a four-week in-service course only.

The careers room operated as a drop-in centre for students especially during the lunchtime when the careers teacher always made herself available. It was well-equipped with a great variety of materials, such as pamphlets and leaflets on careers from the Commonwealth Employment Service, posters displayed on walls, several easy chairs and a telephone. This last was apparently regarded as a luxury as some careers teachers did not have one.

It was obvious that during the lunchtime a variety of girls and boys dropped into the centre for advice either by appointment or spontaneously. The constant comings and goings, interruptions to conversations and phone calls all conveyed an air of business yet informality which seemed to suit the style of the school.

The careers teacher organized a careers day for Year 11 students on a yearly basis. Local industries sent representatives and she tried to select industries in which students would be interested. Occupations were listed according to students' choice and work experience programs were organized for some students in Years 10 and 11 and for all Year 12 STC students.

The careers teacher stated that she puts a great deal of emphasis on encouraging students to find out about jobs themselves, rather than her always finding something and pushing students into going. Every second week on the average she also spoke to all the Year 11 group in assembly about careers, but acknowledged that as there are about 100 students this was not very effective. At the end of the year she tried to give each of these students individual counselling to plan their courses for the following year.

The work experience program for the Year 12 STC group consisted of two or three weeks out in the local industries and with employers. Prior to this period the careers teacher spent considerable time working with students in the group on careers skills such as interview techniques and self-presentation, and also worked on the kinds of skills that would be expected in certain occupations in the work situation. Simulation games and videos were used to put over these ideas. Practice at job application letter writing was also encouraged and done in conjunction with the English and ESL teachers.

Classroom work in the unit on careers education that the careers teacher organized as part of other courses used the booklet, *Take It Away ... a Book for School Leavers*. This was produced by the Central Region Transition Education Committee which was funded by the School-to-Work Transition Program. The book deals with a range of issues of relevance to young people when they leave school and includes not only information on employment and further study, but also such aspects as consumer law and protection, community services, use of leisure and migrant welfare.

The school also ran a 'contact system' which operated in third term at Years 10 and 11. Each staff member at these levels was requested to select four to five students and provide them with counselling regarding their subject and career choices, and also maintain a degree of pastoral care over their well-being. The organization of this system was the responsibility of the careers teacher.

Her basic method of helping students was to 'provide down-to-earth advice' on where to find information about jobs, rather than take students individually for one-to-one counselling. 'For efficiency when giving careers advice you can take a whole class ... but counselling needs one-to-one, you just haven't got time.' Nevertheless this would have been her preferred method:

> I think personal counselling is the most important thing you can do and you have to have time for kids.... Judging from other schools I think that people can get too bogged down with work experience ... to the detriment of personal counselling ... I think it is valuable for an awful lot of kids but you can spend your whole time organizing it too.

The careers teacher also admitted to giving advice slightly differently according to the ethnic background and different needs of the student:

> Yes, I probably do ... probably not consciously so much ... I mean, with a group of Asian students I'll spend a lot more time explaining what jobs are and mean, because they'll ask as well. With kids of Greek background or whatever I'll be briefer and to the point. Very often with them I'm more aware that I'm combatting prejudice ... if I suggest male nursing to a boy, they'll be the ones to say 'oh God, we don't want to do that'. Greek kids will come out with those things much more readily ... sort of a shower of prejudices. ...
>
> Asian kids will think much more carefully.... With the Asian kids it's very seldom that they come to me. Like in Year 12 now ... the Asian kids basically know where they are heading, and they've looked at the tertiary guides, and done all those things ... the few Australian students in the school are in some ways probably the easiest to help, as they are more familiar with the system.

The careers teacher also made use of local employment agencies like the Commonwealth Employment Service and its Youth Officer. However, there was a problem of a high turnover of staff in that office: 'which is a nuisance really because just when you've got one sort of trained — not that they are not helpful, but you can spend six months just telling them what to do initially — they turn them over every twelve months.' So she also used the Careers Reference Centre in the city and the Vocational Orientation Centre. The latter was particularly good, and she employed this quite often as it would counsel individual students:

> Yes, individuals ... kids who are really stuck ... the kids that are semi-stuck I send to the Youth Officer, but kids who are really unsure and I don't know what to offer any more I send there and they are good ... obviously for those kids there isn't a quick solution anyway, but they are a good resource.

In the careers teacher's opinion careers advice should really be integrated with the curriculum, but she did not push this and recognized that it seemed to be difficult in the school. The problems of timetabling had to be recognized. It did involve getting other people to assist and that was not easy. 'People are either too busy or feel they lack skills.' Ideally the careers department could have done with another two or three permanent staff and more cash.

(4)   The Pupil Welfare Coordinator

This teacher also played an important part in occupational socialization. To assist this work he had his own room and an outside telephone — 'very important but not always available in many schools.' He was also a teacher within the school rather than a specialist and took five periods a week at Year 7. His training had been minimal, a matter of fifteen days a year on an in-service basis through the Psychology and Guidance Branch of the Education Department. His background experience was an important prerequisite for this. However, this was probably enough in his opinion, as a psychologist from that branch also came on one day a week to the school and carried out intensive counselling where it was required.

The pupil welfare coordinator worked in close collaboration with the careers teacher, but tended to concentrate on a different emphasis, i.e., students' self-esteem and self-confidence, whereas the careers teacher tended to emphasize the more practical issues of getting a job. The pupil welfare coordinator's task was to know the background and current circumstances of students and through discussions, interviews and continuous supervision to provide support particularly in long-term, time-consuming cases.

He regularly helped visiting counsellors in their work and also maintained close contact and working relationships with the three parent organizations affiliated with the school. These are the Greek Parents' Association, the Vietnamese Association and the Chinese Speaking Parents' Association. He and the careers teacher planned to meet all the associations and get them more actively involved in careers planning.

Observers' Model

There seemed little doubt that the provision of careers advice was inhibited by the current Departmental legislation, warning level coordinators and other non-specialist staff of the risk of litigation if they offer advice to students about their futures. The level of cooperation between the careers teacher and other staff such as the pupil welfare coordinator appeared to be considerable, so it was regrettable that the law as it stood, doubtless with the best of intentions, had the effect of reducing what might otherwise be done.

It seems quite apparent that the school had a well-organized system of careers counselling and 'pastoral care' despite the fact that the careers teacher was not truly full-time. Although some additional provisions for the careers room would be desirable, according to comments we received from the careers teacher careers education was well catered for in the organizational and material sense.

The student clients' perceptions of the careers advice they received from all the sources listed in the questionnaire in Appendix 1 varied according to their year levels and ethnic background. The sources could be divided into three categories: family — those from family, relatives and friends outside school; school — sources provided within the school; community — those from outside school in the wider community, including the mass media.

The degree of use of the sources varied from not having an item available through most helpful or fairly helpful to not helpful. For each of these, Table 3 summarizes the total number of mentions of use made of the kinds of information in the three categories of sources, for the students from Indo-Asian and NES backgrounds discussed above. The responses of the sole Anglo-Australian boy are also listed.

Table 3. Degree of Use Made of Sources of Information about Occupational Socialization

Students	Source Categories	Did Not Use	Most Helpful	Fairly Helpful	Not Helpful
Indo-Asian Boys (n = 5)	Family	9	3	16	2
	School	6	8	16	1
	Community	16	2	6	3
Indo-Asian Girls (n = 4)	Family	10	6	6	1
	School	10	5	13	—
	Community	17	1	6	—
NESB Boys (n = 6)	Family	16	13	4	—
	School	22	9	4	—
	Community	22	6	10	4
NESB Girls (n = 5)	Family	16	6	7	1
	School	15	6	10	4
	Community	17	1	5	7
Anglo-Aust. Boy	Family	2	3	1	—
	School	4	1	1	—
	Community	2	2	1	—

The most obvious feature is the large number of mentions of all the sources in the Did Not Use column. The source that was most neglected is community resources, although there is little or nothing separating this source from family and school in the case of the girls from NES backgrounds, and from school in the case of boys from the same backgrounds. The surprising feature was the large number of mentions indicating that the latter did not use either school sources or community sources, but some did find members of the family, relatives and friends either fairly helpful or most helpful.

In the case of Indo-Asian students the fact that they did not use some members of the family, especially father or mother, could have reflected either that they are dead or still in country of origin. Older sisters, other relatives and friends who have jobs received most mention as being most helpful or fairly helpful by Indo-Asian boys, while Indo-Asian girls mentioned older brother, older sister, other relatives and friends.

Fewer girls than boys from NES backgrounds found their family or relatives either most helpful or fairly helpful, and the majority of girls did not use these sources maybe to resist pressure to conform to traditional female careers. The sole Anglo-Australian boy stated that his father, mother and older brother were most helpful while his older sister was fairly helpful.

When the answers to questionnaires are analyzed in more detail further patterns are evident. Within the school two sources stand out. All but two students mentioned the careers teacher as being fairly or most helpful. She was regarded as most helpful by boys from NES backgrounds and fairly helpful by all the Indo-Asian girls. Indo-Asian boys found her either fairly helpful or most helpful. The sole Australian boy in the sample listed the careers teacher as being fairly helpful in his occupational planning.

All but four students across all groups mentioned information in the form of books and special courses on jobs as being fairly or most helpful. In general, however, apart from these, to judge from the number of mentions in the Did Not Use column, other sources of information within the school were not used. There were some exceptions. Ethnic teacher aides and ESL teachers were fairly helpful to a majority of Indo-Asian girls and boys. The majority of these also listed other sources within the school as being fairly or most helpful in contrast to all other groups who did not use them.

These patterns seemed to indicate that Indo-Asian students were concerned to utilize a range of the information sources in the school as much as possible, and this would be consistent with what was mentioned by teachers about the strength of their aspirations and determination to get on. The careers teacher also referred to the way in which Indo-Asian students utilized as much information as they could find.

Another source that received majority mention by all students as being most helpful or fairly helpful was friends at school. This may bear out the research considered in Chapter 1 which found that this influence is quite high in occupational socialization. Overall, the sources outside the school were least used by all students, and some sources were seen as not helpful while some sources were mentioned as being fairly helpful. These were advertisements in papers, on the radio and television.

Conclusion

The systemic responses to the wants and needs of students reflected quite considerable efforts on the part of the school to cater for the degree of ethnocultural pluralism entailed. From our observer's point of view, there seemed to be little or no systemic discrimination working against the interests of students. What we observed bore out the vernacular model as described by staff and outlined in the various documents we consulted. However, external assessments of this kind are one thing, but opinions of those most directly involved, the students, are another. It is to these observers' viewpoints that we turn in the next chapter.

5 Inner City High School: Ethnic Encounters and Ethos of the School

In the previous chapter we considered the students' attitudinal and behavioural reactions to the way Inner City High School arranged its systemic provisions to meet their needs. In this chapter we compare the views of staff about the kinds of ethnic encounters within the school with the students' perceptions of their own reactions to these features of their occupational socialization.

Tensions between and within Ethnic Groups: The Vernacular Model

(1) Interethnic Relations

The staff we talked to were unanimous that some interethnic and racial tension existed below the surface in the school. At the time of the research they claimed that it was not a major factor, although some years ago strains were more apparent. Then occasional open tensions did occur and this applied especially to students in ESL withdrawal classes, who attracted prejudiced comments from other students. According to one ESL teacher: 'Most of the time it doesn't exist here. The Indo-Asians almost outnumber everybody else — those in the minority would be foolish to try anything. We do a lot to try and foster better relations between groups.' However, this opinion may have been too optimistic as in the year following the research serious interethnic tensions and violence erupted and took considerable efforts to contain.

Generally Anglo-Australian students were said to be the ones to feel threatened and this had led to some leaving the school. However, it would appear that matters were not as strained between Anglos and ethnic students as they were in past years when the graffiti 'Wogs rule, skips [Kangaroos-

Anglos] suck' was common on school walls, probably due to the fact that other targets of animosity had taken their place in the 'ethnic succession sequence', discussed in the last chapter.

Recent entry cohorts of NES and Indo-Asian students from primary school had been very self-confident. In 1985 we were told:

> [They] burst in and took over the school. It was like, y'know, this is our place and now you can go jump. They're really incredibly aggressive and self-assertive. There's none of that hiding behind shell-shock [due to being refugees] or sense of being disadvantaged or concerned that they'll never make it in the world of school.

This kind of comment from one of the ESL staff also applied to the younger Greek students: 'all puppy dogs really, really terribly aggressive and self-assertive.' For this reason, tensions may have been more apparent in lower levels of the school than higher. According to one staff member in the ESL Faculty:

> We find it essential to concentrate on the Years 7 and 8 levels. There is covert racial tension underlying activities in the school ... in the sense that children's attitudes have developed from adults ... and because if you have Vietnamese kids they stick together, and you mix with somebody whose cultural assumptions are the same. Cultural separatism is breaking down but it is still a feature. They are quite willing to talk to each other in interaction in classroom situations. As soon as they go out into the playground there is a tendency for them to separate.
>
> And you can't lump the Asians together either. The Vietnamese and Vietnamese Chinese have been forced to be lumped together although they themselves have some tensions between them.... There is a huge amount of tension between those people who come from Vietnam and those that come from Timor. I think that the Hakka-speaking Timorese Chinese are really annoyed that the Vietnamese Chinese can't speak Hakka, and can only speak Cantonese or Vietnamese. The Vietnamese Chinese, of course, don't really like the Vietnamese, but they have been forced by the Timorese kind of isolationism to join up with the Vietnamese in certain circumstances. I have seen this kind of thing happening in [school] camp ... there are certain leaders of the particular ethnic groups who can cause a lot of trouble. You have to isolate them very quickly.

This was an aspect of the school which many general staff may not have seen, as the special sensitivity of the ESL teachers and their regular contact with the Indo-Asian and NES groups appeared to make them more aware of interethnic tensions. As one ESL teacher commented:

> I don't think the staff are terribly aware of it. And also it is breaking down. Last year you would see those groups completely separate. This year I've noticed that people are outside playing volleyball now or handball ... and there's a tendency for somebody to just wander into a game, and there's a Vietnamese and there's a Chinese, and there's another who's a Greek ... as the kids go up into Years 9 and 10 they become so familiar with that.... I think it is breaking down.

In any case it seemed from several comments that all senior students in Years 11 and 12 had more things on their minds than being racist. Concern to do well in studies and the demands of the STC and HSC courses took over, and there were very few incidents in class that indicated serious racial antagonism. As one teacher put it: 'Any problems have been in the Year 8 or 9 or 10 area ... by the time they get to Years 11 and 12 everybody is sitting next to everybody else, and what they're worrying about is the physics problem ... and the whole racial thing seems to disappear.'

This even applied in the case of Indo-Asian students, whose motivation and dedication to hard work — not usually thought of as major Anglo-Australian values — might have been expected to arouse jealousy among their Anglo peers. According to teachers at the senior level this did not happen. Students worked well together and in some cases the Indo-Asian students stimulated other students to emulate them. They provided 'incentive role models' in one ESL teacher's opinion. Teachers universally commended their attitudes to work and were glad to have them in class as they presented no disciplinary problems, worked hard and were invariably polite and exemplary students.

However, there are tensions between other ethnic groups. Asked how Turks got on in the school, one senior master commented with a laugh: 'They're good at fighting. When Turks and Greeks get together it's a real ding-dong.' From other comments we heard family discipline is possibly at the root of this:

> We seem to have a lot of problems with Turkish kids, behaviour problems, concentration in class ... just in the last year or two this has been the case.... I try to trace it to the home — the severe discipline contributes to the problem.
>
> The situation is far more stern for a girl. The solution for the Turkish girl is often that parents send her back to Turkey.

For the girl more than the boy it tends to be a greater problem. A further reason may have been that Turkish parents did not see their stay in Australia as being permanent. It is after all a Christian country and they might have had the idea of themselves as 'guest workers' who would eventually return to Turkey.

Other interethnic tensions were generated outside the school but were brought into it. Occasionally there were brawls between gangs of, say,

Vietnamese and Timorese in the local community during the weekend, and the Timorese would come to school on the Monday very scared that they would be got at by the Vietnamese kids. Gang violence also occurred among other ethnic groups — Greeks, Turks, Yugoslavs, Anglos — and these squabbles could be brought into school 'not very often, but if something happens outside some kids can get involved in it.'

In such cases the pupil welfare coordinator was able to exercise a powerful mediating and conciliating role with leaders of the various ethnic communities, as he was becoming known to them all and occupied a neutral position vis-à-vis the factions. In consequence there was some evidence that interethnic tensions were slowly beginning to break down. School socials were held during the year and until recently were almost exclusively attended by Greeks and Anglos, but slowly more and more Indo-Asians were coming in and joining them.

Some racial tensions were generated and even encouraged by parental attitudes, and regrettably this appeared to apply mostly to Anglo-Australians. As the pupil welfare coordinator put it:

> In many ways I think the Anglos are the sorriest lot in the school ... for two reasons. Firstly, the Anglo parents were very threatened by what was happening here and a lot of the racism that comes through is a direct 'quote', just like a parent speaking. For example, we had an Anglo child who wrote a very racist note and passed it to a Turkish boy. He was reported to his parents who wrote back. 'I do not believe that my son uses this type of language, because only wogs use this type of language.'

Even when the Anglo-Australian child was clearly in the wrong, the parents laid the blame on others.

> I've had kids who have been given detention, and parents come to school and, instead of helping, say 'my daughter tells me that the Asians never get detention.' I keep saying the Asians don't arrive to school late and do their homework, but they don't see it that way.

Other tensions were generated by common stereotypes about recently arrived Indo-Asians. In the words of the pupil welfare coordinator:

> I hear ... and the thing that distresses me most ... all the Greeks and Italian and Turkish kids saying, and Anglos saying: 'the Vietnamese land here, they're given $1000 ... they've been here six months and they've got better than we have.' The cycle's really reversed ... because I keep saying to these kids I remember the Australians saying that about your parents when you came here, about the Greeks, about the Italians.

Some Anglo-Australian students in particular were said to feel resentful of the fact that the ESL Department took up so many resources. According to the pupil welfare coordinator again:

> And one kid said to me 'all the wogs and Asians get better than we do.' Anglos feel threatened by the presence of Vietnamese shops, languages [and say]: 'Why do they come here ... why don't they speak bloody English?' I once thought of setting up an all-Australian Anglo Parents Association, but felt torn by the idea what if it became a we-feel-sorry-for-ourselves group ... an aggressive racist sort of group.
>
> All the others were set up as a support group for their community and for their kids here. I do think that the Australian parents do need some sort of self-esteem and confidence building. But because they feel the way they feel it's so easy for that lack of confidence to turn to a nasty aggression ... and this is where my dilemma is.

The same attitude affected Anglo-Australian students in the school, with apathy being possibly the most obvious characteristic of the attitudes to school work and care about standards. There was little drive from home or interest in school and responses to letters on the part of Anglo parents. 'They sit around feeling sorry for their position, and blaming anything outside without realizing that there is blame, but it's not the wogs' fault, it's not the Asians' fault.'

(2) Intraethnic Tensions

Tensions were generated by social and cultural dynamics within ethnic groups. They were not 'racial' in the common usage of that term, but nevertheless generated pressures on students within the school that could also spread to relationships between them and teachers. In the final analysis these kinds of intraethnic tensions could have a serious effect on occupational socialization.

The transient nature of the school population already mentioned caused problems. It was difficult to get any kind of welfare and careers program established before some families decided to move on and the program collapsed. Part of this involved parents' misperceptions of the role of careers education. In the careers teacher's opinion:

> Many parents see careers as an interesting part of the school ... but like most European parents they see it as a resource within the school, rather than perhaps as an important functioning of the school. They still see English, mathematics and science being important in the classroom.

Family problems were common, but those in some NES and Indo-Asian families involved excruciatingly human dilemmas that could cause particular difficulties for students' occupational socialization. There was the example of a Vietnamese boy, a brilliant 16 years old in Year 9, faced with the choice of leaving school to get a job in order to sponsor his mother out of Vietnam to Australia, or to continue school and go to university and become a professional and then bring her out. He felt that he was being selfish staying at school and his dilemma was generating behavioural problems in class. The converse could also apply. For example, an apparently straightforward family reunification could cause problems for students. This happened in cases where the father or children may have grown away from the relative who was coming to Australia and tensions would build up at home with consequent side-effects in school.

The high, unrealistic expectations and insensitivity of parents from NES backgrounds were a constant problem and some cases have been referred to above. 'First there are the incredible expectations of Greek parents that "my son will be a brain surgeon or my son will be a university professor or whatever", and often the kid just cannot live up to that.' Secondly there was the general attitude of Greek and Turkish parents towards their daughters. Lots of cases of indifference to or outright lack of support for their education quite frequently came to the attention of the careers teacher and pupil welfare coordinator, when appeals for special consideration in the HSC examination had to be lodged. According to the pupil welfare coordinator:

> You might have a Greek girl doing HSC, and her parents are very traditional and just don't see why she should have any education at all ... and this kid's trying to cope with HSC and dad will come home at one o'clock in the morning, after playing cards or something, and he'll wake up the kid and say 'where's the coffee?' ... and the kid has to cope with those sorts of things.
>
> Or sometimes mum, who's lovely but doesn't understand, says: 'Look, you're locking yourself up in your room all night, come out, have coffee with us, watch television.' And the kid keeps saying 'but I've got to study'. And the parents say 'You're seventeen or eighteen, you don't like us any more, you're not part of the family.'

Indo-Asian girls were said to be not affected in the same way as their parents see education for girls as an important avenue for upward social mobility. As one ESL teacher pointed out women have much more status in Asian society and quite often control the purse strings. In China women hold senior government positions.

In fact, the retention rate at HSC for Vietnamese and other Indo-Asian girls in the school was much higher than for the boys. One reason may have been that the Indo-Asian boys have to go out to work and earn money. They were able to do this as a lot of the Indo-Asian students were much older than stated on paper for school records. If they had stated their real ages when applying for admission to Australia, they would not have been approved under immigration regulations.

In the careers teacher's opinion, pressure from parents and even peers had much more impact than her advice. It was stronger with children from Indo-Asian and NES backgrounds, who were influenced by their parents more than Australian children. As she pointed out:

> The Asian girls are much more affected by parental pressure. Asian kids are much more concerned with their parents' expectations regarding success and monetary gains than any other group of kids I have known. They are much more affected by that than by anything I say.
>
> I have never known Anglo parents to be so dogmatic about what they want as especially Greek parents can be. If their girls want to be a computer operator or something like that, they are very often criticized for it, and get a lot of flak. It's not considered feminine or traditional — girls who want to go and do tertiary subjects have a really hard time, but a lot do still ... it doesn't seem to stop them, but they will still go into very traditional areas. They would not go into engineering or anything like that.

Fortunately this did not apply to all the girls from NES backgrounds. In senior school, according to the careers teacher, there was an appreciable difference between the Greek girls who were born in Australia and were quite assertive, and those born in Greece who had to conform more to the Greek female stereotype. Several of the former Greek girl students had developed feminist attitudes, and had gone to university. They had been exceptionally independent, according to the pupil welfare coordinator, and broke out of their traditional Greek background to 'do their own thing'. Greek and Turkish girls were generally not allowed to go on school camps though there were some few exceptions. One Turkish parent did not even want his daughter to attend the school because there were boys in it.

These aspects confirmed our hypothesis about the existence of 'fossilized' migrant cultures in Melbourne, a point which was also brought out without prompting by the pupil welfare coordinator:

> The other thing that's important with the Greek stuff is that the Greeks who came out here twenty-five, thirty-five years ago have done ... have put on Greek culture in Greece thirty-five years ago and they haven't changed. They go back to Greece and they can't handle Greece because they think that everything in Greece is wonderful, and they see that the Greek kids in Greece are exactly the same as the Australian kids here.
>
> They've broken tradition and they've broken with village life, and they go to Athens and they share flats with their boy friends and things like that. But they [parents] can't cope with that ... because

the only way they survived in Australia was by keeping their Greekness ... and you take away their thirty-year-old Greekness ... and you've broken them.

(3) Sexism

A further cause of tension that affected migrant girls in particular was the sexist attitudes of the boys especially from their own ethnic group. This was very common and affected not only Greek and Turkish boys versus girls but also lady teachers. As we were told: 'A young, attractive lady teacher is going to get hell ... quite often from the Greek boys.'

The pupil welfare coordinator gave an interesting insight into how this phenomenon developed:

> You can see that from the little ones in Year 7.... It's interesting, a matter of dual perception, but little Greek girls always seem to me to be very happy until they get to teenage, then they kind of lose it ... and once you see little Greek boys get to ... y'know, from about eight to nine on they walk around like ... [laughs] like they're gods. A lot of lady teachers get a lot of problems with Greek and Turkish boys and this macho stuff ... it's very difficult.

We were told that male Greek teachers had been deliberately appointed to control groups of Greek boys, who were known to be particularly rowdy and difficult, and likely to give lady teachers a bad time. 'It was thought that a Greek male was needed to handle them and that proved good — I don't think a woman would have coped with that — I mean the boys wouldn't have had the same kind of respect, so that has been a good point.'

However, we were also informed that staff appointments of this kind allegedly had not necessarily increased the degree of sensitivity to this kind of situation. As one female teacher put it:

> Sometimes they are frightfully conservative, and I find it a bit alarming that male teachers can reinforce especially Greek prejudices, and often the female teachers I know get a hard time from the Greek boys, so that possibly makes them not able to function as effectively as they might.

Although the effect on female teachers should not be discounted, the effect of Greek boys' macho behaviour on the Greek girls' self-esteem and self-confidence may not have been as bad as one might imagine. In the opinion of one teacher:

> Well, they cope with it and they accept it ... it's part of what it's like to grow up ... but they themselves accept it, and it's amazing to see how some of the exceptionally bright girls are still lorded over by

some of the moronic boys, who have absolutely no intellectual capacity ... um ... but they're still the boss in a relationship.

Ethos and Interethnic Dynamics: The Observers' Model

(1)   School Ethos

To stroll along a corridor adjacent to classrooms at recess or lunch time was to be immediately engulfed in a jostling sea of boys and girls from obviously different, non-Anglo-Saxon backgrounds. Absence of compulsory school uniform and the consequent colourful variety of jeans, skirts, dresses, jumpers, parkas and shirts added to the cultural kaleidoscope. Some kids were poorly dressed which hinted at impoverished home backgrounds. The chatter in a variety of languges compounded the kaleidoscopic effect.

Individuals and clusters of students from Indo-Asian origins stood out by virtue of their appearance, but also obvious both in appearance and manner were those from Southern European backgrounds. Whereas the senior Indo-Asian students seemed to be quieter and more reserved, going about their business with wary detachment, the Southern European students were more boisterous and even 'pushy'. Some boys taunted the girls and in reply got a quick, saucy retort or a sexy toss of the head. In the quadrangle some Southern European boys were heard to throw mild insults at another boy, who replied with a half-audible comment in which the word 'wogs' could be distinguished. In contrast, the Asian boys and girls seemed more remote from each other, watchful and careful of their personal share of social space.

There seemed to be little discernible tension; mostly the kids were concerned to grab books and bags and get into class or away from the school at the end of the day. Some pushing and jostling were inevitable and apparently good natured, especially between the younger kids who were the most boisterous and occasionally erupted into wrestling matches or mimicked the latest TV karate hero. One moved in and out of the jostling swirl, dodging young bodies and swinging bags, catching an eye here and a tentative smile there especially from students one had interviewed for the research some time previously. Beneath the surface there could well have been tension and almost certainly a 'hidden curriculum', but it was not something one could 'feel' in the way one could in some other schools.

However, the sight of a senior member of staff ticking off a student in one of the counselling rooms outside the principal's office always came as a salutary reminder not to romanticize the kids in this school. They presented as many disciplinary problems as any others. The playground also dispelled idealistic notions. Although some mixed groups of students from Indo-Asian and NES backgrounds played handball or some other sport together, as many others could be seen keeping to their separate ethnic groups. They sat around on benches eating lunches and chatting often in separate sex groups. There was no discernible interethnic tension, but knowledge that it could have erupted at any time was always present in the back of one's mind.

(2)   Students' Perceptions of Prejudice and Discrimination

Discussions with students did not show up the degree of prejudice that comments from staff might lead one to expect. In particular there was virtually no evidence from NES or Indo-Asian students of perceived racial prejudice from members of staff towards students. Most comments concerned relationships between students from different NES backgrounds or the influence of family pressures, and these varied according to the ethnic groups.

(i)   Perceptions of Indo-Asian Students.   For the two groups of Indo-Asians and Timorese we interviewed, lack of or difficulty with English was clearly the major problem. One also needed experience to get a job we were informed, and although several of the students had part-time jobs or had had experience, they still felt that this was a difficulty. 'A lot of our friends leave uni. but still can't find a job.' The economic climate of the times in Australia was a major factor in this situation.

However, more discriminatory aspects were also involved. In the opinion of one Indo-Asian girl, it would be more difficult for girls as they might not be strong enough for factory work. However, another girl felt that some Vietnamese boys could find it harder to get jobs than Vietnamese girls, who could find employment in restaurants or sewing in a clothing factory. She herself had worked in a sewing factory:

> It was not difficult, I know how to sew. Then there is the prejudice when you go for a job. It's not in this school, they are more prejudiced in other schools. We don't think there's prejudice in this school. But when you go for a job people say 'your English is not good enough', and they ask you to go home.

There were no problems with Anglo-Australian neighbours in the flats where they lived as the students rarely talked to them: poor English set up a communication barrier.

In the questionnaire we asked a sentence-completion question: 'When I think about the future I feel ... ', and following it gave space for students to give reasons in answer to a supplementary prompt: 'Because....' How did the Indo-Asian students respond?

It was this group of students who revealed a very high degree of anxiety and uncertainty in their answers to the sentence-completion question: 'I don't know', 'I am anxious', 'I am worried, excited', 'Anything can happen to me', were the main kinds of responses, but no reference was made to prejudice or discrimination causing the anxiety.

However, there were some mild sexist references from the Indo-Asian boys, based on traditional expectations of women's roles. 'If I get a good job, I'll expect my wife to stay home, y'know', was the opinion of one boy, who was the most proficient with English, and acted as spokesman for the group of Indo-Asian boys. He also stated: 'Actually, in my country the girls all stay home when they get married.' Other boys concurred, but difficulty with English and the wish to please us by giving the expected answer may have made their concurrence of doubtful validity. None of the girls referred to similar issues.

(ii) Perceptions of Girls from NES Backgrounds. The group of girls from NES backgrounds at the Year 12 STC level was far different: English was no problem and they were excited, very confident and outspoken. Their answers to 'When I think ...' stressed this confidence: 'Certain I will succeed and have a bright future', 'Very confident and secure about my career', 'Happy, positive', 'I will be very competent and capable of finding a job or being accepted into an institute' were the kinds of answers that contrasted with the Indo-Asian girls.

One girl did admit to being 'very scared', but she was the only one. Her reason was that she did 'not want to get knocked.' The others who gave reasons for their confidence backed it by assertions that stressed personal and social dimensions, such as 'I have confidence in myself to pursue my goal', 'I am certain of exactly what lies ahead of me', rather than economic considerations. There was no mention in these written answers of prejudice, discrimination or even the kinds of family pressures that their NES backgrounds would lead one to expect.

During discussion the girls tended to dismiss the influence of possible prejudice arising from their backgrounds on their choice of careers, and put most reliance on passing examinations and education as the key to getting a job. 'If you do all the work that's required I reckon you've got a good chance of getting into somewhere ... it doesn't matter if you're from a different background. It's the work ... the education ... that's right' [a chorus of agreement]. Another girl said: 'If you go for a job and you haven't done the subjects required that's when they knock you back, not because you're Greek or Italian. In any case you should already have made up your mind by Year 11 level.' Doing STC was seen as an advantage because 'you get offers of jobs earlier than students doing HSC.'

The girls claimed that their families were also behind them, and were happy about their job choices and planning for careers. One girl's family wanted her to be a primary teacher, but she had chosen to be a nurse, 'because I don't like little brats.' Another had planned to be a draftsperson, but when she saw the teaching jobs available in Greece she changed her mind, and now planned to become a teacher of English there. It was obvious how the girls' views differed from those of the staff described above, which stressed the traditional constraints imposed by NES families.

The influences on girls from parents to get married early and have children were quickly dismissed:

> That's in the villages [contemptuously] ... they don't get a chance to know what life's really about. People are really backminded, y'know. If they can't continue in their education that's when they're forced into marriage ... because what are they going to do without education? They've got to have somebody to support them like their husband or something.

Sexist discrimination and Greek boys' macho attitudes were also dismissed contemptuously. These girls exuded confidence: 'We're used to it ... it's something you're used to ... we don't like it [emphatically], but don't really worry about it.' The girls also said that resistance to the macho behaviour and expectations of boys could take the form of defiance. 'That works too, but then they get worse, start fighting ... I think these things can be overcome. It's not a big problem with Greek culture.'

(iii) Perceptions of Boys from NES Backgrounds. The Greek and Italian boys doing STC took a different line. They had mixed opinions about whether girls have the same or different chances compared with boys. According to them, being a migrant girl is not really a difficulty:

> It depends ... depends on the guy ... if the guy's prejudiced, the employer ... some are.
> I reckon girls have the same problems as boys because girls seem to sort of just go for all the usual jobs, secretaries, hairdressers ... they limit themselves, they don't bother to go up against guys for assistant managers, or managers, or company ... they don't think they've got a good enough chance ... they've a good enough chance as anybody else.

All the boys bar one were born in Australia, but it was clear that some traditional values still influenced them though whether answers were exaggerated for our benefit was hard to establish. On marriage and the place of the wife, for example:

> ... she should work full time, have kids ... plan her days and work part-time ... have kids ... I'd lock her up ... I'd want her to be my secretary ... me too to help me around the hairdressing salon [from the boy who wants to become a hairdresser and gets continual ribbing from the others].

We were struck by the bragging immaturity and silliness of the boys compared with the girls. Many of the boys' comments lapsed into mumbles or giggles and it was difficult to see where the male macho arrogance came from in this group.

Their views about the future in answer to the 'When I think ...' prompt stressed optimism more than pessimism. These boys felt: '... that things will change dramatically', 'happy', 'ready for life', 'excited', 'confident'. One boy was ambiguous: '... if I don't become what I want, maybe I won't find a job.' The reasons for their feelings stressed economic aspects more than social or personal aspects: moral positioning seemed to be weaker than was the case with the girls. The boys felt the way they did because: 'Of new technology', 'It's a new type of job that I'm doing', 'If I don't succeed as an accountant I can surely start my own business.' One or two boys had other reasons: 'My relatives will give me a lot of support', 'Others may want the same job.'

Generally, however, there was quite a contrast between both of these groups of established students from NES backgrounds and the Indo-Asians discussed earlier. Confidence was more apparent, particularly among the Greek and Italian girls. English was not a problem — several were very articulate — and perceptions of prejudice or difficulty in the future seemed to be virtually non-existent. There was no way of knowing whether these students were an atypical example, and whether we would have met less confident students at other interviews. It was also quite apparent that the students' views on prejudice from other ethnic groups and the influence of their families differed from those of the staff described above and raised the question as to who was using stereotypes — staff or students.

General Conclusions

The answer could lie in the unexpected characteristics of the systemic influences on the students. The picture that we expected to find in the school, located as it is in a high ethnic density and low socio-economic area with an insalubrious reputation, did not emerge. Instead, the overall and abiding impression of the school was its dedicated, purposeful staff, tight but unobtrusive control and meticulous daily organization. Morale appeared to be very high: there was an obvious sense of purpose and confidence about the place, and the school was buzzing away very busily.

Difficulties there undoubtedly were, but they were not obtrusively evident to us and did not add up to a pattern of chronic disadvantage. More importantly, they did not indicate a staff intent on maintaining a degree of social reproduction and Anglo-Australian ethnocultural hegemony over students from different Indo-Asian and NES backgrounds. The reverse was truer. Much of the curriculum was a direct response to students' expressed needs, especially those from NES and Indo-Asian backgrounds. Systemic constraints from the bureaucracy outside the school were a main source of difficulties, but the staff were trying hard to overcome them in various ways.

What discrimination there was appeared to be largely self-imposed, by the small Anglo-Australian minority on themselves, aided and abetted by their parents. Indo-Asian students were far from discriminated against, as the staff were 'bending over backwards' to help them partly because they are a pleasure to have in class. Some interethnic prejudice and tensions were obvious, but they were mostly at the personal, name-calling level rather than the kind of deeply ingrained, sullen pattern of suspicion and tension that can be found in other schools. Racist graffiti were quite rare and supported this picture.

It would be invalid to generalize from this case study to other inner-city schools, but it may not be so atypical of others, for all its difference from the common stereotype of disadvantaged urban education. It was refreshing to find one example that ran counter to prevailing views about the poor state of the education system in Victoria.

6 Suburbia High School: Curricular Responses to Students' Needs and Aspiratons

Out in the suburbs of Melbourne, as is the case in most other major cities, the ecological context of the schools changes to one of diversity and complexity of ethnic and socio-economic groups. In fact, so big is Surburbia High School that it contains within its student population representatives from all the ethclasses selected for the research on which this book is based. 'The school is like a pot-pourri, cosmopolitan and varied', the principal commented. A drive around the school catchment areas, roughly arranged like the points of a compass, confirmed this.

(1) The Northwest

A depressing drive westwards along a main arterial highway, through a dreary and overcrowded vista of service stations, used and new car yards, old weatherboard houses, the occasional seedy hotel or pub, a variety of small shops and scattered infrequent blocks of flats, takes one into an obviously lower-working-class area of small Housing Commission houses: single or double-fronted brick veneer, others timber weatherboard, many showing clear signs of neglect and poverty. Few of the cars parked outside are recent models; some are 'bombs'. Despite small areas of more substantial and better-off houses, to many observers this could well be tantamount to a western 'Waste Land' (Eliot, 1936).

Further out still are factories, food-processing and car-assembly plants, some of them belonging to major multinational companies. On one side of the highway to the northwest there is a sequence of railway stations, their names made notorious by media reports of violence and vandalism on the trains. Periodically an ambulance or police van screams by, compounding the depression the area generates. It is not supported by adequate services such as transport, social welfare or recreation facilities for youth. There is no local cinema nor theatre, neither is there a local hospital. The lack of such standard facilities is bitterly felt particularly by local youth, one of whom spoke for many: 'They think we're scum.'

A migrant hostel some kilometres away from the immediate area funnels recent immigrants into it, in part because of the availability of low-cost accommodation and possibilities of employment in the local industries. Some 32 per cent of the population in this ethclass were born overseas. Many are impoverished, some are refugees, most are semi-skilled or unskilled and along with permanent residents look to the local factories and assembly plants for jobs.

Three main industries provide these: clothing and footwear (overwhelmingly female employment), transport equipment (overwhelmingly male employment), and other machinery and equipment. Food processing is another local industry. In all there are thirty industries located in this industrial region. But many of these are declining in the economic recession and restructuring of secondary industry partly due to international and multinational pressures, consequently there is very high unemployment in the whole area. This is where the harsh realities of lower-working-class and ethnic background come together to form a severely disadvantaged ethclass.

(2)   The Southeast

In some ways the southeast area is like its northwestern counterpart, being a lower-middle to middle-class residential area, with a high ethnic population, which has grown rapidly in the last twenty years under the stimulus of successive land sub-divisions and quick housing development. Industrial development has also taken advantage of the availability of cheap land so that a string of light industries, car-assembly and other fabricating plants and their related services of all description line the main roads and extend away from them into industrial estates and factory clusters.

Many comparable features are present: a migrant hostel and a Language Centre located further out to the south, a Housing Commission estate, pockets of chronic socio-economic disadvantage. Petty crime and the incidence of jail sentences are high. Lots of homes have videos, but many problem homes also experience physical violence, alcoholism and broken marriages. Fifteen per cent of the parent population are on social welfare benefits, due to being unemployed or single parents. Fastfoods are common elements in students' diets and the area is well catered for in this respect.

Unlike the northwest, services such as good transport, social welfare facilities, entertainment and medical care are available. Consequently the area has not developed the demoralizing features and reputation for severe social pathology that spring to mind when the north western area is mentioned. The southeastern region has not been as neglected by governments, even though in many other ways it provides a broadly comparable ethclass and feeder area for Suburbia High School.

The majority of parents are factory workers, craftsmen, tradesmen, clerical workers, service workers and lower professionals, administrators or managers. Shop proprietors, drivers and labourers are other categories. In general they do not aspire highly for their children, and in the opinion of some staff are quite apathetic — apathy being probably the most frequently mentioned characteristic of the whole area and many students.

(3)   The North

The drive out into the northern area is in stark contrast. This is the 'sherry-and-Tupperware' belt of well-to-do middle- and upper-class residential houses, many double storey, solid brick or brick veneer, set in undulating terrain on one cluster of the sandstone hills that play such a major part in determining the housing patterns (and prices) in Melbourne. No timber weatherboard houses here. There is very little fabricating or light engineering, but a considerable number of service industries related to a large shopping complex and local hospital.

The residents in this area are predictable: middle- to upper-level young executives and professionals, entrepreneurs, 'good people' in the opinion of the principal of Suburbia High School. There is considerable 'leakage' from this area, as many parents are well-off and able to send children to the several private schools that are located in or around it. Despite this, significant numbers from such backgrounds still attend the school, attracted to it by a high reputation for teaching mathematics and sciences, and also a certain element of traditionalism in uniform and discipline.

One result of such a professional and executive background quickly made itself apparent during discussions with senior students. Several commented that they have role models in successful parents or friends of the family who could give advice on similar career options or demonstrate the rewards of economic success and a good education. They also commented that there is no shortage of books and other facilities for study at home.

Contrary to what one might expect, as one does not usually associate such a density with this kind of middle- to upper-middle-class area, the proportion of parents and students from migrant and ethnic backgrounds is surprisingly high. This is because the area has attracted into it upwardly socially mobile migrants who have done well enough economically to move out of the traditional areas of first settlement. Such migrants are typically Greeks, Italians and some Yugoslavs. Other non-Anglo groups in the area are second-generation migrants and well-established ethnic groups who have lived in Australia for many years. Chief among them are Chinese; there are very few if any recently arrived Indo-Asians, although this is the kind of area to which they aspire.

(4) The East

The look and smell of eucalypt-gum trees and semi-rural atmosphere of this area signify that intangible sense of the 'bush' familiar to those who live in Melbourne. But even this rural enclave is suffering changes due to multi-lane highway development that has attracted light industries and modern factories. Despite these, the area is still predominantly residential, with mixed kinds of housing ranging from modern 'trendy' architecture to many surviving timber weatherboards and even the occasional small 'shack', reminding one of the time some thirty years ago when much of the area was used by Melbournians to 'get away from it all' during the weekend.

The population matches the area and is also varied. There are a few parents who are process workers in the light industries, but others are trade-trained skilled artisans owning and running their own businesses. Many others are in service or semi-professional and middle-level executive occupations, such as nurses, teachers, civil servants in state or local governments, who work locally or commute into the inner-city central business district. Many of these, especially those with British immigrant background, have a strong trade union consciousness which made itself felt during discussions with some students and affects parents' negotiations with the school.

Although this is generally an area with a very low ethnic and immigrant population, there are two groups who send their children to the school. The first comprises well-established second- or earlier generation British, Dutch and German migrant-settlers. Their children speak English at home, but maintained during discussions that this does not mean that they are the same as Anglo-Australians, and should be thought of as 'migrants'. The second group comprises religious communities with a fundamentalist orientation; this is the eastern 'Bible belt'.

Despite this, there is a small but significant number of problem homes in the area, due to substantial unemployment, single-parent or broken families. A few homes present complex domestic problems, which have resulted in girls at risk having to be removed and housed in a local refuge house. However, the principal of Suburbia High School also said that most of the students 'come from caring homes.'

(5) The Inner Northeast

Everything about this area spells tradition and conservatism. The suburb is exclusively residential, 'comfortable' middle- to upper-class homes: the kind listed by estate agents as 'highly desirable', with house prices correspondingly high. Most houses are solid brick or of a gracious weatherboard design and slightly old-fashioned, set in pleasant gardens. All is typical, almost stereotypical, of a long-established and conservative Melbourne suburb, with tree-lined streets, grass nature strips and general air of clean, well-kept order. The residential character of the area limits local job opportunity, but this hardly matters, as getting into the university is high on the list of career aspirations for most students and their parents. As the principal pointed out: 'many are not looking to get their hands dirty.'

The proportion of families from migrant and ethnic backgrounds is fairly high as, like the north, this area has attracted into it second-generation migrants who have 'made it' socio-economically and, according to one member of staff, 'improved themselves by moving into the area. We rarely get migrants straight off the boat.' Greek students predominate, followed by Chinese, Italians, and a few Vietnamese Chinese who have been able to shift away from the inner city or southeastern areas of first settlement.

(6)   The Inner Southwest

In some senses a counterpart of this area is located in the inner southwest quadrant, close to the school. It is a lower-middle to middle-class suburb, which has improved socio-economically in the last twenty years or so. A major feature of the area is the local shopping complex of small shops, restaurants, delicatessens and greengrocery suppliers. Most of these bear Greek and Italian names, but a small and increasing number is owned by Vietnamese or Chinese, to judge from the writing on their facades.

The latter reflect the fact that demographic changes are taking place, as they have been doing for many years. Twenty-five to thirty years ago the inhabitants were predominantly Anglo-Australians, but in the post-war period of high immigration the suburb became an area of ethnic second settlement. The predominant ethnic group is now Greek — this is almost a little Athens — served by a local Greek ethnic school that has syphoned students away from Suburbia High, and several Greek churches. Graffiti near the railway station in this suburb advise the reader that 'wogs rule ... skips suck' (skips or skippies = kangaroos, i.e., Anglo-Australians), and are also a reminder that historically this suburb has experienced interethnic tensions and even violence between Greeks and other groups. Although Greeks occupy the same demographic position now as Anglo-Australians did some twenty-five to thirty years ago, they may ultimately give way to the steady influx of Indo-Asians coming out of the migrant hostel well to the southeast after a temporary stay to find their feet. The northern and even northeastern suburbs could be the next destination for the Greeks.

Students' Needs and Aspirations: The Vernacular Model

The cosmopolitan nature of some areas in the catchment of Suburbia High School was reflected in the composition of the student population. This totalled approximately 1100 students. Of these 58 per cent were from Anglo-Australian background, while the remaining 42 per cent came from twenty-six different language groups. Greeks were in the majority (14 per cent of the total population), followed by Italians (9 per cent), Indo-Asian and Chinese (7 per cent), and Yugoslavs (3 per cent). There was also a small and, as the description below indicates. vocal group of students from British origin. It quickly became obvious that the patterns of students' aspirations and needs matched the ethnic categories, and can be discussed in the main groupings adopted below (which we used for the previous chapter despite their departure from strict Education Department terminology).

(1) Anglo-Australian Students

Staff comments clearly demonstrated that in comparison with NES or Asian students, Anglo-Australian students showed different approaches to making career scenarios. However, this did not apply across the board to all Anglo-Australian students, as the level of aspirations and degree of motivation appeared to be correlated with the SES characteristics of the ethclass. This was most marked when the polar cases of the northern area (high ethnicity and high SES) and inner northeast area (low ethnicity and middle to high SES) were compared with the northwestern or southeastern areas (high ethnicity and low SES).

In the former areas aspirations and motivation were generally high regardless of ethnicity. 'People from those areas have all had to get to a level of wealth so that aspirations are similar in degree but there are differences across ethnic groups', one teacher commented. Parents were said to be very ambitious for their kids: 'By Year 12 most middle-class students know where they want to go and persuade their parents.' But even they 'don't stand out as much as migrant parents.'

In this case there were also intraethclass variations, which strengthened the impression of the effect of SES. 'Australians are a mixture. The middle-class group in the northeast have high aspirations and want a good school that adheres to conventional standards. [Students from] the lower-social-class conditions in the newer area [in the southeast] also want to do well but. . . .' The implication given by the accompanying gesture was that aspirations and parental drive in that area did not match those from elsewhere.

In the case of the two high ethnicity, low socio-economic areas the picture was different. Parental and student apathy was one of the most frequently mentioned aspects:

> Parents are factory workers who do not motivate their kids. Students
> at Year 12 are apathetic and don't seek advice. This is a dead flat area,
> and terribly apathetic. Students are low achievers, and some have a
> low level of English. Standard of work is not very high. There are
> few goers, but very few.

Paradoxically, although the general level of English among students from
this area was cause for concern on the part of staff, the number of students
involved in mathematics was very high. Staff could also point to many areas
where students were both active and interested in a wide range of learning
activities. However, very few students ended up by going on to university,
but TAFE colleges after Year 11 attracted some. Students going into business
courses were rare. Those who left mainly went into local factories, shops and
fastfood chains such as MacDonalds.

Supporting opinions were given by staff about the comparable northwestern ethclass area:

> There's a high drop-out rate at Years 11 and 12. Low parental interest,
> kids get away with a hell of a lot at home, they know the limits of
> what we can or can't do. They let off a lot of steam here that they
> can't at home. A tough, consistent teacher earns a lot of respect.

Another comment in a similar vein was that some parents neglected kids and
did not give them enough care and guidance. 'They are ignorant of how to
go about it and are basically incompetent parents.' In comparison, kids from
NES backgrounds, especially girls, were said to be more looked after and
controlled. According to another male teacher:

> Australian kids [from that area] are just content to plod along. They
> don't know the answers to virtually all questions. Migrant parents
> have come to Australia looking for a new life. They work hard and
> [say] 'every opportunity for my kids.' This is very rarely said by
> Australian parents, who are much more flexible and let their kids
> have leeway re job choice, leaving school, etc.

Such parents were more inclined to 'rubber stamp' what their children
decided to do. Such Anglo-Australian parents tended to look more to
apprenticeships or were happy to let their kids leave school early and work in
a supermarket.

These were not isolated comments confined to one area. Repeatedly the
same concerns surfaced from staff and indicated unequivocally that Anglo-
Australians were broader in their aspirations than students from ethnic
backgrounds. Anglo students did tend to be less ignorant about the outside
world and available jobs and were also more realistic about their job chances,
but did not aspire as highly as NES and Asian students. However, they
tended to aspire to jobs that were a bit higher than parents but not
exceptionally so. Boys had higher aspirations than girls: they would not

consider jobs in a supermarket, for example. Pressure from their parents was similarly broader and was less than that put on students from NES or Asian backgrounds and may often have been virtually non-existent.

(2)   Students from NES Backgrounds

Comments about Anglo-Australian students were almost invariably made to point up the degree to which students from NES (and Asian) backgrounds were different and usually superior. Whereas comments on Anglo-Australians tended to be somewhat vague, those about NES students were definite to the point where one must wonder whether they were virtually stereotypes. The implications of this possibility are considered in our final chapter.

Staff comments stressed that many NES parents and some students — Greeks and Italians being most mentioned in this respect — had aspirations that were extremely high and often unrealistic considering the academic talents of the students. 'Compared with Anglos, more pressure is put on NES students so that many aspire to unrealistic professions, e.g. for Greeks it has to be doctors', the Year 11 coordinator told us. One reason for this was considered to be the strong family and community pressure for the students 'to make something of themselves'. In the Greek community, for example, parents tended to compare their children with other relatives that had done well and expected them to do better. Parents thus wanted heavy academic education and exclusively HSC for their children on the assumption that education per se, rather than hard work, was the key to success. They had great awe of and faith in teachers. Education had to be 'facts' oriented. Compared with Anglo-Australians, NES parents tended to help students select subjects and oversee things generally.

However, in some cases parental aspirations often exceeded the children's more realistic assessments of their own capabilities. According to the Year 12 coordinator: 'So many migrant parents have high aspirations. Sometimes students are brain-washed and think that they are better than they are.' There was also an alternative reaction brought about by unrealistic parents' aspirations, while the students were more realistic. This could put students under considerable emotional strain, according to the careers teacher. The student welfare teacher commented that:

> Migrant parents think that the magic formula for a successful job and life is school ... length of time at school equals a job such as doctor, lawyer or whatever. For example, these Spanish parents [in the western area] require this to be achieved, but the boy is really worried that he cannot do it. [There is] no way of breaking this to his parents.

This kind of reaction was not confined to boys, although they were more likely to be favoured and pressured than girls. For example, even Greek girls in Year 10 could be pushed by parents to get to university, especially Melbourne University. There was the case of a girl from the northern suburb coming to the careers teacher in tears because her parents had decided she had to go to Melbourne University to get a degree, but she knew that she would not pass HSC.

Despite the strong emphasis they placed on academic education, some Greek and other NES families did not have relevant study books at home and often made demands on their children that were not in their academic interests. For example, we were told by the careers teacher that for many families from NES backgrounds there were family 'visiting' commitments which ate into study time. 'Even second generation migrants find it difficult to understand the needs of their children. For example, they will lock little Johnny in his room and he'll "work, work, work".'

However, the degree of pressure from NES parents was not ubiquitously strong and appeared to vary for a number of reasons. Firstly, there was some evidence, as in the case of Anglo-Australian students, that SES factors influenced aspirations. NES parents in upper- and middle-class areas pushed their children to achieve, whereas in lower-class areas this pressure varied. For example, according to the vice principal, in the southeastern suburb there was lack of ambition 'even among Greek students ... Greeks are not ambitious compared with those in the northern suburbs.' The degree of general apathy in this area may have had some general influence here.

Parental pressure may also have varied due to the relative size of their local ethnic community. This was one explanation offered to explain the lack of parental ambition among Greek parents in the southeast, where Greeks were not the dominant community as was the case with the southwest area. Another explanation was that many Greek and Italian families were second generation and thus had reduced motivation to get on. However, this did not apply in the case of the northern, southwestern and northeastern areas. Even in the northwestern area there was considerable migrant drive.

An interesting, sociological explanation for these differences, provided by the local community education officer, was that migrant parents' aspirations and motivation to succeed depended on the degree to which they have managed to learn how to 'work' the Western capitalist system: 'Those parents who know Western capitalist culture, once they overcome the English problem, succeed. The low-income people who don't know this culture, don't know how to get on ... [it's] very much a "culture of poverty thing".' It is oversimplistic for us to claim that high parental aspirations applied across the NES board, without also noting that intraethclass variations existed and may have been more related to SES differences than other factors. This issue is taken up in the last chapter.

Staff pointed out that variation was also evident in the reactions of NES students to parental presure. Some Greek students reacted to it by being overambitious in the opinion of teachers, but as a result students found it hard to come to terms with their own lack of ability. They were also restrictive in the courses they aim for: '... it must be uni. and only in the area of sciences. They can't even look at the possibility of failure at Year 12, can't deviate' (careers teacher). It was thus sometimes difficult for staff to place Greek and Italian students in courses that their parents demanded, especially where they would not allow students to do an alternative to the HSC or consider a technical option.

In marked contrast there were the comments providing examples of second generation NES students who tended to be 'laid back and casual'. Greek students from families that had 'made it' were happy to spend the afternoon playing volleyball rather than go home to study. This may have been an atypical or possibly a generational problem, as comments from several teachers suggested that there seemed to be a disproportionate number of low achievers in the second generation students from the northern suburb. According to the Year 11 coordinator: 'First phase are very high; the second phase just sit there.' A similar comment was made about students from the southeastern suburb, although it was also noted that there was always a small group with recognized middle-class aspirations.

(3) Indo-Asian and Asian Students

Students from Asian backgrounds had a number of features in common, although there were some variations due to their countries of origin. Ethnic Chinese were from Indo-China and Timor, and Chinese generally came from such countries as Hong Kong, Singapore and Malaysia. Many of these were second generation. There were also Vietnamese, Laotians, Cambodians and others from the Indo-China region. These were invariably first generation, were found in ethclasses of first settlement and were most likely to pose first-phase learning problems especially in English. A few Asians were from the Indian sub-continent and Sri Lanka.

The great majority of Asians were regarded very highly by teachers and this applied regardless of SES background. Staff stated that they were highly motivated to academic study and were fully aware of its importance for getting into professional careers, which was the ambition of the majority. 'Indian, Singhalese and Asian parents know traditional academic education, and want their children to have a good education' (careers teacher).

Students and parents knew what they wanted from a school and supported moves that would improve its academic facilities. The principal told us:

> The school set up a cooperative to buy computers. The ethnic people who turned up could see what they could get, where they were going ... [they had] clear perceptions and were articulate, e.g., medicine, economics and political science. One Italian family in

particular, likewise Chinese people who turned up. They had very clear ideas.

Staff also perceived Asians as having very high aspirations and being 'brighter' and more motivated than other NES and Anglo-Australian students. However, with some very few exceptions, Asians' aspirations did not seem to be viewed in the same, slightly disparaging way as were those of some NES groups. According to the careers teacher: 'Asians are more recent arrivals here. They have reasonably high aspirations, but not out of their reach. The ones I have placed [in careers] were talented. Many are in the computer field and maths. area.' Despite this, like similar cases from NES backgrounds discussed above, 'some Asian students do have problems with parents whose families have set a path for them to get into, say, medicine, and the student does not feel capable of achieving this or does not want to.'

Chinese students were invariably spoken of as standing out academically from all other students, but it was also conceded that some Chinese students may not have been typical of Asians in general. Many were second generation and, being born in Australia, had fewer problems with English than other Asians.

Chinese students here are second generation and come from upper-class family backgrounds, with many fathers already in professions such as medicine. They are not really Chinese, as they speak English very well. They are a small number and don't stand out as a distinct group in the school (principal).

Other Chinese were private students who had come to Australia as sojourners for one or two years from such countries as Hong Kong, Singapore and Malaysia with the express purpose of getting the HSC qualification and returning home. This was also the aim of Malaysian students who were sponsored by their government. With such clear academic goals in view, the Year 12 coordinator commented, these Chinese and Malaysian students were: '... academically oriented towards training, educationally aggressive and highly geared towards the acquisition of facts ... rote learning is common. Chinese students are here with their families' backing. They tend to take education more seriously then Vietnamese.' It was this Chinese Malaysian group of students who were most likely to have problems with English. 'Their ideas are good but English poor.' Staff felt that this may have tended to make them opt more for the mathematics and sciences, as limitations with English restricted their subject choices. However, it was often difficult for school staff to improve their English quickly, and English classes at school had to be supplemented by attendance at local English Language Centres.

Although Vietnamese and Indo-Asians generally were recent arrivals, it was clear from comments that they too were impressing staff by their motivation and attitudes towards academic work. They were more likely to be in areas of first settlement straight out of hostels, or had only recently shifted out to better suburbs. 'Vietnamese move into new estates but keep up their contacts' (pupil welfare teacher). Comments suggested that they too 'know where they are going' and were becoming influential in expressing their aims. 'Here we have an increasing number of Vietnamese opinion makers, who have ambitions ... and have broadened the school from Greek, Italian, Yugoslav.'

Family backgrounds and prior experiences in their country of origin influenced the aims and aspirations of Vietnamese. Two groups in particular stood out. Those with parents who had a university or academic background opted for HSC and aspired to university entrance. Others with different backgrounds were attracted to TAFE, Colleges of Advanced Education and TOP courses. Personal commitment could also be strong, such as that displayed by a Cambodian boy who was a table tennis champion in his home country, but gave up the sport to concentrate on study.

The class behaviour and attitudes of Asian students received almost universal praise. It was abundantly clear from staff comments that they liked having Asian students in their classes. They were seen as extremely polite, diligent and trustworthy — ideal students in fact:

> With the Vietnamese I can go out and leave the class to get on with work. I'm like a consultant with some of them ... they believe in getting the finger out and doing something. They have enormous self-discipline ... volunteer for things like maths. competitions, fund raising. They are extremely hardworking and polite ... maths-inclined, probably due to language barrier (senior mathematics teacher).

These somewhat eulogistic though nonetheless convincing opinions about Asians must be tempered by the realization that their situations could often be difficult. Parental prohibitions, especially from fathers, could prevent girls in particular obtaining work experience in non-Vietnamese shops with the result that they did not get the experience of speaking English. Some Vietnamese young men were in their early twenties and were virtually self-supporting and had high aspirations, e.g., doctors, university, but no family support and backing, and found the going very hard.

This problem was exacerbated by the break in education caused by the time they had spent in the refugee camps prior to getting to Australia. Such students could be 'drifters' from school to school and were in direct contrast to other Vietnamese students who had stable families. 'The broken family situation greatly affects the Asian students', the pupil welfare teacher told us. Timorese girls had the 'poorest attendance in ESL classes' maybe due to the fact that they had up to four languages to contend with.

A disturbing trend noted about the intake of Vietnamese students from the southeastern area was the effect prolonged socializing in Language Centres had on their aspirations. Together with some recently arrived NES students they originally had an interest in education, but the socializing experiences and exposure to Anglo-Australian culture were destroying it, so that when they got to school they were not interested.

(4)   British and Northern European Students

Despite their relatively smaller numbers in the case study schools compared with other 'migrant' students, those from the British Isles and Northern Europe constituted a significant group even though they did not meet the criteria of non-English-speakers or 'ethnics' as used by the Ethnic Education Survey. Despite the fact that such students were not represented to the same degree as were other 'migrant' students, on both theoretical and empirical grounds it is desirable to include them to complete the composite picture of needs and aspirations.

A supporting reason for including them was the contention from both staff and students that those of British origin were not the same as Anglo-Australians. Staff we spoke to strongly maintained that students of British immigrant background had manifestly different attitudes towards discipline and the authority of teachers. In one case, they had been encouraged by their parents to be very union-oriented: '... these are your rights ... don't stand for this or that' (Year 11 coordinator). It was a group of British and Anglo-Australian students who requested to see the results of the original survey to find out what had been said about them and their views on the presence of NES students in the school. The carry-over of these attitudes into more general aspects of prejudice and discrimination is dealt with in Chapter 8.

Even though they were different from Anglo-Australians, British students paradoxically wanted to be like them. In one senior teacher's opinion this extended to British children trying to be 'more Aussie Ocker than Aussies', by picking up the Ocker speech style and 'worst habits'. This reluctance to accept one's ethnic background — a well-known sociological phenomenon — was not confined to British students. Examples were found of some Greek and Italian students denying their ethnic backgrounds for fear of being 'different' from the predominantly Anglo-Australian majority. One teacher mentioned a German student, who was much better than the rest in a German language class, but would not answer the teacher in German also for fear of appearing to be different.

Staff commented on Dutch students, who were 'well integrated', and German parents who 'want their children to go for it'. Lower-middle-class British-born students and their parents were generally happy with trades as future careers, but aspired generally to a materialistic style of life — good houses, top range of cars, 'Mazdas'. According to another comment: 'Parents want a private school but without the fees that go with it.' A significant number of students did transfer to neighbouring private schools much to the annoyance of the principal.

Some parents would like to see children go on to university and this was most likely with those from upper- to middle-class backgrounds in the northern and northeastern suburbs. For those lacking this level of aspirations general apathy at Years 10 and 11 was apparent, and may have been due to the lower- to middle-class SES character of the areas from which they came. 'They are lovely kids, but lack confidence and don't aspire very highly ... many are social creatures not career aspirants.'

Students' Comments on Their Needs and Aspirations: The Observers' Model

Interviews with students and the results of the questionnaire revealed generally mixed comments on their futures, which only partly matched the comments of staff. A distinct difference between the Years 11 and 12 became apparent.

(1)   General Patterns of Aspirations at Years 11 and 12

Students were asked the question: 'When you leave THIS school, what would you most like to do?' Using opting to go on to professional careers and university or tertiary education as a gross measure of level of aspiration, students in the constructed type groups at Year 11 tended to vary more than students at Year 12. That is, there was less mention by all groups of wanting to go on to university or tertiary education, or wanting a career needing such a qualification level, and more reference to careers in trades, commerce and service industries that did not require a tertiary qualification. Of eighty-five students interviewed at Year 11, thirty-one (36.5 per cent) mentioned going to university, college or careers needing tertiary training. Fourteen (16.5 per cent) were not able to state a career aspiration.

By Year 12, however, going to university or college was clearly the dominant preference. Of eighty-two students interviewed, sixty-nine (84.1 per cent) stated that they wanted to go to university, college or into careers that need tertiary qualifications. Three students did not state a preference. The remaining students mentioned trades or service industries. From this pattern of results it would seem that Year 11 operates as a sifting and sorting mechanism which resulted in Year 12 having a self-selected population of students, the majority of whom were aspiring to go on to university if successful at HSC.

(2)   Interethnic Group Comparisons

Gross comparisons between the totals of students from the major ethnic and NES groups bore out only some of the comments from school staff discussed above. Although their numbers were too small to be statistically meaningful compared with other groups, Asian students at Year 11 had higher levels of aspiration than both Anglo-Australian and NES students. Twelve out of eighteen Asian students (66.6 per cent) wanted to go to university or college compared with thirteen out of thirty-five Anglo-Australian students (37.1 per cent), and six out of thirty-two NES students (18.8 per cent).

This last figure was very surprising as it cast some doubt on the frequent assertions we heard from staff that students from NES backgrounds had unrealistically high aspirations. In our sample of NES students at Year 11, statistically small and unrepresentative though it was, nineteen students (59.4 per cent) opted to go into trades, commerce and service industries. Seven students (21.8 per cent) did not state an aspiration or put 'do not know.'

The figures were surprising in the case of students from the high Greek-density, middle-class southwest suburb, where one might have expected aspirations to be high. None of the NES students (predominantly Greek) we interviewed at Year 11 opted to go to university. Of the fifteen girls and boys, nine (60 per cent) chose trades, commerce or service industries and five (33.3 per cent) did not know. The pattern was basically similar for students from the lower-class high ethnicity northwestern suburb, but here one might have expected it due to the effect of low SES and generally depressed state of the whole employment situation in that area. Of eight NES boys and girls interviewed, only one (a girl) opted to go to college. The remainder opted for trades, commerce and service industries (six) or did not know.

These figures suggest the possibility that staff comments about high aspirations might be a form of stereotyping: 'what everyone knows about NES students.' If nothing else, the figures for Year 11 point to the need for treating such assertions with a degree of caution.

With students at Year 12, however, the pattern of aspirations was more in line with staff comments. Fourteen out of nineteen Anglo-Australian students (73.7 per cent), thirty-eight out of forty-five NES students (84.4 per cent) and seventeen out of eighteen Asian students (94.4 per cent) opted to go to university or college. In effect a form of aspiration–motivation gradient seemed apparent, and this is further discussed in the last chapter.

No definite pattern of the influence of SES on career aspirations emerged from the data. Impressionistically, as might be expected, students from the northern (high SES high ethnicity) and northeastern (high SES low ethnicity) areas stood out as having the highest levels of aspirations to go to university at Year 12, with the former having a slightly higher level (81.5 per cent) compared with the latter (77.3 per cent). The difference may have been due to the 'ideal' combination of SES and ethnic factors influencing students, which were catered for by the strong academic emphasis particularly in mathematics and sciences at the school.

(3)   Aspirations of Girls

A major area of interest was whether girls were aspiring to unusual or non-traditional careers. Unfortunately data did not support this. In total fifty-one girls at Year 11 and forty-seven at Year 12 were interviewed making ninety-eight in all. Of these twenty-five girls from all ethnic and NES backgrounds stated aspirations that could be termed non-traditional. Some aspirations could have been masked by those students who only put 'University' as a career option without specifying what kind of course.

Non-traditional choices did not range very widely nor were any of them of the type usually associated exclusively with boys. Choices were as follows, with the background of the girl given in brackets, i.e., Ang = Anglo-Australian, NES = non-English-speaking backgrounds, As = Asian.

Year 11: Solicitor (NES), Chemist (As), Law (Ang), Police Force (NES), Architect (NES), Cruise Director (Ang), Acting/Journalism (NES), Country Newspaper Cadet (Ang).

Year 12: Accountant/Law (Ang), Medicine (NES), Speech Therapist (Ang), Child Psychologist (NES), Law (NES), Health Administrator/Public Relations/Journalism (NES), Pharmacist (As), Accountant/Computer Programmer (As), Pharmacist/Occupational Therapist (As), University Sciences (Ang), University/Computer Programmer (NES), Retail Sales Management Cadet (Ang), Arts/Law (Ang), University Law/Economics/Language for Foreign Affairs Officer (NES), Medicine (NES), Pharmacy (As), Medicine (As).

At Year 12 in particular non-traditional choices were more likely to be made by NES and Asian girls than Anglo-Australians. The numbers of Asian girls specifying going to university were high compared with Asian boys. Again as might have been expected, students from the northern and northeastern suburbs stood out in comparison with the other areas for the greater number of girls from each choosing unusual or non-traditional careers. It is likely that the high SES component in the ethclass of both with the concomitant availability of professional role models among friends and relatives were the dominant influences in these two cases.

Systemic Responses to Students' Needs and Aspirations in the Curriculum: The Vernacular Model

(1)   General Arrangements for Selection and Content

Subjects offered by Suburbia High School in Year 10, which was considered to be the threshold to the period when thinking about careers usually started, were provided on a core and elective basis. This gave some degree of choice for students, who were able to make up their courses of study by combining choices of electives in which they were interested with the subjects they had to do in the compulsory core.

In practice there was a tendency for students from NES and Asian backgrounds to avoid choosing subjects which had no relevance for Years 11 and 12 courses and their prerequisites. Computer studies and aspects of careers education and work experience had become an important part of the offerings in recent years. The core at Year 10 also stipulated the courses which would provide the foundations for those subjects selected in the following year.

(2) Domination of HSC

The dominant feature of the selection of subjects for the Year 11 and 12 levels of the curriculum was the virtually exclusive preoccupation with providing those that prepared students to take the HSC Group 1 examination. Subjects offered at Year 11 provided traditional academic courses with an emphasis that favoured mathematics and sciences, rather than the humanities and commerce in which the subjects offered were more limited. 'There is little real alternative to maths. science', one teacher commented. School prospectuses were quite explicit that the purpose of this academic orientation at Year 11 was to lead on to the HSC year. Students were also advised to select Year 11 subjects with this and future careers needing HSC qualifications in mind.

Subjects offered at the Year 12 level were those specified for HSC Group 1, again with strong emphasis on mathematics and sciences. It was most uncommon for Group 2 subjects listed for the HSC to be made available or even requested by students or parents. At most two or three Group 2 subjects were provided, such as mathematics at work, advanced typing and psychology. Occasionally, as occurred in 1985, one or two others had been listed, but they had lapsed for want of takers. The reason for the lack of demand from students and parents was made quite clear when we discussed this aspect of the curriculum at Suburbia High School: Group 2 subjects were not recognized for admission purposes by either Monash University or Melbourne University. Consequently 'Group 2 failed for want of support' (Year 12 coordinator).

(3) Lack of STC Provision

No alternative to HSC Group 1 was available at Year 12. An STC stream was not provided although on occasions some thought had been given to setting up one or something similar. However, little serious progress had been made in this direction; always such ideas had been abandoned due to obvious lack of parental and student support. 'I believe if we had tried STC no parents would have wanted it', was the opinion of the principal.

The decision to orient the senior levels of the curriculum to HSC Group 1 was not a unilateral one, but was clearly a response to parental and student pressure. 'The curriculum is a reflection of staff perceptions of what is and should be taught, and is a result of students' wishes re HSC' (principal). If the demand was not there the subject was dropped.

As a matter of general routine decisions on the curriculum were made by a school-based Curriculum Committee, which had a representative majority of staff in its membership. Parents and students did not have full membership of this committee, but could channel their views to it through representatives from such bodies as the School Council, on which parents were more fully represented, and the students' own Council within the school.

Probably the major 'losers' in the selection of subjects for the curriculum were modern languages. These were barely surviving in the face of pressure from other subjects, although Greek at Years 11 and 12 was a recent addition to the curriculum. Traditional languages such as French or German were available up to Year 12, but may have owed their continued existence more to tradition, lobbying from the staff concerned or strong subject associations than to student demand and the ethnic diversity that was present in the school. Demands from ethnic associations, especially the one representing the Greek community, to have their languages increased at lower levels in the curriculum had not been granted.

(4)   Student Evaluation and Promotion

A system of examinations, tests and assessment of classwork such as essays controlled the progress of students up through senior levels of the school. Promotion was not automatic particularly from Year 10 onwards. At the end of Year 10 some examinations were held in key subjects like English and mathematics. Even being permitted to repeat that year in the case of failure was not automatically guaranteed. To be assured of getting into Year 11 a student had to have passed in sufficient subjects to make up a course at that level. Examinations and tests became more frequent in Years 11 and 12.

Promotion into the critical HSC year was the most stringently controlled; it was by no means automatically assured. In general, students had to have an average of eight passes in the class tests and end-of-term examinations in Year 11 to have the best chance of promotion. Marginal cases were discussed by the subject teachers concerned together with the Year 11 coordinator. If Year 11 was not passed some negotiation with parents was possible, but still did not fully guarantee that a student would be promoted.

Where it was considered that a student would not benefit by going on to HSC, parents were advised ('pressured' was one term used by a staff member) that he or she would do better in a TAFE or TOP course. 'We counsel our students and they go off to less academic courses, e.g., the local TAFE, etc.' (principal). A drop-out rate between Year 11 and 12 of about 25 per cent was not uncommon. 'We weed out at Years 10 and 11' was the somewhat cryptic comment of the Year 11 coordinator. He also added: 'kids must not see Suburbia High as the only option they have. We can give advice that the kid leaves school or goes to TAFE.' In consequence, the standards at Year 12 could be higher in mathematics and sciences than in humanities where the 'weeding out' may not have been so strict.

(5)   Special Provisions to Cater for Girls, Asian and NES Students

(i) Equal Opportunity. There was no effective formal Equal Opportunity for Participation and Equity Program (PEP) running at Suburbia High School, although in principle at least it subscribed to an official policy of equal opportunity for girls. The school tended to pride itself on this: 'It is a big plus in this school' (principal).

Despite the lack of any formal program, semi-formal opportunities to alert staff and parents to issues of equal opportunity for girls did arise at career and orientation days and parent-teacher evenings. The main result of these had been to raise staff awareness of the restricted nature of girls' career choices. A staff seminar and subsequent general staff discussions had also heightened awareness of the problems girls faced in class, due to boys putting them down in an attempt to dominate discussions and question time. In general, however, it was left to individual teachers to deal with this as each felt fit. No coordinated program attempted to tackle this problem.

The curriculum and available subject choices were structured on a co-educational basis to give boys and girls equal opportunity to do all subjects together at least in Years 7 to 9. Sport was almost fully integrated, with the exception of heavy contact sports such as football and rugby. In senior school at Years 10 to 12 integration tended to break down as subject specialization became established. Then few girls if any did metalwork and woodwork, and few boys did home economics and typing. Secretarial courses tended to be dominated almost exclusively by girls. The principal made a special point of mentioning two girls from the school who were then studying engineering at Melbourne University, and one boy who was doing male nursing. Despite the fact that these were rare examples, they were obviously considered to be evidence of good intentions on the part of the school.

The majority of attempts to make special provisions for girls and reduce the level of discrimination shown by boys had not met with much success, despite the presence around the school of colourful posters illustrating women in non-traditional careers. In fact, some years ago the possibly premature introduction of a policy of equal opportunity to raise the self-esteem of Greek girls in particular had met such opposition and animosity from boys, especially Greeks, and indifference from some staff that the teacher attempting to foster it abandoned her efforts.

Even the introduction of Women's Studies as an elective at Year 10 had been insufficient to change opinions and had attracted mainly girls, but few boys who could have benefitted from such a course. Girls themselves were inclined by tradition to be oriented to female jobs rather than to non-traditional jobs, we were told, and this was apparently well ingrained by Year 8, showing up in the choices girls made for their work experience program in Year 10.

It must have been difficult for anything to counter the kind of attitude conveyed by one member of staff's comment to us: 'Inequalities are deeply embedded in our social structure. Girls should be typists and it is a good career. We have employers ringing up to get our graduates.' It was thus hardly surprising that even well-assured girls in the school still aspired to go to college and middle-level jobs rather than to university and the professions.

Most opposition to reducing sexism had come from NES groups within the school, especially Greeks and Italians. Examples of them shouting down girls in class and not giving them a chance to speak were common according to staff. This was more likely to occur in Years 7 to 9. Some staff pointed out that although Greeks and Italians were the main offenders there were marked differences between the treatment of boys and girls in all ethnocultural groups. The examples that received most comments were the extreme cases such as the harsh treatment of Greek girls by their brothers, who were invariably spoken of as being thoroughly spoilt at home. Although the example did not occur at Suburbia High School, a new member of staff told us of her experience at a previous school where the pupil welfare coordinator had had to intervene to prevent a Turkish boy from beating up his sister outside the school for daring to talk to boys during recess.

Cultural factors may not have been the sole cause of boys' attitudes. Talented girls were resented by them regardless of their ethnic background and the activity concerned. For example, we were told about a drama class that contained several exceptionally talented girls from Anglo-Australian backgrounds. The boys could not dominate or match them and resorted to sulking and disruptive behaviour in class.

The picture was not entirely negative. By Year 10 and on into the senior level the dominance of boys did tend to diminish we were told. In some classes, such as those for HSC biology and even one or two mathematics classes, girls have been in the majority. This was partly because boys from NES backgrounds could get the opportunity of leaving Suburbia High School when in the senior level to go to a private school as they were invariably favoured over their sisters. 'They are spoilt and let go. The whole world revolves around them' (female ESL teacher). Consequently girls came to outnumber boys in some classes.

(ii) Modifications Due to the Influence of NES Parents. Some parents from NES backgrounds had also attempted to intervene if they thought that

what their daughters wanted to do was not suitable. This applied as much to allowing them to take part in some sports as to choosing their own careers. As the ESL coordinator at Year 12 said: 'We have sent some kids off to TAFE, but it doesn't always work. We had this Cypriot girl — daddy is taking her home [to Cyprus] to marry her off. She's a fifteen-year-old but she's adapted too well!' Although such cases undoubtedly occurred and had the approval of traditional parents, who were inclined to favour sons over girls in the family, it would be erroneous to generalize that this was the norm in all NES groups and families associated with Suburbia High School. Those from upper- and middle-class homes who had 'made it' were likely to be more enlightened and gave their daughters a better chance. Some NES girls themselves had developed a resilience and self-confidence that helped them overcome the put-downs of boys.

We talked to one such group of Greek and Italian girls doing HSC at Year 12. They were most vocal and persuasive that they easily coped with the boys. These supremely assured young women were aspiring to professional careers, and all claimed that they had the backing of their parents. They also spoke of their comfortable homes and well-to-do backgrounds, and it might be deduced that SES factors may have had as much to do with allaying NES parents' fears about their girls as a lessening of cultural traditions.

However, there was still a long way to go in this respect. Even at Suburbia High School there have been examples of Greek and Italian parents not allowing their daughters to go on school camps or join clubs. Very few girls from these backgrounds took part in after-school sport or recreational activities. One incident illustrated how strong this parental attitude can be; it occurred during the practice for a school play after school. The father of a Greek girl in the cast came to collect her well before the end of rehearsal and shouted out from the back of the hall for her to come home. 'It was quite weird ... there was this little bloke standing there ... the poor kid was so upset', we were told by a teacher who was present.

(iii) Multicultural Education. In view of the official promotion of multiculturalism and multicultural education in Australia, it might have been thought that the situations mentioned above could be alleviated by a program that promotes this official ideology in the school. This was far from the case, as there was no official program of multicultural education in the school, but the feasibility of introducing something more formal had been talked about in the past. Some staff felt that something was going on at an informal level, and the following comments may have represented the opinions of several staff especially in the ESL Faculty:

I am unable to point clearly to a multicultural component in the curriculum, but feel it's there. There's no central information, but in home economics they have been cooking ethnic foods, like Greek souvlaki. I say I am multicultural, my groups are multicultural, the way I teach is multicultural. I bring in materials from different cultures, and teachers in history borrow it. Multiculturalism is something that slips away from you if you try to grasp it. We're multicultural because we are (ESL teacher).

In general, multicultural elements in the curriculum were fragmentary and depended on individual teachers' interests. ESL teachers in particular were more supportive than others. Home economics was cited by another teacher as an ideal subject to discuss Asian integration into the school. 'We discuss this in Cooking and when we take the class out to a Chinese restaurant' (home economics teacher). The geography teacher in Year 7 specifically tied part of his coursework in with Greece and classical history. In Year 11 some work on Italy was achieved in a history unit. Teaching French in the school was made the justification for remembering Bastille Day. The principal also encouraged teachers to be aware of the multiethnic composition of the school: 'I try to make teachers aware that we have a fair-size migrant population, so they should use basic English for tests and assignments, but it doesn't always work.'

It appeared to be difficult for the school to go much further than what some staff clearly felt were tokenistic efforts, due to opposition that could come from unexpected quarters. For example, attempts to honour the Greek National Day by flying the national flag or to remember other ethnic festivals 'were a disaster, due to interethnic rivalry' (principal). The attempts had to be abandoned. The issue related to the politicization of ethnicity by some ethnic groups. As the principal commented to us:

> I'd rather not get mixed up with it or know their politics. I resolved from then on that the only flag to be flown would be the Australian flag. This is Australia, and that type of thing does not fit in. So on March 25 there might be Greek dancing and a bit of Greek food but that's all.

A proposal from the Greek Parents' Association to have Greek introduced as early as Year 7 made the French and German teachers feel threatened, so that too was abandoned.

Not all staff in the school were convinced of the merits of multiculturalism and multicultural education. According to the principal there was some passive resistance to multiculturalism, but fairly substantial support for multicultural education. The distinction was an instructive one, as it touched on the comparison made in previous chapters between educating for life chances and educating for life styles. The former has to be organized within an Anglo–Australian perspective, because all ethnic students must ultimately take their places in an Anglo society, while the latter does not need to be. As the Year 11 coordinator at Suburbia High put it: 'It's got to be an incidental thing in a way. We must blend all to be Australian, but keep respect for different cultures. We need to look where we're going. Multiculturalism won't get jobs.'

(6) Organization of the Curriculum for Careers Work

The principal and staff of Suburbia High School organized the curriculum in a way that they considered was in the best interests of students. What was of considerable interest was that the staff and organizational features most directly concerned with 'careers work' appeared to influence differentially the aspirations of students from various ethnocultural backgrounds.

(i) The Style of Careers Work: Referral Roles for Staff. All careers work in Suburbia High School was dominated one way or another by the directive from the Department of Education in 1984, which has already been referred to. Even the careers teacher was restricted in what she was allowed to do. These restrictions and the fear of possible litigation from students or parents were the factors most frequently mentioned during discussions with staff, and in their opinion played a major part in constraining what could be achieved. Even if staff were interested in and keen to assist students plan their future careers, the major result of the constraints was to place all but the careers teacher into referral roles. That is, senior staff who might otherwise have been concerned with helping students make plans for the future were virtually obligated to refer them to the careers teacher, if they wanted to protect themselves against possible litigation. This applied even to Year 11 and 12 coordinators and the pupil welfare coordinator who were most directly involved.

At some time during every one of our interviews, the question 'How are you involved with careers advice?' would produce very guarded responses all to the effect that the staff concerned would be very careful indeed what he/she said to a student. 'It's really not my responsibility. I send them to the careers teacher. We have to be very careful what we do' (deputy principal). Some few members of staff admitted to giving hints and tips to students, but invariably during informal situations such as a chance meeting in the playground or on a school camp for seniors. The general implications of the directive and the constraints it had produced are taken up in our last chapter.

(ii) Year 11 and 12 Coordinators. In view of the directive, the coordinators at Years 11 and 12 in Suburbia High School thus saw that their primary function was to help students plan their academic courses. This they did in consultation with the careers teacher usually some time in third term. If necessary, where borderline cases were involved, other subject teachers and even the pupil welfare coordinator could be brought into a roundtable discussion. This informal arrangement was the equivalent of the more formal pupil welfare committee that existed in some other schools.

According to the two male level coordinators the emphasis was placed on advising students about the logical outcomes that their subject choices for Years 11 and 12 would have on attaining future career aspirations. In effect, the coordinators assisted students to formulate their study pathways rather than their career pathways. Occasionally they would advise parents on the best academic course of action for their children, but usually with the added advice to go and see the careers teacher when career options needed to be discussed.

The Year 11 coordinator would start this activity with Year 10 students in October/November. All students would be interviewed, given the subject choices available and main guidelines for Year 11, and advised to consider the educational requirements of the careers they wanted to follow. For those students who had not taken the relevant prerequisites for subjects at Year 11 this advice usually led to aspirations being modified to some extent. In any case, a student's academic results at the end of Year 10 may have played the decisive part in determining what future courses of action were open to him or her, as a certain standard of results was necessary to be allowed to go on to do some of the subjects at Year 11.

However, the matter did not end there. Although the students were choosing subjects ostensibly for Year 11, their choices were also strongly influenced by the prerequisites for the HSC examination, which would take place the year after. Career plans for some were thus conditional on what would happen in the HSC examination and the subjects they could do for it in Year 12.

In the task of helping students the Year 11 coordinator was directly involved: 'I will advise in terms of subject choices and how they relate to careers only if the parents or kid asks. We can't offer direct advice. That's the career teacher's job.' A saving factor that made up for this was a well-produced, printed handbook setting out the options for Year 11 in detail. A strongly worded preamble advised students to select their subjects with the educational requirements of the vocation they intended to follow in view.

Fundamentally the same routine was adopted at the end of term 3 in Year 11. The Years 11 and 12 coordinators worked in conjunction with the careers teacher to decide Year 11 students' eligibility to go into Year 12. Again the emphasis was on guiding each student into a study pathway. Concern with careers was incidental. As the Year 12 coordinator informed us:

> My role is one of channelling. I have no particular expertise, so I send kids who have problems to the careers teacher. My main job is to interview all Year 11 kids and get some idea of their aspirations and coping ability for Year 12 and the HSC. If they can do the HSC then it's a tertiary course. If not HSC, some kids go to TOP [Tertiary Orientation Program] or leave for employment.

(iii) *Pupil Welfare Coordinator.* The school had a pupil welfare coordinator, who was a female full-time member of staff with additional teaching responsibilities in English at Year 8 amounting to five periods a week. This was a similar arrangement to that set down for the careers teacher, and likewise was arrived at through teachers' union negotiations. The pupil welfare coordinator had CAE course qualifications in social welfare plus an additional twelve months part-time course in counselling at Melbourne University. She had no formal qualifications in psychology.

The involvement of the pupil welfare coordinator in careers work was incidental to her main responsibility of welfare counselling, handling crisis situation cases if possible as soon as they arose and helping parents with social welfare problems and similar matters. For some of these she worked in close collaboration with the careers teacher, but in the main saw her role as being 'pastoral' to make things easier for the students at school. Part of this was to assist isolates to relate to their peers and to counsel others who were 'difficult cases' and not coping well. Like her colleagues she had chosen to refer most specific career problems to the careers teacher, but dealt with questions from parents and students when they cropped up incidentally during her other work.

(iv) *The Careers Teacher.* The careers teacher was also a female member of staff. This was quite common as the tendency was for women rather than men to be in careers education, because it was not a good career pathway for those who aspired to senior level positions. The careers teacher was relatively young (another common feature), had some training in methods of guidance from an Educatian Department in-service course run over twenty weeks for one day a week and was doing a part-time Graduate Diploma in Careers Education at a local CAE. She also taught at least five periods a week, in this instance Year 9 English.

In discussions, the careers teacher saw her role more as a resource person to provide students with as much information as possible often quite informally so that they could make their own decisions, rather than to be directly involved in intensive counselling. In her view there was a need in the school for a more formal back-up system of pastoral care as a team effort of form teachers operating in conjunction with the pupil welfare coordinator. However, she also said she recognized that the current Education Department legislation worked against this. Despite the multiethnic composition of the student population, she did not believe that multicultural education was an opportunity to promote careers education: 'It's not an ideal vehicle, especially the way we have it in this school.'

Providing students with information and experience relating to careers was attempted in a variety of ways. A careers education course was timetabled for all students at Year 10, for one period a week over a whole term. Part of this was a two-week work experience program, which the careers teacher coordinated. Students were encouraged to be actively involved in the preparatory work of writing or telephoning for appointments and taking as much responsibility as possible. However, work experience provisions did not assist some students from Asian backgrounds, as they tended to be placed in jobs related to their own ethnic community, and did not get the chance to practise English or relate to a wide range of non-Asian persons. The careers teacher followed up every student after the two weeks. However, because of the demands of other subjects a similar arrangement could not be made at Years 11 and 12. No careers education was timetabled for them and work experience could not be arranged.

Another function of the careers teacher was to arrange a careers orientation night each year in conjunction with the local branch of Rotary. This usually covered some eight-five occupations, but involved close to 100 per cent male speakers rather than women. Lack of female role models was obvious. To the careers teacher this was not of major concern: 'It doesn't matter here. Most of our kids have very traditional job aspirations; there are very few aiming for non-traditional jobs.' Parents' attendance at this function was generally very good, but the other parent-teacher nights did not attract many. In particular Asian parents did not attend in numbers commensurate with the Asian students in the school. The careers teacher suggested that this could have been due to communication difficulties.

The facilities that enabled the careers teacher to function effectively had only recently become fairly adequate. Until two years previously she shared a room with the pupil welfare coordinator which made private interviewing difficult. In 1985 she had her own room, a telephone and equipment. The major resources consisted of incomplete sets of pamphlets on careers from the Commonwealth Employment Service. Handbooks from the universities in Victoria, the Victorian Universities Admissions Committee (VUAC) and Victorian Institute of Secondary Education (VISE) were also available.

The careers teacher was also slowly building up sets of slides and a few videotapes on careers, but had to rely on the uncertain availability of a videotape player from the main library to use the latter. Another major resource used in the careers education courses during Year 10 comprised sets of booklets on planning careers put out by the Department of Employment and Industrial Relations (DEIR), and the *Life Skills Program* published by the Commonwealth Banking Corporation. Despite the availability of these fairly substantial resources, we were told that students did not use the careers room as much as they might have done, but tended to buttonhole the careers teacher in informal settings such as the playground and corridors or at lunchtime. Not all students did this, and Asians were often too shy to contact her in this way.

(v) The ESL Teachers. The three female ESL teachers at Suburbia High School were responsible for classes in English as a Second Language mainly for Indo-Asian students, who were new arrivals, and some NES

students. Work with the latter was often of a remedial nature rather than truly ESL. Classes were run on a withdrawal basis in Years 7 to 11.

All the ESL teachers we spoke to were emphatic that ESL was crucial for helping students' careers. Indo-Asian students in particular needed considerable support from their peers when going on school excursions. According to the ESL coordinator ESL teachers were a 'little involved with Year 11 students' job applications. Some Asian students in particular need help.' However, they felt that they should not get too involved — 'it's not really our role' — and should try to refer students to the careers teacher where possible. The principal also commented that part of careers advice was extra help for NES students and this too comes from the careers teacher.

However, one ESL teacher was more forthright: 'Yes, I do use my work to talk about careers and feel that's inevitable in much ESL teaching, as we try to stress practical things.' She had begun to advise her students at Year 10 to be realistic about their futures and make a wide choice of subjects. She would advise against doing subjects like legal studies or anything with technical English if the student was just out of the Language Centre or a new arrival.

Conclusion

Suburbia High School was a fairly typical, if large and cosmopolitan, high school, and many like it could have been found in the state. It was fairly conservative and, as portrayed in a vernacular model, appeared to cater adequately for the academic needs and aspirations of its student and parental clientele. The ethnic diversity was given some recognition, but little was done through the curriculum to cater for individual needs. The diversity of ethnic backgrounds and numbers may have worked against this, but over all there was the constraint imposed by the Departmental directive against making careers advice freely available from all staff.

A vernacular model is one view, but needs to be balanced by the observer's model comprising the views of external research observers and students. This takes up the next chapter, with some unexpected results.

7   Suburbia High School: Students' Perceptions of Systemic Provisions

The views of all groups of students concerning the career planning assistance from the school and community are considered in this chapter. In particular, the aim is to establish whether students from NES and Asian backgrounds considered that they were discriminated against in their attempts to formulate career scenarios.

Perceptions of Systemic Influences: The Observers' Model

(i)   The Most Influential Groups of Systemic Factors

The influences on students' career scenarios and sources of information they could draw on were grouped into three categories: family and home influences, school influences, community influences. Considered as a whole, the students were quite clear about the way they ranked these three groups on the basis of their helpfulness. Family sources were seen as by far the most helpful with positive (most helpful, fairly helpful) comments substantially exceeding negative (not used, not helpful) comments. School influences were the next most helpful, even though negative comments outweighed positive comments. Community influences and resources were seen as the least helpful and either were not consulted at all or were not helpful for the majority of all students.

The same ranking of the groups of influences still held when Year 11 and Year 12 students were considered separately, but a difference was apparent in the degree of helpfulness accorded to the school. The family was still seen to be far more helpful than not helpful by both these groups of students. However, the school was regarded as much less helpful by the Year 12 group than by the Year 11 group. It is possible that this difference was due to the fact that Year 12 students may have formulated their career scenarios by that stage of their lives, and no longer needed the same kind and amount of advice from the school as Year 11 students. The majority of students in both groups still maintained that the resources available from the community were either not used or were not helpful.

There was some but inconclusive evidence to suggest that Indo-Asian students in both year levels found the school resources to be more helpful than did either Anglo-Australians or students from NES backgrounds. Supporting data for this were available in the views of all students on the relatives they considered to be most helpful. It would appear that Indo-Asian students lacked strong family backup resources — a not unwarranted assumption as many lost relatives in Indo-China or came to Australia unaccompanied — and thus were forced to place more reliance on school resources.

(2) The Most Helpful Resources within the School

The way the groups of students regarded the sources of careers advice in the school was somewhat surprising. For all students the three most or fairly helpful sources in descending order of preference were information from school such as books on jobs, etc., friends in the school and the careers teacher. These three far outweighed all the other resources within the school. Least helpful were ethnic teacher aides.

A difference in the ranking was apparent when the first three choices of the students in the two year levels were compared. At Year 11 information from school ranked first, closely followed by the careers teacher, then friends at school some way behind, but still well ahead of the next most helpful source, the Year 11 coordinator. At Year 12, information from school ranked first, followed by friends at school some way behind and the careers teacher some way behind again.

These results were significant for several reasons. Firstly, it is logical that the careers teacher ranked well ahead of other teachers in view of the current Education Department regulations that advise against them giving careers advice and make referrals common. Secondly, 'neutral' sources of advice in the booklets and other kinds of information made available in the school could be seen in the same light as a replacement for teachers who were unable or unwilling to give advice. Thirdly, by Year 12 many students were committed to HSC and possibly tertiary studies and had already made up their minds, so that the careers teacher was somewhat superfluous, and was ranked lower than is the case at Year 11. Fourthly, the strength of friends at school was an interesting support for the research findings mentioned in the first chapter, which also stressed their importance in the occupational socialization process.

(3)   The Importance of the ESL Teacher for Indo-Asian Students

Students' comments also revealed some interesting and not unexpected differences among the three groups of students at each year level. At Year 11 Indo-Asian students ranked the careers teacher ahead of all other resources, followed closely by the ESL teacher, information made available in the school and then friends. The high importance given to the ESL teacher supported what we were told about her offering advice to students on careers.

We might thus again question the wisdom of the Education Department's directive in the case of Indo-Asian students. By insisting that they could only be given careers advice by the careers teacher, it could have deprived them of a source of information, i.e., the ESL teacher, to whom they related naturally and often informally in the normal course of her work. In other words, some systemic discrimination could have resulted against Indo-Asian students if the Departmental directive were adhered to rigidly.

(4)   The Importance of Impersonal Resources

Students from NES backgrounds at Year 11 ranked sources of information and the careers teacher equally ahead of friends at school. Anglo–Australian students at Year 11 gave a similar ranking. For students of NES backgrounds at Year 12, sources of information were ranked first followed by friends and the careers teacher in that order. Anglo–Australian students at Year 12 followed a similar pattern.

These findings suggest that for senior students at least a careers room and library well stocked with booklets, pamphlets and other kinds of material on careers were essential and highly valued components of effective careers work. To judge from the preferences of Asian students and others from NES backgrounds discussed below it might have been highly desirable for such material to include newspapers with large sections on employment.

(5)   Limited Support for Work Experience Programs

A small number of students at both year levels gave 'work experience' as one of the sources from which they gained help. However, these mentions were confined to Anglo–Australian students and those from NES backgrounds. No Asian students mentioned this source of help. Although there were insufficient data to go on, this could indicate that work experience programs may have had limited usefulness for Indo-Asian students. This was supported by the opinions of staff and comments of these students discussed below. It would appear that they tended to find work experience in businesses run by relatives and thus did not gain the experience of contact with Anglo–Australians. In any case, many Indo-Asian students had part-time jobs out of school, which would give them more experience than the school could organize.

(6) The Most Helpful Sources in the Community

The resources in the community outside the school and family that were ranked most highly by both year levels were newspaper advertisements. Experience from part-time jobs was ranked next by both levels, and in the case of Year 11 students this was equal second with television as a source of informaton. The Commonwealth Employment Service (CES) office was ranked fourth.

If one compares the three groups of students, it was noteworthy that NES students in Year 12 placed more emphasis on all community resources than either Asian students or Anglo-Australian students, who placed least emphasis. At Year 11 the stress on newspaper sources was greatest for Indo-Asians, followed in order by students from NES backgrounds and Anglo-Australians. At Year 12 the students from NES backgrounds placed greatest stress on newspapers, followed by Asians and Anglo-Australians in that order. At both Year 11 and Year 12 a similar ranking was followed in relation to television advertisements. The order of ranking was completely reversed in respect of the CES at Year 11. More Anglo-Australians favoured its use than either students from NES backgrounds or Asians in that order.

From this pattern and the preferences for newspapers and television mentioned above it seemed that sources of information which did not involve face-to-face contact were more likely to appeal to Indo-Asians and students from NES backgrounds, at least in Year 11. A similar pattern was not so evident in Year 12.

(7) Help from the Home and Family

Students were asked to state which family members had most influence on their career plans. Anglo-Australians and students from NES backgrounds gave most credit to 'parents'; a few Anglo-Australians rather endearingly referred to 'mum and dad'. However, although parents were most helpful for Indo-Asian students at Year 12 brothers were most important for Indo-Asian students at Year 11 regardless of sex.

Within each of the three groups of students there were some variations of emphasis. For Anglo-Australian students at both year levels mothers gained equal (Year 12) and more (Year 11) mentions by girls compared with fathers or parents. Mothers were also important for boys at Year 11. At Year 12 sisters were most important for Anglo-Australian girls. The groups of students from NES backgrounds showed other variations. Fathers were marginally more important for boys than for girls, and mothers were much more important for girls in both year levels. At both year levels sisters gained more mentions by boys than by girls. This may reflect the comments on the spoiling of boys from NES backgrounds by their sisters, which was referred to frequently by staff. Variations in the Indo-Asian groups were not so obvious, as numbers were small. However, there seemed to be a tendency for sisters to be more important for girls than for boys in both years. Brothers were marginally more important for girls than for boys at Year 11. Parents did not receive many mentions in this group. This may have indicated a lower level of parental support than the other ethnic groups enjoy. Brothers and possibly elder sisters had to act *in loco parentis,* and may have needed boosted support from such systemic resources as counselling, parent/student nights and the pupil welfare coordinator. Interpreter services could also be needed in such cases and any reduction of this facility in the school and community could be seen as a form of discrimination.

Perceptions of Systemic Discrimination: Observers' Model

As at Inner City High School students' own views of possible systemic discrimination could be gained from questionnaire data backed up by interviews and discussions. We anticipated that they would indicate whether racism or prejudice existed. What we obtained in replies was surprising.

(1)   Students' Feelings about the Future

Although the questionnaire prompt '... about the future I feel' may have made students assume that they should answer in a way that expressed their feelings, the number of students who did so was close to 75 per cent at both year levels. Most students gave answers that indicated either optimistic or pessimistic feelings about their futures and then followed up by giving reasons for these feelings. Of them, 47 per cent at Year 11 were pessimistic in emphasis and the remaining responses were optimistic. At Year 12, 57 per cent of the responses in this category were pessimistic and the remainder optimistic.

Commonly used terms indicating pessimistic feelings at both year levels were: 'insecure', 'frightened', 'scared', 'worried', 'uncertain', 'unsure', 'nervous', 'confused', 'frustrated', 'anxious', 'apprehensive'. Terms indicating optimistic feelings were: 'confident', 'comfortable' and 'not apprehensive', 'excited', 'positive'. Two or three students were ambivalent about their feelings at both year levels. Examples of optimistic and pessimistic comments at Year 11 were: 'I feel scared that I won't be able to get a career due to lack of knowledge' (Anglo-Australian girl); 'I'm happy and confident so that I want to start my career. I really like what I have chosen' (girl from NES background); 'I feel happy and nervous ... language is the biggest problem for me' (Asian girl); 'I have to be a success. I have to be better than I am now' (Anglo-Australian boy); 'A bit uptight. I don't know what to do or expect to do in the workforce'(boy from NES background); 'Unconfident ... I don't know whether I can get to uni.' (Asian boy). Some examples of answers from students at Year 12 were: 'I'm curious and sometimes a little frightened. I don't know what the future has in store for me' (boy from NES background); 'Scared and worried as I have no experience about looking for jobs' (Asian girl); 'Uncertain of myself and distrust my own ability: I may end up doing what I don't like just for survival' (Asian boy); 'Excited ... I'll be majoring in a particular subject, and am curious what will happen to me' (Anglo-Australian girl); 'I feel violently ill and lost, because I have to make a big decision that will affect my future' (Anglo-Australian girl); 'Frustrated ... can't get job I want. Marks are higher than I expect to get' (Anglo-Australian boy); 'Confident and a bit worried ... excited about course and career [Fashion Designing at RMIT]' (girl from NES background).

Other types of comments did not fall clearly into one or other of the emotional states, but still indicated that students had quite deep-seated concerns. Typical of these were: 'A sense of danger and a longing to be happy with my children ... a fear of war and weapons' (Anglo-Australian girl, Year 11); 'I feel like going to uni. I want to earn a degree and get a good job' (Asian girl, Year 11); 'A big jump from school' (Asian girl, Year 12); 'Lack of time to consider options' (Anglo-Australian boy, Year 12). 'I feel as though I have to decide on one definite direction ... there are so many occupations I would enjoy and believe I could do' (boy from NES background, Year 12); 'What will happen, will I live long, will I marry or who. I just don't know what will become of my life' (girl from NES background, Year 11); 'I must be careful of what I do, as I wish to have a happy and secure future' (boy from NES background, Year 11).

(2)   Students' Reasons for Their Feelings about the Future

At Year 11 the employment situation and current lack of jobs were clearly the major concerns for the majority of students except Asian girls, and received more mentions that were negative than positive. One is struck by the tone of quiet despair pervading many answers. A selection of examples indicates their range: 'I'm confident, but job positions are scarce' (Anglo-Australian boy); 'Worried, unsure — there may not be a position at the end of my studies' (Anglo-Australian girl); 'Quite depressed — I don't think there are job opportunities around' (Anglo-Australian girl); 'Unconfident — other people with experience or HSC will be considered first [before me]' (boy from NES background); 'I'll be alright at getting a job. It's not hard to get into nursing with good marks' (girl from NES background); 'Unsure — if I can't get the job, then all the years of work will have been wasted' (girl from

NES background); 'Terrible — don't know whether I will get a job or not' (Asian boy).

At Year 12 a significant number of students 'don't know' what is going to happen to them, and appeared to have a kind of free-floating anxiety, rather than a specific reason for their feelings. However, apart from them, the dominant concerns for the majority of students were passing HSC and the employment situation. In the latter category, comments were basically similar to the examples at Year 11 and were predominantly pessimistic. Only a small number of students were optimistic. Comments about their HSC chances were also predominantly pessimistic and apprehensive. Some examples of the latter were: 'Fear of failing. A lot depends on results' (Anglo-Australian boy)'; 'Insecure, frightened how I will go and what will happen to me' (Anglo-Australian girl); 'If I fail HSC there won't be much hope for me' (boy from NES background); 'Confident if I work hard and get good marks' (girl from NES background); 'Unconfident, uncertain — my future all depends on how I go in exams' (Asian girl); 'Comfortable and not at all apprehensive. I have to concentrate on my studies and worries are the last thing I need' (Asian girl).

(3)   Some Implications of the Students' Views

The pattern of responses above is very clear. Regardless of ethnic background, many students saw the future in a very pessimistic and uncertain light. Also of interest is the fact that students' views of their futures revealed weak moral positioning, i.e., futures were seen predominantly in instrumental and economic terms, rather than in terms of moral cues and social skills (strong moral positioning).

This pattern has implications for systemic provisions in careers guidance, as it suggests there is a necessity to provide as much down-to-earth information as possible about alternative career scenarios and life skills. More generally at the transmission level of the curriculum, adopting the kind of 'mental health' or 'social welfare' orientation, which implies an emphasis on strong moral positioning, could be counter-productive as it does not address the reality of the socio-economic and political constraints that are limiting career opportunities in Australia. Politicizing this issue along lines suggested by Bullivant (1981a) might be a more realistic orientation.

Perceptions of Causes of Difficult Careers Planning

Some reasons why students thought that careers planning was hard related to family influences and the effects of society and the school. Although such comments were relatively few, they did give some indication of the other problems facing students from NES and ethnic backgrounds, and even pointed to aspects which could be interpreted as discrimination and cultural reproduction.

(1) The Influence of the School

Blocking of subjects seemed to cause some problems, as it reduced options. 'You choose a subject at school and have to keep going, can't change' (Anglo–Australian girl, Year 11). However, a Year 11 boy from NES background thought that planning for the future was easy because 'I have been able to get all the subjects I want with no trouble.' At Year 12 lack of information available in the school was mentioned by two boys from NES backgrounds. Two Anglo–Australian girls felt they had not received enough help. One wrote: 'Personal interest is not taken at school with our future.'

In one or two instances success or failure hinged on which aspects of the school were involved. For example, a Greek boy at Year 12 'had a dream to be a PE teacher', but found by the time he got to Year 12 that he lacked the science subjects necessary to get into a CAE course of teacher training. This was because he had chosen the wrong subjects to study at Year 11 and had ended up with only biology. As he commented to us sadly: 'It [his dream] just went down each year.' However, another Greek boy at Year 11 with a similar aspiration had more success. He wanted to be a gym instructor and found that planning was easy: 'I got a lot of help from my PE teacher'.

Little should be generalized from such comments, but it is worth speculating whether they hinted at the kind of impersonal situation that might result in Suburbia High School, if the Education Department's regulations on giving careers advice were followed to the letter by all teachers except the careers teacher. Then students might well have been justified in thinking that nobody except her took a personal interest in their futures.

(2) Influences from Society

Some students felt that society was against them and in some cases their comments hinted at possible discrimination. One Asian boy at Year 11 wrote that he was not being given a fair go: 'Some people don't let you have a chance in any job, like disabled people. They think if we work for them now, in the future our skill will be better, we will be richer.' Another Asian boy at the same level also found planning hard. 'I'm nervous, worried — some people don't let us have a chance.'

Four boys from NES backgrounds at Year 12 also commented on the influences of society to explain why they found planning hard. Their reasons referred to pressures or demands from society and the uncertainty caused by social changes. One comment might touch a responsive echo in some: 'Society demands that I work when I don't want to.' Society could also seem to be indifferent to some students and this made their career planning hard. The comments of Asian students indicated how isolated they felt: 'I have no support from anybody, and have to stand on my own two feet'(Asian girl, Year 12). 'No one to talk to, am very much on my own. I'm not sure if my decision is right' (Asian girl, Year 12).

The way 'society' could bring out anomic feelings of powerlessness and loss of control over the future seemed to be at the bottom of these comments. To us, this reinforced the need for units in the curriculum related, say, to social studies, that present a politicized interpretation of Western industrial society in an attempt to give students more insight into the dynamics that control their lives. The need Asian students had for Australian friends referred to above was an indictment of the indifference Anglo-Australians feel towards those from different cultural and racial backgrounds.

(3) Family Influences

The family could exert influences that made planning both hard and easy, to judge from students' comments. 'It is hard to plan', commented one Anglo-Australian girl at Year 12, 'because parents and other relatives expect me to do a better job than teaching.' In contrast, an Anglo-Australian boy at Year 11 found planning easy: 'I can depend on my parents for help.' Two girls from NES backgrounds at Year 11 also found planning easy because of family support. One of them said that she depended on her brother for most advice.

Other girls at Year 12 from NES backgrounds also had mixed feelings about the family. A Greek girl complained that planning was hard because: 'Father wants me to do medicine not fashion designing, which is what I want to do'. She also commented that she could not do the subjects required for medicine and that made it worse. The power of the family came out in the comment of one Asian girl at Year 12 that planning was easy: 'My family explained the advantage of being a pharmacist, and I accepted it.' Another Asian girl found it hard because: 'I can't get much help from family members.'

That the family can exert both positive and negative influences is the obvious conclusion we can draw from the above. The comments should dispel simplistic stereotypes: not all Asian families are supportive, for example. Neither do all Anglo-Australian families have medium–level aspirations for their children, as the comment of the girl whose family wanted her to aspire higher than a teaching career indicated. The control NES families could exert over their girls' aspirations may have been at the bottom of the Greek girl's complaint about being stopped from choosing a career in fashion designing. It certainly supported the views of some staff concerning the strong influence on career scenarios exerted by these kinds of families.

Comments in Group Discussions on Career Planning

The fears and hopes about the future came out most strongly in the discussions with students. Differences among the various ethnic groups emerged that indicated basic insecurities, many of which pointed to the systemic sources of prejudice and discrimination in both school and society.

(1)   Anglo-Australian Students

(i)   Job Opportunities and the HSC Hurdle.   Many Anglo-Australian students at both year levels pointed out that job opportunities were limited and the careers they wanted were not going to be achieved easily. Although there were several students of both sexes, particularly those from middle- to upper-middle SES backgrounds at Year 12 who exuded confidence, most students were apprehensive or not very confident about what is ahead of them. They also thought that HSC was a big jump in standards and demands on time, a comment echoed by most of the other Year 12 groups we talked to.

At Year 12 the need to have HSC as a basic qualification for getting a job received frequent mention. 'If you get a high score in the HSC you've got a better chance of a good job' (Year 12 girl). Without it the chances of getting something good were thought to be slim, and even with it there was no absolute certainty. The comments of several students were summed up by one boy's remark to the effect that some of his friends had HSC, but still could not get into the careers they wanted. We sensed a disturbingly general feeling of frustration and despondency when such examples cropped up in discussion, despite the bright confidence and brave face that many students put on.

(ii)   Limitations of Work Experience Programs.   Many students at both year levels maintained that it was necessary to have had prior experience to get a job, but it was clear that they had had very mixed success in obtaining it. This was very off-putting. For some, the school's work experience programs at Year 10 and at Year 11 helped, but for others they were a dismal failure. Two weeks were thought to be not long enough for such a big step into the workforce. Most caustic remarks were reserved for the pittance that is provided: 'Work experience has helped. We got paid $3 a day — that's an experience! It doesn't even cover your fare into the city' (Year 12 boy). The general laughter that greeted this comment and the way it was echoed by other groups made it clear that the comment was not unique.

Students at both levels mentioned that work experience was used by some employers to exploit their labour without really teaching them anything. 'All I did was sweep floors. They didn't let me handle any of the machines or learn anything. You don't really do serious work' (Year 11 boy who went to a metal fabricating workshop). On the other hand, for another boy from Year 11 the work experience program had decided him on his career in the building trades. 'I did this work experience as a tiler, and liked it, so I've decided to be a plumber and stay in the building trades.'

More seriously, several students mentioned that some part-time work experience had been humiliating and suggested apparent discrimination from the employers. Some of the major supermarket chains came in for several comments from students. 'The management there treats you like dirt' (Year 12 girl). Anglo-Australian students were sometimes not accepted by European immigrant business owners in high migrant density areas because of their prejudice against Anglo-Australians.

Where there were high densities of Indo-Asian immigrants in the area students went to, management preferred supermarket check-outs to be manned by girls from similar backgrounds so that the ethnic language could be used. Anglo-Australian girls felt discriminated against in such cases. However, boys were almost invariably employed in the rear of the supermarkets where their strength was an asset shifting boxes and stacking crates. Consequently they did not experience comparable feelings of discrimination. In such instances, knowledge of English which is virtually mandatory elsewhere did not help.

Several comments suggested that work experience was too general, and often did not help one get experience in a future career. As one Year 12 girl put it: 'Work experience only offers a short range. Like, if you want to go into physiotherapy, you are not offered it … you can't opt for what you want to go into. So you've sort of got to do the jobs you don't want to do.'

(iii) Mixed Opinions about Parental Support. Most Anglo-Australian students claimed that the support of parents had been a valuable factor in their career planning. However, the idea of students invariably benefitting from adult role models was queried by one mature girl at Year 12, who claimed that they could be an incentive, but could also put one off: 'I think it is good to have people to look up to, so you can say "Well they have got that so maybe I can get it too", but you can also have doubts, like I am not good enough — I just don't know.'

(iv) Inadequacies of School Facilities. Although there were some inevitable adverse comments on the school's inadequacies, the personal limitations of the careers teacher in particular and restrictions on subject choices due to blocking, the career advisory resources were generally commended. However, there were still sufficient adverse comments to suggest that some systemic aspects could be working against some students.

The careers night came in for several adverse comments. Adult speakers from the business world and some of the universities 'talked down' to students, failed to give them real information and just passed them along to another source of advice. The result was that students could waste a whole evening trekking from one source of advice to the next and end up by getting nothing. Limitations on the number of advisers students were allowed to talk to also caused frustrations.

(2)   Students from NES Backgrounds

The comments of students from NES backgrounds reiterated many of those already mentioned, however, there were some variations that were due to the students' different cultural backgrounds. These were of interest, as they gave us some insight into the special problems these students faced.

Impressionistically and in very broad terms, it seemed that girls from NES backgrounds had very confident outlooks on their futures and careers more so than the boys from similar backgrounds. But even they were usually confident and outgoing. In comparison, many Anglo-Australian students seemed to lack such exuberant confidence, although there were some exceptions, especially among those from the middle-to-upper-middle SES parts of Suburbia High School's ecological context.

(i)   The Strain of HSC.   The HSC year was felt to be particularly hard and there were more comments to this effect from NES students than from Anglo-Australians. The following comments were typical of several. 'It's a depressing year. Such a big jump from form 5, it's unbelievable. The workload now is really getting on top' (Year 12 Greek girl).

(ii)   Work Experience.   For some of the students work experience was relatively easy to obtain, as it could be done with relatives or members of similar ethnic background. However, this could constitute a form of discrimination against those from a different ethnic background. The statement of one Italian girl was one of several comments on this kind of situation: 'Well, the person that I worked for was a bit racist against Anglo-Australians. I only got the job because I had an Italian background. He was Greek and would not take an Australian in. I don't think he would have taken one.' Boys from NES backgrounds at Year 11 also thought that being migrants did make a difference when it came to getting a job.

> It depends on your work and employer, and whether he's prepared to give you a go. Maybe he doesn't like migrants and won't give you a go. Maybe he's a migrant and knows what happens to you if you're a migrant, and you might be from the same country. So he would give you a go.

However, it appeared from other comments that coming from a different background could be a disadvantage. 'The boss I worked for was a bit [racist], but most of us that were working there were Greeks or Italians, and he treated us a bit rough' (Year 11 Greek boy).

(iii) Careers Night. Comments on the value of careers night at school echoed some of those made by Anglo-Australian students. One group of Year 12 Greek and Italians girls appeared to have derived little from the experience:

> I went, and every person I went up to — I went up to the medicine bit — I asked all the questions, and they would say 'I can't help you with that you will have to ask the next person', and they would say 'I can't remember that far back' . . . they couldn't answer one of my questions, I was so frustrated (Year 12 Greek girl).
>
> I had the same. Actually I got from some of them, they were really old [general laughter from group]. I just wasn't impressed, and thought I will never go to one again. It was just a waste of a whole night (Year 12 Italian girl).

(iv) Influence of Parents. Students had mixed feelings about the help they received from parents, although most claimed that it was generally positive.

> They have seen the hardships and they condition you (Year 11 girl). Your parents push you a lot. They hate working in factories. They say 'listen, don't get into overalls, get into a suit, wear a tie, get home at 3.30. If you don't pass it'll be a factory job, you'll cut your own throat' (Year 12 boy).

However, it was also pointed out that parents were not always able to help due to lack of English or ignoranc about the demands of the HSC:

> It's an advantage [having migrant parents] in one way, but it's a great disadvantage in another way. Because at home we all talk Croatian, my parents don't talk Australian, maybe a few words. If they would talk Australian it would probably help us at school (Year 12 boy).

Career planning could also be affected by other factors associated with the family. In the opinion of one Greek girl at Year 12:

> Well I haven't got much help from my parents, they don't really understand the concept of HSC. They know that I have to pass it but they don't know — like I don't go home and tell them I did well in a test or that because they don't really understand. They would understand, but it doesn't concern them much. So I do career planning by myself. I have got an older sister and she is doing second year college, but she doesn't have much time so I manage myself.

Lack of parental help could also cause indecision. This was mentioned by many students and in ways that eloquently conveyed their mixed-up feelings. As one Year 12 girl put it:

> I'm definitely going to get my HSC, that's about the only thing I'm sure of. I may become a social worker, but again ... I have my parents' influence and [they say] 'no, there's not many of them these days and couldn't I become a doctor or lawyer'. But I've always had these different careers. I wanted to be a nurse, now maybe a doctor. Lot's of ideas ... I don't know where I'm heading.

Cultural factors appear to have played a more important role in the career aspirations and education of students from NES backgrounds than those from Anglo-Australian backgrounds. This pointed to the desirability of careers advisers acquiring a sound background knowledge of the main cultural features of the various ethnic groups in the wider society. This issue is further discussed in the last chapter.

(3)   Asian Students

Asian students reiterated many of the previous comments. Like the students from NES backgrounds, Asian students' parents frequently could not help due to lack of English and knowledge of the HSC system. 'My parents encourage me to do HSC, but that's all. They care about me but cannot help' (Vietnamese girl, Year 12).

(i)   Systemic Influences on Career Planning.   The importance of the HSC made it crucial that the school facilitated students' attempts to achieve this goal. The Asian students were very reluctant to make any verbal comments about the way the school helped them in this and other aspects of their career planning. However, there was one exception to this kind of reticence.

A very ambitious and apparently bright Cambodian boy (almost a young man) had not been put into the HSC year as he wanted when he arrived at the school, on the grounds that his English was not of a standard to cope with work at that level. He had vigorously campaigned to be allowed to attempt HSC, but had been put into Year 11. Even this was a concession as the school staff wanted to put him into Year 10. As a result of his complaints and the fuss he created about being deprived of a chance to do HSC immediately, he appeared to have alienated the sympathies of staff concerned and had gained the reputation of being something of a troublemaker. This seemed obvious from comments of the staff.

As for the boy himself, it was very clear from our discussion with him that he still felt bitter about what he saw as discrimination and said so strongly. His personal feelings were aggravated by his domestic situation. He had no parents, as they were both killed in a purge. He lived on his own in Melbourne and consequently he had to make all career decisions himself and felt, rather compulsively it might appear, that he had to succeed as soon as possible.

There was an additional factor in this situation. The student pointed out that most Cambodians were working in factories as they had peasant backgrounds. Academics and intellectuals were killed in the purges, so that even those adults with whom he had contact were not in a position to understand and advise him on going for a career needing academic qualifications. In contrast, he explained that ethnic Chinese students in Melbourne were in a better situation. They tended to have the academic backing of their families, who did not experience the purges and often had good education or understood what it meant, and encouraged their children to pursue academic studies.

(ii) Work Experience. We were told by other Indo-Asian students that work experience was hard to find as students' language difficulties often put Anglo-Australian employers off. As a result there was a tendency for Vietnamese especially to get work experience with compatriots. The distinction that the student from NES background brought out about there being two kinds of employers, the racist ones and the non-racist, was also mentioned by two Asian students.

As the following transcript indicates Asian students also had an optimistic faith in qualifications that was not fully shared by other students:

Q. Do you think Australian-born Australians have an easier time getting jobs than people from migrant backgrounds?

A. I don't really think so, because it all gets back to the qualifications you have. I think now most employers, I don't think they're as concerned whether you are Chinese or whatever, more whether you are capable of doing the job (Chinese boy, Year 12).

A. I think there are some cases though. I think there are two scenes, one where they have prejudices — those who like Australians — one that likes ... migrants, because we work harder (Asian girl, Year 12).

As with the students from NES backgrounds, the comments of Indo-Asian and other Asian students revealed strong influences from cultural backgrounds operating on occupational socialization. Apparently minor organizational decisions could be perceived as discrimination, even though it was unintentional and merely followed the 'rules'. Students' adverse reactions could also be partly due to the strong value placed on the maintenance of 'face' and also to a strength of academic motivation that was not typical of Anglo-Australian students. How this appeared to affect more personal ethnic encounters is taken up in the next chapter.

8 Suburbia High School: Staff and Student Perceptions of Prejudice and Discrimination

To some extent, prejudice and discrimination exist in the eye of the beholder; what appears to be prejudice to one person may not be seen the same way by another. The vernacular and observers' models of these aspects of Suburbia High School illustrate this kind of contrast, and enable some assessment of the degree of cultural reproduction that was occurring.

Staff Perceptions of Ethnic Encounters: Vernacular Model

(1) The General Pattern of Prejudice

The usual comments from staff were to the effect that in general there were some interethnic tensions in the school, but that they were usually latent and episodic, flaring up from time to time. They were not always between the same groups and may have been governed to some extent by the changing student composition of the school. How far they influenced students' career scenarios was not certain.

Views of the staff were often past-oriented, i.e., their comments almost invariably alluded to periods 'two or three years ago' when rivalry between ethnic groups was severe. For example, we were told: 'Greek versus Italian antagonism is not so vitriolic now as it was two years ago. Then there was gang warfare between them. We're a melting pot of a school, but that's not to say there are not periodic tensions' (Year 11 coordinator).

It was probable that Indo-Chinese and other Asian students may have become the most recent and main target for prejudice and discrimination. However, views differed on how severe they were. 'A few Asians haven't related well ... there are language difficulties and they keep to themselves, but haven't been discriminated against' (deputy principal). 'There's some underlying hostility towards Vietnamese students, but it doesnt't amount to much more than name calling' (principal). 'The Asians are tolerated rather than liked' (Year 11 coordinator). 'There's some evidence of antagonism towards Asians from Australian students, but it's not bashing or real taunting, just name calling' (careers teacher).

Other staff supported the opinion that prejudice most commonly consisted of name calling with 'wogs' being probably the usual epithet, though 'slant eyes', 'flat face' or 'slitty eyes' were used to refer to Asian students whatever their background. One blackboard had 'Chen sucks' scrawled over it. How long this comment had been there was uncertain, but it said something about the school that it had not been immediately erased.

(2) Causes of Prejudice and Discrimination

(i) Jealousy over Academic Ability. Reasons for the hostility were not entirely clear. It may have been more apparent in junior and middle school rather than in senior levels, and could be related to a form of rivalry between ethnic groups over the amount of work that should be done. The ESL coordinator described sitting in on a group of Year 9 Italian and Greek girls who were having a 'fascinating discussion' about the Chinese students in the school. The Greek and Italian girls 'don't like them, they said they work too hard and study too hard.'

Yet at the more senior level of Year 12 HSC it was said that Asians were respected in class if they were doing well. Year 12 students tended to work more together and there was no apparent jealousy, according to the Year 12 coordinator. Outside class, Asians tended to isolate themselves, but there was some integration of ethnic groups especially for lunchtime sports and recreation. However, he also commented that some Vietnamese aroused jealousy especially in the junior grades, and mentioned the example of the Vietnamese girl who got poor marks in a test. When the marks were read out publicly the rest of the class, which included a majority of students from NES backgrounds, cheered and reduced the girl to tears.

It was an indictment on those responsible that such antagonism would not be reciprocated. The ESL coordinator mentioned that some comments by Asian girls in her classes indicated that they placed high value on getting Australian friends and were elated when they did. Anglo-Australians may not have perceived that Indo-Asians needed friends, particularly if there were enclaves of them in the area. This could occasionally generate antagonism from Anglos, who thought that 'the place is swarming with them ... all those ninety-seven Vietnamese in the one house', as one Anglo-Australian student put it (Year 11 coordinator).

(ii) Interethnic Antagonism. Other comments revealed that intolerance could come from surprising quarters. The pupil welfare coordinator referred to the attitudes of some Greek students towards Italians: 'They call them peasants ... some of those who have been here some time can be more intolerant towards other migrants than Anglos.' An extreme example

concerned a non-Anglo boy calling an Indian student a 'black bastard', despite the fact the boy who used the term had a skin that was darker than the other.

(iii) Influences from Home and SES Backgrounds. Staff suggested that a great deal of the prejudice originated in the homes of students and were understandably keen to exonerate the school. 'I'm sure families affect students, but the discrimination is not through school structures. We do our best to stamp out prejudice here' (principal). His view about the lack of involvement on the part of school structures was echoed by the deputy principal.

The ESL coordinator commented that an Anglo-Australian student in middle school had said to her: 'My mum's on a pension, and she can't get a home loan, but Vietnamese can easily get them. That's why I don't like them.' Another junior Anglo-Australian boy habitually called all NES and Indo-Asian students 'wogs', and when pulled up by one of the staff defended himself on the grounds that his father called them all wogs so why shouldn't he. Such examples were not isolated incidents. As the pupil welfare coordinator commented: 'The problems in the school result from the homes, not the school, but are inflicted on us.'

The kinds of prejudice and discrimination described in (iii) may have been indirectly related to the socio-economic backgrounds of prejudiced students. There were some grounds for thinking that they were more likely to come from lower-working-class and broken homes than from those which were more well-to-do. The feelings of inferiority and being hard done by through adverse socio-economic circumstances may have triggered off a transfer of jealous hostility towards scapegoats such as Vietnamese and Asians in general, who were highly visible targets and were thought to be more successful. However, this did not explain the attitude of former migrants such as the Greek students towards Italians, the 'peasants'.

It is difficult not to fall back on theories of social closure discussed in the second chapter to account for such phenomena, and this issue is taken up in Chapter 9. It should also be apparent from the above examples that the whole question of prejudice in school was highly complex and could not be reduced to neat categories and thus simple solutions such as those proposed in much culture contact or self-esteem theory. Where prejudice originated from homes or was due to socio-economic forces outside the school, it was hardly likely that such curricular palliatives would be effective.

Students' Perceptions of Prejudice and Discrimination: The Observers' Model

In contrast to their written responses, students' comments often revealed a deeper perception of reality and maturity. Due to the size of Suburbia High School and the fact that its catchment area included a variety of socio-economic suburbs ranging from lower-middle to almost upper SES, the views of students were correspondingly varied.

(1) The General Pattern of Comments

As a general rule, Anglo-Australian and Australian-born students were the most outspoken about students from ethnic backgrounds. Their comments ranged from sensible and balanced assessments of the difficulties those from NES and Asian backgrounds faced to some obviously prejudiced views. The latter usually came from students at Year 11 level. Students at Year 12 from middle- to upper-middle-SES Anglo-Australian backgrounds, who had non-Anglo-Australian acquaintances of the same SES level, were the most balanced and least prejudiced in their views. Students from NES and Asian backgrounds tended to be more restrained in their comments and rarely if ever indulged in personal prejudice.

However, one group of students stood out from all others for the crudity of its outbursts against Asians. It was composed of Year 11 students, with one or both of their parents who were long-established, former migrants from Western and Northern Europe (e.g., Germany, Holland, Britain) and from lower-middle SES backgrounds.

(2) Factors Influencing the Views of Anglo-Australians

There were several major recurring themes in discussions with Anglo-Australian groups that suggested some of the possible grounds for the prejudice and discrimination.

(i) Competition as a Major Cause of Prejudice.

The theme that stood out as probably the main cause of prejudice against students from NES backgrounds and Asians was jealousy about the competition they provided for Anglo-Australian students in the classroom, especially in Year 12 HSC groups, and more generally in the workplace. The competition was felt to be due to several causes: more language skills, better brains, willingness to work harder than Anglo-Australians, the benefit of pressure from parents. Not all comments were negative. Frequently there was grudging admiration, particularly from Year 12 students, of the ability and capacity for hard work of students from NES and Asian backgrounds. In fact, such comments from the Anglo-Australians demonstrated wry insights into their own shortcomings.

The following comments from a group of Anglo-Australian students at Year 11 clearly focused on the theme of competition. About migrants in general: 'Well, you feel like they are going to take over our jobs, and there will be nothing left because there are so many of them here' (Year 11 girl).

Another girl gave a more balanced view: 'I feel that if they've got a better qualification than me then they should get the job over me. I shouldn't get the job just because I am Australian and they are Asian.'

In general the comments of Anglo-Australian students at Year 12 were less prejudiced. One group of confident and articulate students in particular made a number of positive comments based on migrants of their acquaintance. However, it quickly became apparent that they did not think of migrants at the school in the same way as the 'different' migrants from what they frequently referred to as the 'western suburbs'.

> You can't really compare the migrants from our school with the migrants from the western suburbs, because the migrants from our school are more likely to be behaving the way that we are than others, and the ones from the western suburbs are liable to be behaving like the rest of them, like not high hopes and things like that (Year 12 girl).

(ii) Perceptions of the Effect of SES. For this group of students an interesting class-focused type of analysis took the place of the usual themes about prejudice towards migrants:

> I don't know so much whether it's speaking English [that gets good jobs] but I do think that the area you come from makes a difference (Year 12 boy).

> I think it does, but it shouldn't (Year 12 girl).

> It shouldn't, but I believe it does. It shouldn't make any difference how you present yourself and what background you have but it does, because someone's more likely to employ you if you look well presented, you speak well, have a good background, good schooling than if you've been from some western suburbs or something. I'm sure they look at that, they shouldn't but they do (another Year 12 girl).

Sadly, the comment of a Greek girl from such a lower-working-class 'scum' area mentioned below appeared to confirm this.

(iii) Influence of Teachers on Perceptions. The implication in the above statements of 'there but for the grace of God go I' was explained by several in the group. It threw an interesting light on the way misconceptions about migrants could be built up inadvertently and with the best of intentions, even though some would not agree with them on pedagogical grounds. As the following exchange of questions and answers revealed, it transpired that the western suburbs had featured heavily as a form of 'bogey-man' in teachers' attempts to motivate the class:

Q. Have you been doing a unit on the western suburbs, you seem to know a lot about them?

A. We hear about it, we always get told about them by the teachers. They're shown as an example. Last year we did economics on unemployment, the teacher was saying 'that'll be you, don't worry about it, unemployment is for you' (Year 12 girl).

A. Yes, that's what we're going to be doing when we leave school. Our teacher had the uncanny ability to make you feel very low ... it was 'oh forget it, you're going to fail anyway.' You don't have that many patting you on the back, saying don't worry, calm down, you're going to pass (another Year 12 girl).

(iv) Envy of Language Skills. Jealousy over the extra language skills of students from NES backgrounds and the competition for jobs this could cause produced the following prejudiced comments by Anglo-Australian students. They resented Greeks and Italians speaking to each other in their own languages in class and complained that they could not get jobs in places where these languages were expected. Job chances were better if you knew two languages:

Q. Do you think it's an advantage being an Australian in this society?

A. No, not in Melbourne, no way ... many of the shops, you look at them and they're Italian or Greek, and if you don't speak Italian or Greek you're lost, because most of the people around this area do. So it's really unless you do languages it's us without the advantage because ethnics have two languages. A lot of the kids that go to school with us speak two languages. What annoys me is that they speak Greek in class (Year 11 boy).

(v) Effects of Ambivalence about Ethnic Identity. There was an interesting ambivalence about Anglo-Australian students' ethnic identity in some cases. As the extreme case discussed below suggests, such ambivalence may have influenced the prejudiced views that a few students, who could have been confused about what it meant to be a migrant, held against others from NES backgrounds. For example:

Q. I get the feeling that there is a kind of competition between you and the Greek kids, is that right?

A. There is, like you don't think of your friends like that but it is (Year 11 boy).

A. Like, I look Greek and walk down the street, and I look Greek and no-one knows that I am Australian, and I can say things in Greek. Everyone thinks I look European but both my parents are Australian. But when you come to think of it, it's also in the way of clothing and the way you dress because of fashion and the way your hair is ... if you're dark skinned or dark (another Year 11 boy)

A.   It's funny, I work sometimes for MacDonalds and we get these 'old mamas', and it's lucky I can understand a bit of Greek, because they're trying to ask for potatoes, etc. They should be made to learn our language (Year 11 girl).

(vi)   Jealousy about 'Brainy' Asians. Comments about Asian students were varied, with the more prejudiced coming from Year 11 students. In particular it was clear that they were jealous of their 'brains'. A discussion with one group of Year 11 Anglo-Australian students about the job situations facing Asians produced the following comments:

... [they will have] no problem. Well the Asian kids here are pretty smart (Year 11 boy).

Brains! ... well we could probably be just as brainy if we were prepared to put in just as much work. I've got three Asian friends and they are forever doing homework and study and that (Year 11 girl).

It comes from their parents, because their parents are usually more strict than ours, we're not pressured as much (another Year 11 girl).

My parents, they try to pressure me, but you say 'I have done half an hour's homework and that's it, I'm going out'. I get pressured, but I just do a little bit (second Year 11 boy).

(vii)   Competition from Asians at HSC Level. Year 12 students were usually more tolerant, and even showed grudging admiration of Asian students' capacity for hard work. Asians' good 'brains' also came in for frequent mention, though students had mixed opinions about the competition they generated in class. As the following excerpts illustrate, some Anglo-Australian students were obviously well aware of their own shortcomings.

Q.   What do you think of Asian students in class?
A.   In form 3 they're doing form 5 work, way ahead of us. They don't talk much. Like in chemistry, I don't think I am the dumbest in chemistry, but I talk all the time, and all the smarties sit at the back and wait for me to make a fool of myself and then they get the answers (first boy).
Q.   Is it only chemistry they concentrate on?
A.   No, everything, pure and applied, sciences, you find very few

doing English Lit. etc. They're good at everything (first boy).

Q. Do you think Asian students face the same problems as you about the future?

A. More so, I reckon ... like, if a Chinese kid goes for a job — this is probably a generalization too — but they say they are Chinese — oh, I don't know — I think they would have more trouble getting places than we would (first girl).

Q. How do you think they could overcome those problems?

A. I think they have to work harder than we do and get better marks, so they would have better qualifications, and that would put them a step ahead of us (second girl).

Q. Do you think that is going on?

A. Yes, especially with Asians [three girls nod in agreement]. I think that parents tend to push them a bit ... you know, like the ones that have just come over ... but they are just naturally pretty brilliant (fourth girl).

A. There are usually two types of Asians, the delinquent one and the smart one — they are either very smart, or you don't see them after form 4.... There is not really an in-between Asian person. They are usually either really smart, or otherwise they leave, and the victimization of Asians is usually on the delinquents, never for the smart ones (second boy).

(viii) *Ambivalence towards Asians.* Although Anglo–Australian students thought that competition was undoubtedly one aspect of their relationships with Asians, it seemed clear that they experienced some ambivalence about them, as the following excerpts illustrate. They occurred during a discussion with Year 12 students:

Q. How do you feel about working with Asians?

A. The Chinese are dogmatic. If it's them versus you then they won't help you (boy).

Q. What do the girls think of the competition? You say there are a few Asian girls in your class.

A. Good luck to them. I mean, if they work hard then good luck to them (first girl).

A. Maybe it's weakness, but I'll help them (second girl).

Q. What if you and an Asian girl were going after the same job?

A. Different, I suppose (first girl).

Q. In what way different?

A. I would treat them the same way as if it was an Australian going for the job. I think that racism is really strong in Australia. I think that the younger generation is more tolerant because they are growing up in it — the multicultural thing — like, my grandfather would never buy anything Japanese because of the war (second girl).

A.   I agree with K——— about going for jobs. I would feel the same way about anybody if they got a job before me. I would probably hate them but it wouldn't matter whether they were Australian or what (third girl).

(ix)   Asians' Difficulties with the English Language. A group of Anglo-Australian Year 11 students from a lower-middle SES part of the school's area were of the opinion that English was the major problem facing Asians. As one girl summed up the issue:

It [job opportunity] would depend on the employer, whether he was prejudiced against Asians or not. It is also the communication gap, their English, how well they speak English. A lot of jobs you require proper English, so they could be disadvantaged.

(3)   Australian-Born Students of British and Northern European Background

(i)   Racist Comments. Regrettably not all comments were so thoughtfully put. One group of Australian-born students at Year 11 had quite extreme views, and our first contact with them gave some warning of what to expect. We had finished talking to a group of students from NES backgrounds and, as they filed out of the classroom, a Year 11 student in the group of Australian-born students who were waiting called out loudly 'go away you ethnics. How's fishing in Uruguay?'

Their comments during the ensuing discussion were little better and descended to a disturbing level of stereotyping, crudity, personal denigration and viciousness. The main target was Vietnamese, but Chinese and other migrants came in for attack. This was the only group of students to use personal terms of abuse and denigration about them. As the following excerpt shows, many of the fears and prejudices that we have already discussed were present:

Q.   Did you find the Vietnamese students were very good students?
A.   No they weren't ... they were pains (first girl).
A.   From an academic point of view (first boy).
A.   Well they were — all they would do would be to run around the school and speak in their own language. I mean if they come over here they should be prepared to speak English in the schools. If they don't speak English they should stay in their own schools ... they come over here and they don't want to take on any of our customs ... they just blabber in their own languages, and they don't worry about what you think. The only time they will speak English is to a teacher, otherwise they just run around and blabber their own language (first girl).

Q. Do they swear at you?
A. Oh yes, in their own language! I mean I could tell you ten thousand in Greek and Italian and Vietnamese and all the rest of it (second girl).
Q. Did they do well in class?
A. No, not all of them. They were just the same as us — you have some people high and some people low. Most of the wogs were dumb (second girl).

There were many other and worse remarks in similar vein. How can one account for them? Revealing comments from several students in this group gave us the feeling that they were very unsure of their own identities. Although born in Australia, some had parents who were former immigrants from Northern European countries such as Holland or Germany, but had been in Australia for many years. Others were born of Australian-born parents, or had English-speaking parents formerly from England or other English-speaking countries. Such lack of firm identity may have provided one clue to the viciousness of some of the comments, particularly about Asian and Vietnamese students. The group also came from the eastern catchment area, which has few recent migrants such as those from Indo-China, and could have been ignorant about them or were reiterating the comments of their similarly prejudiced parents.

(ii)   A More Mature Set of Opinions.   However, a group of students with similar SES and parental backgrounds but at Year 12 had more mature views especially about Vietnamese students. This may suggest that the age and personal maturity of students could have had a bearing on the degree of prejudice they showed. The greater maturity seems evident in the following:

Q. What do you think about Asian students in the school?
A. I don't know, but there always seems to be something or somebody prejudiced against another person. If it's not their colour or race, it's their disability, or something else. If people want to be prejudiced against you they will find something that they don't like (first girl). [Several other students nod in agreement.]
A. Yes — there is a lot of prejudiced people around the school. Oh, they just ignore some of the Vietnamese. Some of the kids have had a few fights — I saw one in the corridor yesterday (boy).
Q. But is this prejudice or just that they may not like each other?
A. They don't try to get to know them. They just seem to have a set against them (second girl).
A. Well, like, the Australian boys don't get to know the Asians (second boy).
A. Some English-speaking people hate the migrants, but after a while they get used to them (third girl).

The influence of other factors such as peer pressure and parents on students' prejudice also came out in the same discussion group, as the following comments on hate against migrants illustrate:

Q. That's a very strong word, hate, isn't it. What do you think about it?

A. Yes, well a lot of people do hate migrants and that, but to me they don't take the time of day to get to know what is really inside that person or their personality (girl).

A. It sort of follows from generation to generation — if one person says they hate somebody, then their friends are going to say they hate somebody. Just say you have a mob of people, and just say the leader of that group says he hates somebody — don't you reckon the rest are going to say that? (boy).

A. Sometimes the parents tell their children ... it's often the case where the parents say, oh like the Vietnamese, they have come over here and [done well] and we're still poor, and the children begin to hate (second boy).

Q. Have you heard of things like that?

A. Yes, well I have been in a situation like that with my mum. She doesn't like Vietnamese, and I nearly said that I don't like them, but then I thought why should I say that. I was nearly caught in a situation where my mum doesn't like them, but now I have realized I should think what I think, and not follow what she said because I was nearly influenced by what she was saying (third girl).

A. Once you get to our age, or say a bit younger, you start thinking for yourself. Just because your mum hates Joe Blow, you don't hate them. Once you start thinking about it, you get your own thoughts and it is different (third boy).

(4)   Students from NES Backgrounds

Not unexpectedly NES students were more reticent about prejudice in the school and society generally and at least in the group discussions never descended to the level of the previous examples of prejudice. This was understandable, as they were talking to two obviously Anglo-Australian interviewers, who could have been representatives of the school authority for all they knew. Despite this, students from NES backgrounds provided some interesting insights into the way they perceived their encounters with those from different ethnic backgrounds.

(i)   Poor Opinions about Anglo-Australian Students.   Although some students commented that they were insulted in the school by name-calling,

their most common opinions about Anglo-Australians concerned their laziness and unwillingness to work hard. One even sensed a sort of contempt, which might have surprised some Anglo-Australians, even though it was clear from the self-critical comments cited above that they too perceived themselves to be lazy in comparison with ethnic groups.

The following are representative comments from a variety of NES students and provide an insight into some of the experiences of migrants in a Western society like Australia:

Q. What do you think of Australians?
A. Like, the Australian wouldn't give up his Sunday afternoon to work. My dad works. Like, last week he worked twelve hours a day, seven days a week, whereas an Australian wouldn't usually do that. Mainly because the Australians have not seen the hardship that we've been through (Greek girl, Year 11).
A. Education is what it comes down to. They [parents] have it so hard, they say you must get educated at a really young age.... I think we want to finish school. Australian kids, because they have the option, their parents say 'well it's your life, if you decide to leave' ... so they just leave. They [my parents] say 'get a job, because I don't want to see you working in a factory the way I sweat every day.' My mum works in 50 degree heat. I know she's exaggerating, but she works where they burn these little parts, and she gets burns all over her, and it really makes me do my homework (second Greek girl, Year 11).
A. Australian kids take too much for granted. The Australian kids do (Yugoslav boy, Year 12).
A. I think there's more Australian kids out of school than there is in, because the ethnics are more keen than the Australians. All the Australians I know, they give up in form 5, because their parents aren't so hard on them. They don't mind them dropping out sometimes. As for the ethnics, if I told my parents I was going to drop out of school, they'd kick me out of the house, they wouldn't understand (Greek boy, Year 12).

We heard no prejudiced remarks against Asian students, though as the comment from one Asian boy cited below indicates it did exist.

(ii) Comments about Prejudice from the School System.   There were few statements which revealed that students from NES backgrounds felt that the school system discriminated against them. However, as the following excerpt illustrates this could happen when school staff may unwittingly discriminate against some students or could be perceived as doing so, even though they were only enforcing the rules as they saw them.

The incident occurred during the lunch break. It concerned a group of girls from Greek and Italian backgrounds, who were told to move away from an area which they were allowed to use for social relaxation, because staff claimed that their chatter was disturbing Asian students who wanted to use the computer room nearby. Again the reference to Asian students' 'brains' is obvious.

Q. Is it the brainy kids you feel strongly about?
A. I think they get more attention, I think, from the teachers (Greek girl).
Q. Is it any particular group you're thinking of, these brains? What sort of advantage have they got?
A. It's the Asians. They're back every lunchtime doing that [computers] (second Greek girl).
A. I think they might be a bit prejudiced or something like that ... we've got a social area where we can do work, and we were sitting there, we had a free lesson, and this girl was actually trying to get her work done, and she went in and told the coordinator, and he came out and told us off. But then during lunchtime a couple of days ago, when we were doing our work, they were making so much noise and we couldn't do our work. I don't know whether she did that because she really couldn't do her work or it was because of us. I don't know (third Greek girl).

We weren't making that much noise. The coordinator came and said 'you've got plenty of work to do, you shouldn't be playing around like babies.' You can't spend all your time working [other girls agree emphatically]. They tell you off — say 'go do your work.' You study at home, you study at school! (first Greek girl).

An element of sexist discrimination on the part of the male staff could also have been involved in this incident.

Q. It sounds as if the boys might have it a bit worse?
A. Yes, they do, maybe because they answer back — they stand up for themselves (first Greek girl).
A. We just have to stand there and take it. We get told off and take it (Italian girl).

(iii) Prejudice from Anglo-Australians in the Wider Society. The opinions of students from NES backgrounds varied on how much prejudice there was in Australian society. One Italian boy claimed that it didn't really matter how many marks one got for the HSC, you could only get a good job opportunity 'if you're anonymous, because there are a few prejudices out there.' A girl claimed that it was not so much a matter of one's ethnic background so much as the suburb one came from. If it happened to be a

'sort of a scum area, that is where all the scums and vandals are' an employer might not take you on (Greek girl, Year 11).

Comments from several Year 11 and 12 Greek boys illustrated how sensitive some NES students were towards being accepted as Australians:

Q. Are you Australians?
A. I was actually born here (first Year 12 boy).
Q. And how do you feel — are you Australian or Greek?
A. Well, I'm not really sure. I just see myself as an individual. I am just part of Australian society. I don't think I am an Aussie Ocker or old-fashioned Greek (second Year 12 boy).
A. My parents are Greek but don't speak it ... Greek doesn't worry me ... you have a lot of Greeks with jobs and they get things like phone calls because they speak Greek. And then a few of my friends are really thick, but they got jobs with their relatives (Year 11 boy).
Q. And J____ what about you?
A. Yes [I was born here] I suppose we are referred to as Greek, but you know ... (second Year 11 boy).
Q. You are not referred to as Greek — but some other way?
A. Well there used to be a name for them but not any more (third Year 12 Greek boy).
Q. Why? Is it because people have grown up here or what?
A. I think that before people used to just accept it, but now there is sort of a new generation of us — because we are the children of migrants, and there is just more of us, and they just accept us now (second Year 12 Greek boy).

(5) Indo-Asian and Asian Students

If some of the students from NES backgrounds were wary and reticent, the Indo-Asian and Asian students were even more so, and this too was understandable both on cultural and 'political' grounds. Culturally, they may have been trying to give us the answers they felt we wanted to hear. As we tried to avoid putting leading questions on prejudice, Asian students could have been at a loss to know exactly how to respond. Politically, as for students from NES backgrounds, we were obviously authority figures of some sort, and the short period we spent in Suburbia High School gave no time to build up the necessary high level of rapport for doing research into sensitive issues like prejudice and race relations.

In fact, at one of the schools used to construct this composite case study, we were not able to interview any Indo-Asian students. Our policy through-out the research was to ask the principal or vice principal of each school to invite selected groups of students to participate in the interviews rather than coerce them, on the assumption that willing interviewees would be better than unwilling ones. At the school in question, located in the northwestern area of severe social and economic pathology described above, a group of Indo-Asian boys was asked to speak to us but flatly, if politely, refused. They gave no reasons and the principal could not insist.

(*i*)   *Comments on Prejudice in Society.*   It was apparent that students had differing views about the difficulties Asians face. In general there was a marked contrast between the opinions of students that correlated with length of time in Australia. Well-established Chinese students especially from middle- to upper-middle-SES homes spoke of having few problems.

Indo-Asian students who were more recent arrivals had different opinions. They considered that it was difficult to get a job without good English — probably the most common complaint — and that Anglo-Australian employers 'dominate people' (Vietnamese boy, Year 11). Girls had a better chance of getting a job than boys, especially on checkout counters in big stores in areas of high Indo-Asian population where the ability to speak the language was an asset.

Some Indo-Asian students thought that it was important to have connections or even relatives in the company to get a job. 'You can't get a job immediately, there must be a relationship' (Year 11 boy). An Asian's appearance also had some influence on job prospects we were told by a group of boys at Year 12, and this kind of prejudice was of concern, because it lies at the heart of racism.

The experience of a friend of one Cambodian boy at Year 11 had obviously coloured his perceptions of discrimination in Australian society, because it involved an institution — a major Australian bank — that one might have considered would be ultra-careful in its relations with prospective employees. According to his account, the boy's Asian friend had approached one of its branches, and had asked for a job. The reply was given, in so many words: 'We need Australians, we don't want Asians as we have to have people who communicate easily in the _____ bank.'

It should be emphasized that the boy's personal history and experiences in Australia, after fleeing the purges in Cambodia where both his parents were killed, could have accounted for the bitterness with which he told us about the incident. It could also have been inflated. However, the point at issue here, in line with the logic of the phenomenological emphasis in our models of socialization and prejudice, is that this boy's perceptions were genuine even if misplaced. As long as they remained they would colour his whole relationship with future employers.

(*ii*)   *Prejudice in the School.*   From the guarded comments of the Asian students it was apparent that they had experienced prejudice in the school. Friendship was important to them, and one Chinese girl in particular missed having friends among Anglo-Australian students:

Q.   What are things like in this school?
A.   The kids here, if they're in a group, they won't accept you [several girls nod in agreement].
Q.   Do you think Australian girls are jealous of you?
A.   Only in study-wise. I know Asians usually get higher marks ... since I came here I have worked much harder, and usually get higher marks, I think (Malaysian-Chinese girl).
A.   Girls, if they're in a group, they all do the same. If one picks on you, they all do ... but on their own they are okay (third Asian girl).

There was an interesting twist to the experience of one of these Chinese girls. Initially she had not been accepted on first arriving at the school, but when students learned that she came from England and had lived there for many years they became friendlier.

Asian boys were not immune from experiencing prejudice, but in this example some of it apparently came from students from NES backgrounds. The Asian students obviously considered that there was safety in numbers and size:

Q.   Do the boys have the same problem? Do they get picked on?
A.   Not if you're a big size. Not really. I suppose it's because I've been here since form 1, maybe I've been with them longer (first Chinese boy).
Q.   Do you think other migrant groups have the same problem?
A.   I think Greek and Italians not so much, because there are quite a lot of them, so when the new ones come, they go into a group. But with the Chinese, there aren't so many (second Chinese boy).
A.   Greeks and Italians try to pick on us too, so we call them 'wogs' back (first Chinese boy).

Finally, probably the most disturbing comment came from a Year 11 Fijian Indian girl, who had obviously travelled widely and had lived in several countries. The comment came during a discussion with a Year 11 group of girls from the eastern suburb, with its predominantly British and Northern European population:

Q.   What do you all feel, are you Australian or not?
A.   I don't feel like it. I am not welcome as an Australian. I am known as someone who has come from another country and treated like that.
Q.   How are you treated?
A.   Because of my colour, they treat me like someone that is not

welcome. I mean I am not Australian. I am a foreigner, which doesn't worry me. I am proud to be what I am, but it hurts. [In the USA] your colour didn't matter, the same as in Fiji. But when I came here it was really different. I was really disappointed.

Perceptions of Sexism

To judge from students' comments sexism may have been a bigger issue in Suburbia High School than anti-ethnic prejudice. There were many statements to the effect that sexism existed, but little clear indication of how serious it was or how it affected career scenarios. Students from Anglo-Australian and NES background were the most outspoken on the issue with girls from Greek and Italian homes being particularly candid in their comments. Within the wealth of data a number of themes could be identified.

(1) Anglo-Australians' Comments on Sexism during Lessons

Most comments were made about the sexism that occurred in class. Girls complained that boys tried to put them down by smart and derogatory comments. This was most common in junior levels, and was not completely absent from HSC classes, although one Year 12 girl maintained: 'I think we've all grown out of it by that stage.' However, the comments of other girls indicated that she may not have been entirely correct. Evidence also suggested that there was a difference in maturity between Years 11 and 12. Comments from boys in particular at the former level were more brash and often sillier than comments at Year 12.

Many sexist comments from boys were also said to occur during sport or physical education lessons, where girls had to put up with their derogatory remarks about poor performance. 'Like we used to have a girls' cricket team, and the guys used to stand around and say — you know, make comments — I think a lot of it is in fun, it's not very serious' (Year 12 girl).

At year 12 the standard of discussion about sexism was usually mature and sensible. A certain idealism was present, and some of the comments came over as refreshingly naive without the cynicism that can creep into discussions about sexism at more mature and often ideologically biased levels such as university and college. Girls could be surprisingly magnanimous towards boys. They acknowledged that their behaviour could be crude and off-putting at times, but also said that it didn't really worry them in class. Some girls did not take it seriously and obviously regarded it as a fact of life in school.

Many boys were prepared to acknowledge their own shortcomings — 'mucking around' received frequent and often boastful mention — and even admitted to girls' superiority in some aspects of education. The following excerpts from Year 12 discussions illustrate these themes of brashness, idealism and tolerance:

Q. Does it affect your relationships in class to have boys there?
A. I don't think so. I have found that girls and boys are very friendly, they have the same interests, and are equal, and they think the same way (first girl).
A. Well, I think that's one of the advantages of a co-educational school — you treat boys just like other people, you don't worry about what sex they are, they are just people. You treat them just like you would your girlfriends and things like that (second girl).
A. I just find boys are boys and girls are girls. I don't find them any different in class (third girl).
Q. What about the standard of work?
A. They [girls] have a higher pass rate (first girl).
A. Apparently girls do. I don't know whether girls work harder. Why do you think they have a higher pass rate? (first boy).
A. Because the guys muck around in class (second girl).
A. I think they work harder ... the nature between boys and girls. The girls aren't so boisterous as the boys. They don't tend to concentrate as much. The girls are more conscientious than the boys (second boy).
Q. It doesn't seem to make you feel very worried about this?
A. By this stage you realize that you have to work to get anywhere. The earlier bit where you're just competing with other guys who can embarrass the teacher the most, whereas the girls are just trying to get the best marks all the way through (second boy).
Q. They've got a head start?
A. Yes, because they've been working all the way through (second boy).

(2) Ethnic Groups' Perceptions of Sexism in Class

Examples of sexism cited by Greek and Italian girls in particular introduced a cultural dimension into discussions. They focused most on the macho behaviour of boys and even a few teachers from these ethnic backgrounds and girls' reactions to it. Girls also criticized the sexism inherent in parental influences, and such comments provided often dramatic insight into the persistence of fossilized cultural traits even in Melbourne. Most of the girls put a very brave face on things. However, a certain undercurrent of bitterness and hurt was also evident in some comments and this was cause for considerable concern. Some of the girls' observations might provide food for thought about official reluctance to criticize some fossilized ethnic customs, due to ideological bias or belief in naive cultural relativism, and whether this is necessarily in the best interests of young people who have to grow up in a very different Western world.

The girls claimed that they could cope with the macho arrogance of boys in class, and even admitted that some girls could get a bit arrogant in class too, but not as much.

> We get it in class sometimes, they're a bit smart. I just ignore it. Then if you remark back they get really angry. They can't take it. They can't think of anything better to say, they get really upset. Especially if you say something about them physically ... they're very vain (Year 12 Greek girl).

The following extended transcript illustrates how some Year 11 Greek girls felt about the emphasis given to boys and males generally, both in the school and in the home:

Q. They had a kind of equal opportunity course here didn't they?
A. That was for the teachers so they could become aware of sex discrimination in the form, like letting the boys get away with murder, and not letting the girls because boys are meant to be rowdy and boisterous and the girls are not (first girl).
Q. Do you think they are?
A. Yes [emphatically from most girls in the group], Mrs _____ she lets the boys get away with everything. She let them swear, sometime she lets the girls get away with things too ... when you think about it the girls don't fool around as much.... In Greek families it [spoiling boys] exists very much (second girl).
A. When I say things like why can my brother go out [they say] 'he's a boy ... and can't get pregnant', and that's it (third girl).
Q. Do girls get resigned to this if they're from migrant backgrounds, or do they fight about it? How strong is the feminist movement?
A. It's quite strong ... getting stronger. Equal opportunity is quietly strong among Greek women (first girl).
A. Our modern Greek teacher, he's the biggest chauvinist in the school. Last year A—— and myself we were so feminist and sticking up for our rights, we got into so much trouble. He thinks that women should stay at home and have kids every couple of years or so, and do the housework and that's it. I bet if he had a daughter he would probably drown the poor baby (second girl).
A. In Greece, like, they have sons because they don't have to leave

them any dowry, and the son can have the second name (fourth girl).

A. My mum was telling me there are two daughters in her family. Her parents couldn't hack it because there were two daughters, and they always wanted a son, and it makes you feel unwanted (third girl).

Q. And that still affects your lives here? I didn't think it was still going on.

A. Not so much, but in some families. It goes on in my family. There's a word like child in Greek, *'pedi'* which is a non-sexist word for child, and in my family the *pedi* this and the *pedi* that means child not only the boy. And, like, I'm a child, but they always classify that as a boy only (second girl).

A. My dad says 'I'm not going to sell my daughter, she can be educated and has that to offer' (fourth girl).

These girls were also able to rationalize these problems in a mature way and with a degree of insight that would have done justice to a trained anthropologist. This from a Year 11 Greek girl:

A. Could I just make one point? It's really hard to know if it's because you're Greek or whether it's because they're like that, and they're just being parents. Is it the way they grew up and the way they were brought up is the way you're being brought up? The thing is the Greeks now in Greece are given so much freedom now that we would not think of having, and just because our parents came here and they brought their customs here, and that's why it's only the Greeks in Australia ... they came with traditions that are really old, and they come to a new country where it's really free. They are really vulnerable so they stick to those things. It's only the Greeks in Australia or Melbourne in particular. They're scared to change.

Comments on Official Measures to Reduce Sexism in the School

Unfortunately, measures taken by staff seemed to be unsuccessful or provoked amusement and even mild ridicule. Even the careers teacher was candid enough to admit that she pushed equal opportunity 'but boys won't listen anyway and girls think it is a bit of a laugh.' Such opinions were not confined to staff. As one Year 12 girl commented, as equal opportunity program that attempted to stress the value of mathematics for girls was 'a dumb thing to do.' Another girl admitted staying away from lessons on feminism run by another teacher: 'I spent more time out of class than in it' (Anglo-Australian girl, Year 12).

Comments from two Greek boys at Year 12 may suggest that such programs were counter-productive:

I think equal opportunity is pushed onto us too much, because now I'm sort of scared to speak up. I think that a male could do the job much better than girls, but we're scared of a backlash from the chicks (first boy, said with a laugh and apology to the girls present).

An international males' day is needed (second boy).

Sexism in the Workplace and Work Experience

Whether they were from Australian or NES backgrounds most girls criticized the barriers against their entry into certain occupations. For example, in one discussion we were told that girls could not become ambulance officers or firemen, and this seemed to make two Year 12 girls from Greek background very resentful. Another girl at Year 11 had chosen to be a policewoman and had her parents' permission and encouragement, but realized that getting in would depend on the qualifying examinations, and this could be difficult in view of language. In general, there was a touching faith in the power of education and qualifications and, for girls, physical appearance for getting jobs. Most boys seemed to think that they had no natural advantage over girls provided qualifications were the same. Some boys suggested that girls had a bigger range of jobs to choose from especially in the service trades.

It was also evident that boys still thought in stereotyped terms about women's jobs as the following illustrative excerpt from a discussion with Year 12 male and female Anglo-Australian students illustrates. It is not untinged by a degree of cynicism:

Q. Do you think there is a difference between, say boys and girls about getting jobs?
A. It depends on what kind of job (first girl).
A. It depends on the qualifications too. I feel that girls with lower qualifications can have an easier time obtaining a job. There are more jobs for, say, well not untrained, but lower trained (boy).
A. It is changing. They claim that they pay equal wages now, they just call the women's jobs different names so they can pay them less (second girl).
A. There's a reason for it. If you employ a woman and spend a thousand dollars training her, there's a reasonable chance she is going to get married, then has kids, then it knocks her out of the workforce, and you have to replace her (first boy).
A. But it's not fair, she can always come back again (second girl).
A. But in the meantime they have to replace her, which is more

expensive, so overall it would be better to employ the man possibly not so well qualified, and train him, bring him up to standards, and have less chance ... (first boy).

Q. How much discrimination is there against girls?

A. Well, in some jobs but people might traditionally believe that a lot of people in power or seniors believe that a woman's role is in the home (boy).

Q. Does that influences certain plans? Do you think of yourself, oh, I'm only a woman and my chance of getting a job are pretty poor?

A. No, we like to prove them wrong (girl).

Boys from NES backgrounds had the same kinds of opinions as Anglo-Australian boys, but they were also coloured by cultural overtones and macho arrogance.

A. Well, I would say experience combined with education is very important for finding work (Year 12 boy from NES background).

Q. Would you find it easier to get jobs than girls?

A. I think both male and female have the same sort of opportunity to get jobs I suppose ... females there is a lot of secretarial work and things like that, and a lot of girls go into that and boys who have a high education standard they sort of go into the clerical work and management and all that. I think it's about the same (Year 12 boy).

A. I think it's easier for girls ... it depends on what job you're looking for. If you're going for a job as a secretary, you're not going to find a guy going for it (Year 12 Italian boy) [General laughter from the other Greek and Italian boys].

Q. What do you think of the girls' chances if they come from ethnic backgrounds?

A. Depends on whether they're married or not. Depends on whether they are pretty or not. That finishes that! (Year 12 Greek boy) [All the others laugh, and discussion on that topic falls flat].

One boy's opinion about the force of cultural influences on girls' lives verged on a parody, as this example from a Year 12 Croatian boy demonstrates:

I think that the migrant female role is predetermined by the parents, because parents sort of sit there and say you're going to school, and then you're going to be a housewife, and we'll marry you off to some nice lawyer or something. She's got the decision, like they say, this guy comes into the house and they say 'do you want him, yes?' And the father says 'yes or no?' And if she says 'yes', the wife comes and they get married.

An interesting comment with cultural overtones closed the discussion with that particular group. One Greek student pointed to this possible future: 'Go back to a village, buy a little shop, run a taxi, and you've got it made.'

Unfortunately, girls also tended to see getting a job in stereotyped terms:

Q. If a boy went after a job and you went after the same job, how do you think you would get on?

A. Depends on what sort of job. I was working on the holidays in a shop, small business, and the owner wanted a part-timer, and he didn't put male or female. Whenever males came for the job he would say he wanted females, he just preferred to have a female serving (Year 12 Greek girl).

Q. Do you think girls get on better with the public in that kind of personal contact job?

A. Yes, I think we're stereotyped into the idea that we're very good at talking to the public, and they're very good at being mothers, and to have relations with other people such as touch and contact, whereas men aren't expected to do that ... it's very difficult for a man to say 'that looks good on you', etc. (second Year 12 Greek girl).

Q. You're thinking of a particular job. Would that be for hair-dressing?

A. Clothes shop — they want women. If it's a women's shop they want women. If it's a man's shop, they want men (second Greek girl).

However, girls from NES backgrounds in particular disputed that their roles were predetermined, and made many confident assertions that they would not bow to the dictates of culture. As one Greek girl stated emphatically: 'If I get married my husband better know that I am going to work. I am not going to stay home and have babies and wash up and that.'

General Conclusions

This chapter has presented numerous examples of the views of students from a variety of backgrounds on prejudice, racism, sexism and discrimination in the school and society. That they existed is undoubted, though to what extent they played a major part in influencing students' career scenarios was not clear. It may be that many accepted them as part of life, 'that is the way the world is.' We take up this issue in the last chapter.

9 Dimensions of Ethnocultural Hegemony and Resistance in School

The case studies discussed in the previous chapters clearly show that students from ethnic minorities were not inevitably disadvantaged by factors in the school systems, or from the wider community and during ethnic encounters. In fact, findings pointed to ways in which students were able actively to resist some of the forces. We cannot generalize beyond the sample, but as we point out later in this chapter there is growing evidence from Australian, British, American and Canadian research that some ethnic groups succeed in establishing themselves economically and socially even in the face of prejudice and discrimination from the host society. There may be some universal process at work in all multifaceted pluralist societies which enables some ethnic groups to resist the forces of ethnocultural hegemony. The discussion in this chapter leads towards a possible explanation for this resistance in terms of social closure theory.

Forms of Prejudice and Discrimination in Ethnic Encounters

(1) Systemic Factors

To demonstrate the existence of systemic discrimination, that favours some students and disadvantages others, it is necessary to assess a number of factors. One cannot point to apparent occurrences of discrimination in the curriculum or any structural aspect of a school, without also assessing who is disadvantaged, who gains, who might have 'engineered', sought, or intended these outcomes, or whether they are occurrences without hegemonic intent on the part of those in control.

Opportunities for staff to exercise hegemony were available at all four stages of the curriculum. The selection of curriculum content and experiences could be so arranged that Anglo students would benefit, but those from ethnic groups could be disadvantaged. Organization of resources in terms of staff, timetabling, equipment and facilities could similarly disadvantage ethnic students if the school system aimed to exercise hegemonic control over their life chances. In effect, were they the 'poor cousins' and deprived of facilities which were available only to Anglos? Methods of evaluation provide unique opportunities for staff to influence promotion of students into the critical examination grades of Years 11 and 12. Only by assessing both the vernacular and observer's evidence described in the previous chapters can one assess the effects of the above factors.

(2)   Personal Factors at the Transmission Stage of the Curriculum

Although the other curriculum stages do depend on the motivations and values of staff, it is during the actual transmission of the curriculum content and experiences at the teaching–learning interface that more personal kinds of prejudice and discrimination are involved. They are quite difficult to establish beyond reasonable doubt and their deleterious effects cannot be assumed, as the theoretical discussion about the limitations of self-esteem and culture contact theories in Chapter 2 indicated. The terms 'prejudice' and 'discrimination' are also subject to loose, emotive and often ideological usage, which frequently clouds discussion on the whole issue of interethnic relations and calls for some clarification of the terms before employing them in any analysis.

(i) *Prejudice: A Realistic Group-Conflict Perspective.* There are numerous definitions of prejudice as each tends to follow the emphasis of its parent academic discipline, and little will be gained by reviewing them in detail. As Banks (1985) has rightly pointed out the phenomenon of prejudice is a complex one that combines psychological and sociological factors. Although Banks does not consider this, it is also possible that prejudice has deep roots in socio–biological drives (Dawkins, 1976; Bullivant, 1981a:54) which relate to what we term a group's 'survival imperative'.

Following these kinds of interpretations, the theoretical framework that guided our research extended the ideas of 'realistic group-conflict theory' (Le Vine and Campbell, 1972:29–42) along lines suggested by Max Weber, Banton and others. Our view of prejudice rejects purely psychologistic interpretations, while recognizing that some individuals may be more predisposed to be prejudiced than others. Even when this appears to be the case in an isolated situation such as a school, the societal context of prejudice and discrimination needs to be recognized. As Barton and Walker (1983:8) point out: 'Both racism in schools and conflict in the community are not simple products of isolated episodes or of individual interpretations and whims; rather they are rooted in the well established and deeply entrenched institutional routines of group life.'

Realistic group-conflict theory assumes 'that group conflicts are rational in the sense that groups do have incompatible goals and are in competition for scarce resources' (Le Vine and Campbell, *op. cit.*). In our view, scarce resources can be both economic and social rewards such as others' esteem and increased status. Individuals and groups strive to maximize these gains and advantages and promote their sense of self- or group-satisfaction, in competition and occasionally conflict with other individuals and groups. To legitimate their 'right' to greater access to such rewards and satisfaction it is necessary for groups to establish grounds for claiming that they are 'different' from others and therefore entitled to such privileged gains.

These tendencies are likely to be magnified in a society that is characterized by multifaceted pluralism, as the social, political, economic, historical, racial, gender and other diacritica provide more grounds for claiming differential access to rewards than is the case in homogeneous societies. Strategies of 'social closure' discussed in Chapter 2 utilize some or all of these diacritica. A sociological definition of prejudice that fits within this view has been proposed by Theodorson and Theodorson (1970:311):

> [Prejudice is] any oversimplified and overgeneralized belief about the characteristics of a group or category of people, either favorable or unfavorable. Prejudice then means to prejudge any individual in an out-group on the basis of his supposed similarity to the stereotype of his group. In this sense the person who sees all the members of a persecuted minority as uniformly kind, generous, noble, etc., rather than as ordinary fallible human beings like those of his in-group, is prejudiced; the oppressed minority is denied ordinary human characteristics.

(ii) The Dual Nature of Prejudice. The dual nature of prejudice, i.e., that it can be both negative and positive, has been commented on by others (see for instance Milner, 1975:218) and is important to bear in mind. It is not unknown for simplistic educational solutions to minority group problems to have been adopted for reasons that had more to do with emotive, positive prejudice than any logical rationale. This tendency, which appears to contradict the basic tenets of realistic group-conflict theory, can usually be explained by searching for the ideological, political, economic and other motives behind the actions of those who are positively prejudiced. They stand to gain in some respect, even if only by a reduction of feelings of guilt for the historical mistreatment of a persecuted minority, fear of legal sanctions against negative prejudice which makes them overreact, the need to maintain the respect of others — on the world scale, the international community — or pure altruism, a relatively rare phenomenon.

(iii) The Fallacy of Assuming Moral or Normative Equivalence. The tendency for an observer to take such a view is often due to adopting what I term an assumption of normative equivalence, which is analogous to Wolfe's

(1985) concept of 'moral equivalence'. That is, an observer uses his or her own normative frame of reference when interpreting and judging an event involving another culture, and assumes that it abides by the same moral code. Normative equivalence takes account of both the norms and sanctions in a substantive or descriptive sense that are operating in a situation and those that ought to or should prevail in a prescriptive sense as the bases for understanding social relations. Instead, during cross-cultural encounters, a more interpretive view of social relations should be taken and assumptions not made that they are all equally governed by similar normative codes.

However, this too runs certain risks. The assumption of normative equivalence is on one polar side of a continuum and its corollary is the idea of universalism, i.e., that all cultures share universal characteristics. On the other side of the continuum is what I term naive cultural relativism. Originally cultural relativity was a doctrine which maintained that part of a culture should only be evaluated and studied within its 'parent' society and culture. Its corollary is contextualism. However, due to what were often ideological reasons the idea of cultural relativity has been used to maintain that no cultural feature should be criticized by members of another society using value judgments which are not appropriate to the feature. In effect 'anything went' cross-culturally. As our ensuing discussion suggests the polar ends of the continuum can pose dilemmas for a teacher when faced with cultural practices very different from his or her own.

(iv) Discrimination. Prejudice is the attitudinal precursor of discrimination, which conversely is the behavioural or action outcome of prejudice. Discrimination can be defined as: 'The unequal treatment of individuals or groups on the basis of some, usually categorical, attribute, such as racial, ethnic, religious, or social-class membership' (Theodorson and Theodorson, 1970:115). The value of this definition is that it can encompass discrimination in favour of an individual or group, which is the result of positive prejudice towards them. Favouritism towards pupils in school is a well-known example of this phenomenon.

To stress the complex relationships between prejudice and discrimination, Rose (1974) has developed four ideal types (see also discussion in Banks, 1985:71–2):

1. The unprejudiced nondiscriminator;
2. The unprejudiced discriminator;
3. The prejudiced nondiscriminator;
4. The prejudiced discriminator.

Rose's typology is an essential corrective to simplistic ideas that people's prejudiced attitudes towards others must invariably result in discrimination. We should also extend the typology to include the categories that follow from the existence of positive prejudice and its corollary, positive discrimination.

(v) Legitimate and Illegitimate Discrimination. Prejudice is one of the conditions that give rise to discrimination, but the existence of discrimination does not necessarily mean that prejudice was its precondition. To appreciate this, it is useful to distinguish between legitimate and illegitimate discrimination. The latter results from prejudice, while the former is universal. 'Whether or not discrimination is considered as illegitimate depends on societal values, and social rank and social stratification are based firmly on discriminatory principles' (Theodorson and Theodorson, 1970:116). Given the unlikelihood and socio–biological undesirability of achieving an egalitarian utopia, such a situation will always be with us, and from the point of view of a group's survival imperative we must accept the inevitability of legitimate discrimination (see discussion in Bullivant, 1981a: Foreword and Ch. 2).

(vi) The Need for Gradations in Use of Terms. On occasion the use of such broad and uncompromising terms as 'prejudiced' or 'racist' may be far too sweeping and question-begging, because they do not allow for finer shades of meaning. Their use also risks otherwise rational and innocent individuals being labelled as 'prejudiced', just because their views about members of an ethnic group do not happen to accord with official ideologies, political pressure or prevailing conventional wisdom. To avoid this kind of situation, Banton has suggested (1985) that gradations in terms are needed in certain circumstances. He has proposed that the term 'antipathy' should be adopted in place of prejudice, in some contexts, to reduce the kind of blanket generalizations that are too frequently used about people's unfavourable reactions to others.

Prejudice, Discrimination and Resistance in the Curriculum

(1) Selection of Curricula

(i) Inner City High School. Inner City High School selected two clusters of subjects and content for Year 12 students. The first cluster comprised HSC Group 1 subjects, which was a trong academic emphasis. No Group 2 subjects were provided. The second cluster comprised STC subjects, which were much more 'liberal' in emphasis and provided a broader vocationally oriented education. Both HSC and STC were terminal qualifications and were accepted by the great majority of tertiary institutions for entry purposes, although the two major universities in Melbourne did not recognize STC.

Some students claimed that this hampered their future career plans, as their decision to do STC had resulted in them being shut out from both these institutions. To that extent it might appear that they were disadvantaged.

however, it was a form of legitimate discrimination built into the admission regulations of both universities. It also applied to all students regardless of ethnic background, and was out of the school's control. Thus it cannot be interpreted as deliberate systemic ethnocultural hegemony, even though it disadvantaged some students from an ethnic background.

It is also difficult to establish a case that hegemonic control was being exerted through the content of curriculum selection. As we observed the school constructed the curriculum only after what appeared to have been an exhaustive process of establishing the needs and preferences of students at the end of each academic year. 'Blocking' was then use to maximize their choices. More generally, they were able to make their wishes known through their Students Representative Council.

Staff claimed to be highly responsive to students' needs, and there was no apparent evidence to suggest otherwise. In fact, the current structure of the curriculum at Year 12 with the inclusion of sciences and mathematics owed its establishment and continuation to the decision of staff in the late 1970s not to drop these subjects. They took it partly on ideological grounds that even students from lower-SES backgrounds should be given a chance to go on to HSC and tertiary entrance if they wished.

Student and parental 'resistance'.   The decision can also be interpreted as resulting from a form of NES and Indo-Asian parent and student 'resistance'. In part, it had acceded to their demands for high-prestige mathematics and science subjects, which they considered would open the door to university entrance and professional careers. This last fact makes it extremely difficult to establish a case for ethnic hegemony in curriculum selection which worked against the interests of students from NES and Indo-Asian backgrounds, and in favour of Anglo-Australian students. The reverse was more likely. The availability of HSC Group 1 subjects favoured those students who were academically motivated and looked towards university entry, namely those from NES and Indo-Asian backgrounds, rather than Anglo-Australians. The majority of the latter came from lower-SES backgrounds and, according to the evidence, were said to be less motivated academically.

Limited multicultural provision for ethnic students.   There was only a very limited and tokenistic provision of curriculum content appropriate for multicultural education. What there was appeared to stress ethnic life styles, although staff claimed that they were teaching survival skills to enhance life chances of students from NES and Indo-Asian backgrounds through units in commerce, social studies and related subjects. However, these were obviously of the additive variety and could not be claimed to provide an integrated approach to multicultural education infusing the whole curriculum. Most of the purely multicultural content was in the ESL courses, but stress on these could go only so far in preparing students from NES backgrounds for social and economic survival once they had left school.

Student and parental resistance to multicultural education. The lack of a comprehensive multicultural education program was largely due to decisions of staff to concentrate on the HSC and STC at Year 12. Like the concentration on the HSC itself, it is thus not possible to claim that this constituted some form of discrimination, as parental and student demands were clearly for academic courses, which they considered would provide better survival skills than multicultural education programs.

This was a 'Catch 22' situation as there was little opportunity in an obviously very full curriculum for staff to give more time for the approach called 'politicized multicultural education' (Bullivant, 1986b) even if this had been demanded, as some HSC subjects might have had to be dropped. In such circumstances, teachers might have resisted such an emphasis and opted for the more tokenistic form of multicultural education stressing life styles. Such an approach would then have left teachers open to the criticism that it was little more than a subtle kind of cultural capital or habitus, which perpetuated Anglo dominance and offered little that would enhance the life chances of students from ethnic backgrounds.

(ii) Suburbia High School. In contrast to Inner City High School, Suburbia High School selected only one cluster of subjects, those oriented exclusively to the HSC Group 1, with at most three other Group 2 subjects. Attempts to expand the number of the latter failed due to lack of parental and student support. Although there was a wider range of non-academic subjects. available at Year 11, it was seen as a preparation for HSC, and students were advised to keep the prerequisites for that level in mind when they made their Year 11 subject choices. In effect the HSC dominated both years.

Despite the fact that such an arrangement was clearly disadvantageous for those who did not aspire to an academic or professional future, this selection of the curriculum was demanded by students and parents, and these demands were channelled to the school staff directly and through the School Council. Equally clearly, the possibility of providing the STC option failed through lack of parental support.

Who stood to gain from the selection of HSC Group 1 subjects in Suburbia High School? Obviously, it was those students who were academically motivated and aspired to tertiary education and professional careers. It was not possible to say who these were with as much certainty as was the case with Inner City High School, due to the greater variations of the SES component in the ethclasses which were the feeder areas for the school. However, our evidence suggested that those who most demanded the HSC Group 1 emphasis in the curriculum were students from some NES (particularly Greek and Italian), and Indo-Asian (particularly Chinese) backgrounds, together with higher-SES Anglo-Australian students and their parents. They were the most academically motivated and would benefit by the concentration on HSC Group 1.

Those who were most likely to be disadvantaged were inter alia Anglo-

Australian students from lower-SES backgrounds, along with students from NES and Asian backgrounds who did not aspire to tertiary education. The numbers of the latter dropped off in senior levels due to them leaving the school by Year 10, to seek alternative education in TOP and TAFE courses. Whether they were disadvantaged, or would have transferred due to perceived lack of ability or preference for such education anyway, is a moot point.

As in Inner City High School, there were a few instances where students considered that the range of subjects available to them did not enable chosen career options to be pursued. The example of the student who was 'locked out' of his 'dream' of becoming a PE teacher was probably the most memorable in this respect. Apart from such isolated instances, it was not possible to state with any certainty that the selection of the curriculum discriminated by exerting hegemonic control over the life chances of academically motivated students from non-Anglo-Australian backgrounds. The reverse was truer: those were the students most likely to be advantaged.

Lack of a multicultural curriculum for ethnic students. There was some evidence that official policy at Suburbia High School was not in favour of multiculturalism. From comments of the principal it was also apparent that he was not keen for more modern Greek to be introduced into the curriculum, despite the demands of representatives of the Greek community on the School Council. He seemed determined to resist them if possible. Whether this constituted discrimination that would disadvantage ethnic students' career scenarios is open to question. A language such as Greek would not be regarded as a high-status subject for university entrance requirements, even though it has a high intrinsic value for maintaining ethnic life styles. To that extent the decision not to allow Greek could be interpreted as a form of ethnocultural hegemony, but in the wider context of studying it to enhance life chances this is debatable. To establish such a case it would be necessary to show that possession of multicultural knowledge and a community language was likely to improve survival skills in a society dominated by English as a common language of commerce and social interaction, and by meritocratic accreditation through Year 12 examinations. In such a societal system legitimate discrimination is inevitable and a case for the opposite would be hard to sustain.

Students' indifference to multicultural education. There was no indication from students in either case study that they were concerned about the lack of multicultural education as a factor in preparing their career scenarios. We might expect this to have been the case, as evidence from Britain, Canada and the United States (Bullivant, 1981b; Sowell, 1986) has suggested that interest in language and cultural maintenance surfaces in the established ethnic second generation once it has overcome economic difficulties. With those concerns settled, it can begin to concentrate on a revival of ethnicity and culture that have been neglected in the struggle for survival. We might expect ethnic groups in Australia to be similar.

In this respect, with one qualification, we can agree with Sturman's (1985:82) conclusion from a comprehensive review of the literature that

> ... research evidence indicated that it was not in general the new arrivals who saw the need for multicultural aspects to the curriculum. Rather, new arrivals were more concerned with what might be termed survival skills, such as English proficiency, and it was later-generation immigrant Australians who were likely to support multicultural aspects of curricula including language maintenance.

Our qualification stems from Sturman's unclear use of the term 'later-generation' rather than the customary term 'second generation'. If by later-generation he means second generation, i.e., children born of former immigrants, then his assertion is scarcely tenable. Children born of established immigrants are 'new arrivals' in the sense that they ultimately have to become established in the workforce and society, and while young may not have time or desire for multicultural education and ethnic revitalization. This has to wait until they are securely established in economic terms as adult second generation migrant–settlers. From the findings of our research NES and Asian students' preferences in education were clearly for obtaining survival skills including HSC qualifications that would lead on to tertiary education. Multicultural education scarcely featured in their aims.

(2)   Evaluation for Entry into Senior Levels

According to classic cultural reproduction theory, one way of controlling the life chances of students is to prevent their promotion into the higher year levels, which are the gateways to tertiary academic futures and the professions. As Lakomski (1984:153) has noted: 'They [cultural reproduction theorists] argue that schools effectively perpetuate the existing social structure in that they promote those students who enter equipped with cultural privileges and progressively eliminate others whose cultural capital differs significantly from that of the dominant group.' What evidence pointed to this process in our study?

Both Inner City High and Suburbia High operated a system of evaluation by term examinations for controlling entry into the Year 11 and 12 HSC streams. In general, students must have passed the stipulated number of subjects at the Year 11 level, especially in the prerequisites laid down for the HSC examination. Lack of them could effectively act as a barrier to going on to some subjects, thus limiting the career options available.

In both schools the Year 11 and 12 coordinators, assisted by the careers teacher and others called in if necessary, were in a position to exercise a channelling role in deciding who went on to HSC. In effect they operated a filtering system, through which students had to pass towards their chosen careers. Conceivably the discussions about each student's 'promotability' that occurred at the end of each year provided one opportunity for exercising hegemonic control over the aspirations of those who wanted to proceed to university and on into the professions. However, 'filter papers' or examinations — to pursue the metaphor — were built into the system through the prerequisites set down for HSC, and were thus largely outside the control of the schools. Despite this, the possibility always existed within either school for the promotion system to be used to discriminate against students.

Student Resistance at Inner City High School.   There was always the possibility that such moves could be resisted. At least in Inner City High School the dual structure of senior courses provided a flexible way of promoting students and gave them an opportunity to resist staff decisions on promotion. There were no prerequisites nor examination barrier to entering the STC stream, but entry to Year 12 HSC was not automatic. Students must have passed satisfactorily at the semester examinations in Year 11 and have had the necessary prerequisites. The staff sometimes felt that a student should not attempt HSC and advised against it. In theory this was one way by which a student's ambitions could be curtailed.

In practice, however, students could get around staff advice not to attempt HSC, provided they could establish a case and had the prerequisites. Those students who wanted to do mathematics and sciences were specially favoured, as their ambitions were backed by the directive from the Regional Director of Education that no students were to be excluded if they wanted to do these subjects, the major route to prestigious academic tertiary courses. From the evidence such students were more likely to be from NES and Asian backgrounds, so again it is difficult to see how they were being discriminated against, compared with Anglo-Australian students. Prima facie it would appear that as much as possible was being done to cater for their career ambitions, even though some staff felt that their unrealistic aspirations worked against them.

Limitations on Student Resistance at Suburbia High School.   A similar system of promotion through examination results and staff consultations operated in Suburbia High School. However, they were not governed by a Regional Director's directive to favour those who wanted to do mathematics and sciences, so a way was at least available for staff to restrict the promotion of some students. The rules regarding promotion also appeared to be somewhat tougher compared with Inner City High School. The preoccupation of staff with assisting students to determine their study pathways, rather than career pathways, was obviously a potential source of limitation for some, but hardly discrimination. The advice from staff that resulted in non-academic students being weeded out at Year 11 and leaving school for the local TAFE college may have been discriminatory, but applied to all students rather than to those from NES and Asian backgrounds. It was not outside the bounds of possibility that discrimination could have been exercised in the way tests and examinations were assessed, but this was impossible to establish.

A 'grey area' existed in the case of some Indo-Asian students for whom it was not always easy to recommend promotion. They often had difficulties with English, which could hamper their progress, even though their standards in other subjects such as mathematics and sciences were satisfactory. The ESL Coordinator played a significant part in such students' promotion, as of necessity she could recommend against it in what she perceived to be their best interests. De facto legitimate discrimination may have resulted in such cases but may not have been perceived as such by those who failed to gain promotion. There was only one example of how this affected an Indo-Asian student's prospects, namely the Cambodian student cited in a previous chapter.

There may well have been similar cases that were not observed, and their complexity admits of no simple solution. The dominant academic motivation of Asian students has the corollary that it necessitates a high degree of dedication and even compulsion to work hard, which may be outside the range of most Anglo teachers' experience. Such teachers might fail to empathize with such drive and also not understand the considerable loss of face for these students when high goals are not achieved. Lacking such deep understanding, staff are always at risk of adopting policies towards Asian students, which may be completely rational and even non-discriminatory, but are nonetheless culturally insensitive.

(3)   Organization of the Curriculum for Careers Advice

In both schools the personnel involved with providing careers advice and guidance were the careers teacher, Years 11 and 12 level coordinators and, for students from NES and Indo-Asian backgrounds, the ESL teachers. In addition there were impersonal, written sources of information such as career guides, brochures and other material. Of these systemic sources, the evidence showed that the written sources and the school careers teacher were seen by students as the most helpful. Asian students tended to consult her more than others and also preferred to consult written sources of information, but this was probably because they 'know where they are heading', in the words of the careers teacher at Inner City High School. It cannot be assumed that it indicated discrimination.

Limitations on the financial provisions for all facilities were present in both schools, and this was most obvious at Inner City High School. The most serious was the lack of funding for ethnic teacher aides and the interpreter service which severely limited the back-up available to teachers. These factors could be interpreted as a form of ethnocultural hegemony, but were more likely due to the deficiencies in the centralized, bureaucratic control by the Education Department.

(i) *Effects of the Referral System.* A more serious factor was the stress on referring students to the careers teacher because of Education Department regulations. This placed considerable responsibility on her to give advice that was appropriate for students' needs. In effect the careers advice 'buck' stopped at her desk. The reluctance of other senior staff to give advice except in an indirect way relating to subject choices was obviously a self-imposed limitation on the avenues open to them to influence adversely the career scenarios of any students, let alone those from NES and Indo-Asian backgrounds. Equally it could provide uncaring staff with a convenient excuse not to help students they wanted to discriminate against, but there was no evidence that this occurred.

The operation of the 'referral system' in both schools placed considerable importance on the careers teacher's skills, sensitivity and understanding of students' needs. We found no firm evidence, either written or verbal, to suggest that students from NES and Asian backgrounds claimed that there were prejudice and discrimination in her help and advice. However, the careers teacher at Inner City High School did admit to advising students from Indo-Asian backgrounds differently from NES and Anglo students, but no evidence suggested that this was discriminatory.

Some comments from students in both schools indicated that they did not find her advice helpful, that they could not contact her, or found that she was inadequate or a waste of time consulting. However, the few comments of this kind were spread across the board and were not confined to students from NES or Asian backgrounds in a way that might have suggested that they were being discriminated against. The opposite impression was the case. In both schools we observed several instances where the careers teacher obviously went well beyond the call of duty to assist students: being available in the careers room during the lunch hour to see them; making the careers room a casual drop-in centre especially for students from NES and Asian backgrounds; taking students on weekend camps or visits into the community to improve their awareness of jobs; being available after school often quite late at night to see parents and students.

In principle, there was the possibility that the careers teacher might have been less sensitive to the needs of NES and Asian than Anglo-Australian students. At both Inner City High and Suburbia High the careers teachers were Anglo-Australians, and made no mention of being able to speak either a European or Asian language. Research by Davis (1986) has shown this to be the case in the great majority of schools throughout Australia. This situation has prompted her to comment (1986:49, 83–4):

> Unfortunately ... this lack of language skills also reflects a lack of real familiarity with non-Anglo cultures. This is a clear danger sign

in a multicultural society which is endeavouring to ensure that migrant and refugee youth are not disadvantaged in terms of careers education and counselling.... At best, counsellors may have, in a few instances, offered some extra time for counselling, but the norm was to offer essentially the same program as that offered generally. Schools seem to acknowledge that there are special needs but, whether because of a lack of appropriate material resources or a lack of staff expertise, little is being done.

There was also evidence in both schools that senior staff took advantage of informal situations such as school camps or educational excursions to chat to students and give them careers advice. Such opportunities may have been denied to some students from NES backgrounds who were not allowed to attend by their parents. This occurred in both schools, but obviously cannot be attributed to discrimination on the part of the staff, as it was a parental decision whether or not their children should participate in extra-curricular activities.

Parental resistance to school assistance. Despite the efforts of staff to meet parents in informal situations, they were not always reciprocated. For example, on one occasion at Suburbia High School we attended a well-organized meeting in the evening which aimed to attract Italian parents for a discussion on their children's careers. The careers teacher, principal, ethnic aide, community education officer and an interpreter all gave up the evening to be present. Well-presented and appropriate refreshments were provided. The event attracted six Italians. Four were from one family — mother, son and two daughters. Another was the president of the Italian Association who would have been there anyway. Many reasons can be adduced to this kind of result, and it could be too sweeping to label it 'resistance' even though its effect was similar.

(ii) *The Helping Role of ESL Teachers.* The special responsibilities of the ESL teachers in both schools brought them close to NES and Indo-Asian students, in a way that may not have been the case with other staff. We found no evidence to suggest that the ESL teachers were lacking in sensitivity towards the aspirations of students from NES and Indo-Asian backgrounds. As noted above, there were some occasions when they had to be realistic and suggest that a student not be promoted to the next grade, because of lack of familiarity with English. However, exercising the professional responsibility and judgment that are part of the systemic role expectations cannot be construed as illegitimate discrimination.

Our evidence suggested that ESL teachers did give advice on careers, and it is difficult to see how they could avoid doing so if they were concerned to equip young NES and Indo-Asian students with more than the bare essentials of language skills. It did place ESL teachers at risk legally, but was in line with a general pattern noted by Davis (*ibid.*, p. 83):

> As regards migrant and refugee youth specifically, only 15 (7.8%) of the sample of schools indicated that they offered *any* special careers education and counselling, and then usually only within the ESL stream. Indeed, there is some evidence from the questionnaire that, to a very great extent, the ESL teachers, because of their language and communicative skills, fulfilled a great many other educational roles for migrant students, including careers education, guidance and counselling.

Had the ESL teachers at Inner City High and Suburbia High Schools kept to the letter of the law it is likely that many students from NES and Asian backgrounds would have been discriminated against, but the ultimate responsibility for this must be attributed to Departmental regulations rather than the teachers themselves.

(iii)   Other Sources of Information.   Impersonal sources of information such as pamphlets, guidelines and other written material also played their part as logistical support for staff. Our evidence indicated that they were highly valued, especially by students from Asian backgrounds. When assessing whether discrimination existed in the way this kind of logistical support was provided it is necessary to bear in mind that neglect or shortages in some areas could have been errors of omission. Shortages of information there certainly were in both schools: some pamphlets were lacking in the careers room, and the library in each case could have had more information in ethnic languages to assist students from such backgrounds. However, there was obviously a financial limit to what could be provided, and only perfectionists would argue that there could never be enough material to assist students in this important area. To establish the case that lack of them constituted deliberate discrimination, i.e., errors of commission, would have been extremely difficult if not impossible.

(4)   Transmission of the Curriculum

(i)   Little Evidence of Overt Prejudice by School Staff.   It was in teaching-learning interfaces at the classroom level that prejudice and discrimination were most likely to occur. But with few exceptions, it was not possible to do the kind of fine-grained research that would have been needed to establish this. There was some evidence from NES girls in both schools that some members of staff from similar backgrounds were 'chauvinist'. For example, there was the incident described in a previous chapter where a group of girls from NES backgrounds in Suburbia High School felt that a member of staff had unfairly asked them to stop making a noise during their

lunch hour so that Asian students could use the computer room in peace and quiet.

In such a sensitive area as race relations the term 'racist' can be employed in an ill-considered way that is often little more than an emotive term of abuse. We expected to find the term used about members of staff in both schools, but this did not occur. It was used by students from all backgrounds about employers in the community, and by some few students from NES and Asian backgrounds about Anglo-Australians in general. But this was the limit of perceptions of so-called 'racism'.

(ii) Staff Preference for Asian Students in Class. We found very little if any evidence that staff were prejudiced against Asian students. The converse was very much the case. They considered them to be exemplary students, quiet, diligent and highly motivated, and valued their presence in class. The only contrary opinion we heard was during an informal discussion at the pilot school, when a female member of staff commented half in joke that Asian students were so successful that very soon Australia would find itself taken over and run by Asians.

The perceptions of staff in both schools about students from NES backgrounds focused on their high aspirations, macho attitudes and sexist comments about girls. The reactions of some staff to these features were adverse, but whether this would lead to systematic discrimination is debatable. However, as a corollary, the frequency of the remarks suggested that Anglo staff might well have held strong stereotyped views about NES students which may have had several adverse effects. Firstly, it may have caused some staff to treat the aspirations of students from NES backgrounds less seriously than they warranted, because 'everybody knows' that their ambitions are too high. Secondly, macho behaviour may have produced a labelling effect which made staff assume that all students from NES backgrounds treated girls in a disparaging way. In any representative group there would have been exceptions, but they may have been labelled and treated accordingly along with those who were sexist.

(iii) Self-Disadvantaging Behaviour of Anglo-Australian Students. Staff may not have deliberately discriminated against Anglo-Australian students — something that would run counter to ethnocultural reproduction theory — but ironically Anglo-Australian students even from higher SES backgrounds probably may have invited discrimination by default against themselves. This would most likely have occurred if they belonged to that group of students, who by their own admission 'mucked around' in class, attempted to challenge teachers' authority, made sexist comments about girls and generally, again by their own admission, did not work as hard as students from NES or Asian backgrounds. This paradoxical situation, producing what we term a self-deprivation syndrome, contributes to the model of the aspiration-motivation gradient discussed below.

Prejudice, Sexism and Discrimination

The incidence of interethnic prejudice and tensions was rarely so intrusive as to show out in dramatic ways, with the exception of one group of prejudiced students from British and Northern European backgrounds. However, it was clear from the evidence that staff in both schools knew that interethnic tensions existed outside in the community and could lead to violence between members of ethnic groups, which was then brought into the schools. Internal 'territorial' ambitions by some ethnic groups to control particularly favoured playing spaces on the campus of Inner City High School occasionally triggered off serious tensions and ugly violence. Some of the students we talked to also commented on this aspect of their lives. Given that tensions were present, how seriously did they affect the life chances of students from NES and Indo-Asian and Asian backgrounds?

(1) Prejudice between Students

There was considerable evidence of negative prejudice leading to overt acts of discrimination on the part of students towards their peers in both schools: verbal abuse, name calling, violence between ethnic groups. Whether these kinds of discrimination affected students' ability to plan and work towards career scenarios was extremely debatable. As the old adage has it: 'Sticks and stones may break my bones, but names will never hurt me.' In other words, adopting Rose's term, some students may have been prejudiced non-discriminators.

    The case that such prejudice did lead to discrimination that affected students' academic attainment or aspirations rests on a very tenuous set of causal assumptions. It must first be established that prejudice does adversely affect a person's perceptions of his or her own worth, i.e., self-esteem. Even if this is the case, it does not necessarily follow that academic achievement will fall. Even Coopersmith, one of the architects of self-esteem theory (1975), has acknowledged the tenuousness of the relationship between self-esteem and academic performance. The likelihood that poor self-esteem will adversely affect career aspirations is similarly debatable. In our two case studies we would suggest that these relationships were 'not proven'.

(2) Prejudice during Work Experience

All groups of students claimed that they had experienced prejudice and discrimination in the workplace, during work experience programs and part-time employment. As a result of this some students claimed to have been put off their career plans and disadvantaged. This was not confined to those from

Asian or NES backgrounds. In fact, in areas of high ethnic concentration Anglo-Australian students felt that they were disadvantaged and cited examples of discrimination from ethnic employers. One or two examples suggested that Asians experienced prejudice and discrimination that amounted to racism. There was no clear difference in these patterns of discrimination between boys and girls. In some occupations girls felt discriminated against and claimed that boys had an advantage. In other occupations boys felt discriminated against and claimed girls had an advantage in casual employment.

(3)   The Effect of Socio-Economic Status

There was some evidence that disadvantage may not have been solely a function of ethnic and cultural differences, but that these factors were augmented or even exceeded by SES differences. This complicating factor operated especially in the case of some students from lower to lower-middle SES homes. Regardless of ethnic backgrounds, they tended to be more apathetic, less confident of their career plans and did not aspire so highly as students across all ethnic groups from middle- to upper-SES backgrounds.

However, there were important exceptions to this such as Vietnamese in lower-socio-economic areas of first settlement, who have upwardly socially mobile aspirations and move out as quickly as they can. Cultural factors may be more important in this case. It lends some support to Sturman's (1985:76) opinion, based on a comprehensive review of research studies of immigrants' levels of achievement in Australia: 'As was the case with educational aspirations, occupational aspirations were less closely linked to socioeconomic status for ethnic groups than other group in the Australian population.'

Generalizations should not be made from the limited data, but one tentative conclusion in the case of some ethnic groups is that under certain circumstances SES factors in the schools may have 'washed out' ethnicity and cultural difference as a correlation of either actual or perceived disadvantage. But the inmterrelationship of these factors is highly complex, as Sturman has also pointed out (*ibid.*, p. 81)

(4)   Sexism

The relationship between boys and girls that indicated sexist prejudice showed several patterns. In general sexism occurred more within ethnic groups (intraethnic) than between groups (interethnic). There was also some discrimination based on gender criteria in the workplace and within the school system itself.

(i) Sexism within Ethnic Groups: Culturally Legitimate Discrimination?
When analyzing sexism that affects girls from ethnic backgrounds it is
important to recall the two kinds of discrimination discussed in the first
section of this chapter. Within an ethnic group there may be what can be
termed culturally legitimate discrimination. To an external observer from a
different culture this may appear to result from sexist prejudice, and such
evidence as macho arrogance from Greek boys when putting Greek girls
down may be interpreted in this light. However, the girls may not see it in
the same way, and some of their comments suggested that Greek and Italian
girls did not feel put down by the sexist, macho behaviour of boys from the
same ethnic backgrounds. Girls claimed to be 'used to it,' and even
responded by 'rubbishing' the boys. Some girls' comments also suggested
that boys' sexist remarks stimulated them to try even harder, 'just to show
them.'

Culturally legitimate discrimination may also have occurred during the
discussions with Vietnamese students, especially at the pilot study school.
The senior boys — virtually young men in some cases — were apparently in
a position of some authority, and the girls deferred to them. It is possible that
this was a function of their relatively recent arrival in Australia, whereas
those who had been in the country longer may have had a less obvious
pattern of deference. The point at issue, however, is that this too could have
been another form of apparent discrimination that is culturally sanctioned. To
interpret it as discrimination in the illegitimate sense of sexism could have
been an oversimplification.

We did find examples that indicated more extreme forms of apparent
sexist discrimination. The Turkish girl, who was beaten up by her brother
outside the school, was one such example. However, if this kind of sibling
control over a sister's sexual integrity is customary in Turkish culture, as
indeed it is, then once again it may be insensitive to label it as sexist
discrimination. In Western culture such behaviour cannot be condoned, but
when faced with it a teacher can be trapped in the dilemma discussed above.
On the one hand, by adopting a form of naive cultural relativism, the teacher
may decide not to interfere in a matter that appears to be culturally
sanctioned, and run the risk of ignoring what could be a serious matter. On
the other hand, by making an assumption of normative equivalence, the
teacher would have to intervene even if he offended ethnic community
sensitivities.

(ii) Resistance to Sexism. This is not to claim that girls from NES
backgrounds passively accepted the culturally legitimate discrimination they
experienced within their families. They were quite prepared to speak out
against it, and some have managed to break away and get into professional
careers and tertiary education. Comments indicating the existence of
'fossilized cultures' within some NES communities cropped up several times
and cast some doubt on official policies that encourage their maintenance,

which can have such a deleterious effect on the aspirations of girls from NES backgrounds, who ultimately have to take their places in a modern Western society.

(iii)   Sexism in Class and School.   General sexism in the school and classroom undoubtedly existed to judge from comments across all ethnic groups. It was more prevalent in junior grades, but tended to diminish in the senior classes where common concern to prepare for the HSC examination may have reduced its impact. However, sexist prejudice by name calling and macho behaviour is one thing, but discrimination that affects planning career scenarios is another. Evidence suggested that some male staff were 'chauvinists', and in one or two instances the girls concerned were disturbed by occurrences of apparently insensitive male behaviour. The adverse comments about the careers evenings noted above were mostly made by girls, and it may be that their perceived gender made the male advisers they attempted to consult intolerant and unwilling to help.

Apart from these relatively isolated examples, there was little to suggest that girls felt so put down that their career planning suffered. No comments to this effect appeared in answers to the questionnaire. Considerable evidence was available that boys were sexist during mixed sport and PE, but to claim that this could affect career scenarios would be stretching things too far.

(iv)   Sex Discrimination in the Workplace.   There was little doubt that girls were discriminated against in the workplace on the basis of their sex. Comments about barriers to getting into some jobs came from Anglo-Australian, NES and Asian girls, so it is difficult to sustain a case for discrimination against girls from specific ethnic groups. Against this it should be noted that in some jobs their sex was a positive attribute. An attractive girl manning a checkout counter in the foodstore was apparently considered to be preferable to a boy, especially if she could speak one of the ethnic languages used in the surrounding area. This generated some adverse comments from boys, and in several instances they obviously had stereotyped views about girls' employment. However, as we have noted above in other contexts, whether this generated the level of prejudice and discrimination that worked against NES and Indo-Asian girls' career scenarios is debatable.

(v)   Resistance to Combatting Interethnic and Sexist Prejudice.   There appeared to be no systematic attempts in either school to use programs based on culture contact theory to reduce interethnic tensions, even though their effectiveness is highly questionable, as was pointed out in Chapter 2. Inner City High School used tokenistic multicultural symbols such as commemorating ethnic national days, flying national flags and decorating some rooms and corridors with sayings and signs written in ethnic languages. Some books in ethnic languages were available in the library. Suburbia

High School was basically similar, but did not allow the flying of national flags, and commemorated only one national day, the French. Given the agreement noted above about the ineffectiveness of even well-conducted programs of intercultural learning, it is highly questionable whether any less tokenistic efforts would have been effective.

Both schools had attempted to organize equal opportunity and anti-sexism programs to alert staff and boys to the effects of sexism on girls, but with mixed success. Even the careers teacher at Inner City High School was dubious about their effectiveness, while the teacher in Suburbia High School gave up the attempt in despair. Some boys, especially those from NES backgrounds, actively resisted the anti-sexism programs, and comments from girls indicated that they considered equal opportunity programs a waste of time and even a 'bit of a laugh'. In the face of such evidence it cannot be claimed that the absence of such programs constituted discrimination against girls.

Towards a Theory of Ethnic Aspirations and Motivation

(1) The Evidence from the Case Studies

It was not feasible to do a longitudinal study that would have ascertained how many students actually achieved their career or tertiary education goals. Even if this had been done, it would still not be possible to say anything about prejudice and discrimination, as many students from NES and Asian backgrounds could have achieved their goals despite such handicaps. Indeed, a significant number of NES and Asian students in both case studies had done very well academically, gained tertiary entrance, were dux of school, or attained comparable types of success. They could scarcely have been disadvantaged.

What was very clear in the school was the way teachers ranked students in a descending order according to their degree of motivations, achievement orientation, hard work and aspirations in what we refer to below as a form of aspiration-motivation gradient. Chinese and some other Asian students ranked high on the scale together with some Anglo-Australian students from middle- to high-SES homes and similar neightbourhoods. Greek, Italian and Yugoslav students tended to be ranked lower on the scale and after them came students from such ethnic backgrounds as Britain, Europe and other countries. Anglo-Asutralian students were also placed in these rankings usually according to their SES backgrounds. It was most apparent that generally they were not regarded as the high achievers, and some teachers even went so far as to say that some of them were a 'sorry lot' and by implication somewhat disadvantaged.

(2)   The Supporting Evidence

Independent evidence now becoming available supports both the above findings and the many other studies that have been carried out on the high aspirations of NES and Asian students referred to in Chapter 1. A study comparable to our own of a number of Melbourne schools carried out by Tsolidis (1986) on behalf of the Ministerial Advisory Committee on Multicultural and Migrant Education in Victoria has corroborated our findings in respect of students from Greek, Italian, Yugoslav and other NES (non-Asian) backgrounds.

More general evidence also supports the case that many students from NES and Asian backgrounds are succeeding. It further suggests that the conventional picture of the inevitably 'disadvantaged migrant' must be abandoned or at least modified. On the basis of his comprehensive research review, Sturman (1985:83) has concluded:

> In summary, with respect to the educational experiences of immigrant Australians, although there is a lack of data relating to certain aspects of disadvantage, in connection with educational outcomes (participation and performance) there is no indication that the immigrant groups are disadvantaged in Australian society.

Burke and Davis (1986) have demonstrated from detailed statistical analysis that greater proportions of second generation students from NES and Asian backgrounds are gaining tertiary education places than are Anglo-Australian students. The numbers of Greek students have shown a dramatic increase, as have those from Italian backgrounds to a lesser extent. Burke and Davis summarized their conclusions (1986:128):

> There is some suggestion in recent data that the extent to which participation of students of non-English-speaking background [in higher education] exceeds that of those of English-speaking back-ground, has grown. Some recent data suggest a disproportionately high enrolment in universities, whereas data from the late '60s and early '70s suggested a disproportionate enrolment in CAEs.

Comparable research by Clifton and Williams (1986) and Mistilis (1986) has also supported this general picture. Closer to home and involving one of the universities to which students in the case study schools aspire, Birrell and Seitz (1986) used first-year enrolment figures from Monash University to show that the proportion of students from Italian, Greek and Asian back-grounds has increased over the last ten years, while the proportion of stu-dents from Anglo-Australian backgrounds has decreased. Also, significant numbers of the NES students attending the university were upwardly social-ly mobile, coming from lower-SES homes, while the majority of students from Anglo-Australian backgrounds came from middle- to upper-middle-SES homes. In other words, many first-year students from NES and Asian backgrounds had 'made it' against all cultural and socio-economic odds.

> The magnitude of the migrant achievement can be appreciated when we compare the occupational background of Monash students' families. Whereas hardly any Australians were from blue collar families, the majority of Greek and Italian students came from this background (Birrell and Seitz, 1986:24).

(3)   The Bases of the Aspiration-Motivation Gradient

(i)   *Qualifications to the Model.*   We recognize that the model merely confirms the findings of the numerous studies discussed in Chapter 1. In addition it must be stressed that adopting blanket terms, such as 'NES', 'Asian', 'Anglo-Australian', carries with it many dangers of oversimplifying matters and even of creating new stereotypes, which is not our intention. These groups are not homogeneous and contain within them many variations. There are bright and achievement-oriented Anglo-Australian students with high aspirations from lower-SES homes, and dull uncaring NES or Asian students with low aspirations from middle- to upper-middle-SES homes.

The aspiration-motivation gradient does not fully represent the complexity of the way those from ethnic backgrounds see their futures in a society that is characterized by syncretic multifaceted pluralism. However, we cannot ignore the consistency with which the factors constituting the gradient were emphasized by staff and substantially confirmed by discussions with students. Neither should we dismiss the implications of the other researchers' conclusions given above.

(ii)   *The Self-Deprivation Syndrome.*   Rather, we wish to extend them by suggesting that a significant number of second generation students in some ethnic groups have higher achievable aspirations and motivations than many Anglo-Australian students and are no longer the disadvantaged in schools, as has been conventionally assumed. Instead, it is highly probable that significant numbers of Anglo-Australian students are at risk of becoming a new category, namely, the self-deprived, in the sense of inhibiting their own life possibilities and career scenarios. Some students from British and Northern European migrant-settler families also come within this category.

What can be termed the self-deprivation syndrome is partly due to these students' own lackadaisical attitudes towards the value of education, and disinclination to work hard to achieve their goals. In essence they are influenced by what we can call a shirk-work ethic. It also appears to be due to lack of parental encouragement and drive, which in contrast are so apparent among parents from NES and Asian backgrounds. It would further appear that a number of British migrant-settler and Anglo-Australian parents and students, particularly from lower-SES areas encountered in the case studies, chose to shift the blame for their own inadequacies on to those from NES and particularly Asian backgrounds — the classical scapegoating strategy — or take a militant attitude against what the school is trying to do for their children. It may not be stretching matters too far to suggest that most of these aspects form part of the general Anglo-Australian value system.

(4)   The Bases of Ethnocultural Resistance to Hegemony

What has to be explained is the process by which some ethnic groups are able to resist dominant groups' ethnocultural hegemony and succeed in the face of apparent disadvantages. Recourse to social closure theory provides part of the explanation. Attempts at social closure by the dominant group in society can be resisted by reciprocal strategies of inclusion and exclusion, which are employed by subordinated groups. The aim of such collective types of reciprocal social closure is to usurp a share of the dominant group's socio-economic resources and rewards. This is based on the principle of 'solidarism'. As Parkin comments (1974:10): 'Solidaristic efforts are always directed at the usurpation of resources in the sense that claims to rewards, if successful, will normally result in some diminution of the share accruing to superordinate groups.'

Both social closure and usurpation are enacted by institutional agencies, i.e., organized groups carrying out particular institutional functions (Theodorson and Theodorson, 1970:207). For example, schools are institutional agencies carrying out the functions of education, which is part of the wider institution of enculturation, i.e., cultural transmission. To operate effectively institutional agencies are programmed by the relevant parts of the culture or sub-culture of the society or a sub-group of it which they represent. Thus state or government schools attempt to transmit as representative a selection of the common culture as possible. An ethnic or socio-economic sub-group within the society may not agree with what is being transmitted and will establish its own institutional agency such as an ethnic or private school. This can be interpreted as a form of usurpation or solidaristic attempt to resist dominance by the mainstream school system, and in Australia Jewish and Greek ethnic groups have adopted this strategy with obvious success.

A further feature of the evolution of successful ethnic groups may be connected with their gradual shift from areas of first settlement into better areas as their economic situations improve. Upward mobility in socio-economic terms is symbolized spatially. In turn this may entail a corresponding shift out by those who were in the area first. In effect there is a form of serial usurpation as one ethnic group succeeds another. Given gains in economic security, newly established groups can give more attention to encouraging their children into higher education, which they recognize is the route to further successes. Groups such as the Greeks, with a reputation for being able to use political lobbying with considerable effect, are able to succeed in this kind of usurpation. Their second generation children reap the benefit and are able to aspire to higher occupations than their parents in the knowledge that they have a secure economic base from which to achieve them.

However, other ethnic groups do not manage to achieve this and one example in Melbourne is the Maltese community. Possible reasons for the comparative lack of success have been suggested by Chetcuti (1986:74). Maltese apparently have not maintained a 'greater Malta overseas', but some aspects of their culture could have been affected by a 'cultural freeze'. Despite this, 'one cannot exclude the possibility of Maltese in Australia being socially and ethnically inert, a proposition consistent with the reputation that Maltese have for "assimilability".'

Other groups may succeed by erecting particularly strong barriers against assimilation and 'contamination' from Anglo values denigrating drive and success, and are aided in this resistance by their own strong values towards such institutions as education and family ties. The Jews and Chinese are examples of such groups: in effect, their usurpation is strengthened by conscious ethnic coalescence focusing on symbolic markers of self-ascribed ethnicity. However, it may be that this is still not enough to prevent deleterious influences from other value systems. Ronald Taft has commented to this writer that in the United States evidence is accumulating which suggests that third-generation Jewish youth are not motivated by the same degree of drive that was characteristic of their parents, but are inclined to rest on their parents' laurels and economic achievements.

A further example provides some indication that even the aspirations of Chinese students may be at risk of being affected by length of stay in Australia. A doctoral study being undertaken by Helen Chan (n.d.) suggests that Chinese students can also be ranked in a gradient. Those who are temporary overseas HSC students are the most committed to achieve academically and are also most committed to their own culture. Chinese students from migrant-settler backgrounds or who were born in Australia have lower aspirations and are less committed, but are still very achievement-oriented. Refugee Vietnamese Chinese have slightly lower vocational and academic aspirations, but are at least as hardworking as overseas students. In contrast, Asian students from migrant-settler and Australian-born backgrounds spend an average of four hours less per week on study than overseas students.

Chan hopes to identify the effects of length of stay in Australia and weakening maintenance of Chinese cultural values on educational aspirations and achievement. She predicts that length of exposure to Australian values and loss of Chinese cultural values, especially those concerning education, have a deleterious effect on aspirations, motivation and achievement. There is some early evidence that this prediction will be fulfilled.

Explanations for what we can term the ethnic success ethic cannot be viewed in isolation, but must be assessed against the backdrop of conditions in the receiving or host society. For example, negro groups in the United States have resisted assimilation, even to the extent of using slogans such as 'black is beautiful' as phenotypical markers of their ethnic identity. Yet historically strong institutional racism has resisted the majority of negroes' attempts to achieve solidarism and usurp fairer shares of economic resources and rewards.

In contrast and in another context, institutional racism was defeated. Until the early 1970s in Australia, the so-called 'white-Australia policy' provided an official basis for excluding Chinese and other 'Asians' (see Bullivant, 1981b, 1984). Since it has been abandoned numbers of such settlers have increased. However, it would be wrong to attribute this to unalloyed altruism on the part of the Australian government and public. Sensitivity to world opinion especially in the forum of the United Nations, a historical turning away from the 'old country' of England, desire to foster new commercial markets in Asia, changing views of former wartime enemies and a host of other factors all caution against giving a single explanation for the phenomenon of the successful ethnic group.

(5) Challenging Conventional Wisdom about Ethnic Disadvantage

The models of the aspiration-motivation gradient and self-deprivation syndrome present an interpretation that challenges assumptions about ubiquitous ethnic disadvantage, which have influenced much of the thinking about pluralist education in English-speaking societies. Too many data in all of them are indicating that the conventional wisdom that students from NES and Asian backgrounds must be disadvantaged is no longer tenable and should be abandoned. The more the proportions of ethnic groups increase in English-speaking societies, the more will the reverse become obvious: many second-generation ethnic students are resisting the forces of ethnocultural reproduction and are achieving better than their Anglo peers.

This has an important corollary. The doctrine of multiculturalism should mean that the contributions of all ethnic groups within a pluralist society are equally valued, including their high academic aspirations and the socio-economic contributions to society and rewards these can achieve, even if this means that the dominant Anglo majorities are challenged and displaced through processes of usurpation. The problem of maintaining ethnocultural justice among a society's constituent groups has yet to be solved, but if a country like Australia is a to prosper and benefit fully from the ethnic success ethic solved it must be.

Bibliography

AMIR, Y. (1969) 'Contact hypothesis in ethnic relations', *Psychological Bulletin*, 71, 5, pp. 319–42.

AMIR, Y. (1972) 'Contact hypothesis in ethnic relations', in BRIGHAM, J.C. and WEISSBACH, T.A. (Eds), *Racial Attitudes in America: Analyses and Findings of Social Psychology*, New York, Harper and Row.

AMIR, Y. (1976) 'The role of intergroup contact in change of prejudice and ethnic relations', in KATZ, P.A. (Ed.), *Towards the Elimination of Racism*, New York, Pergamon.

ANDERSON, D.S. and VERVOORN, A.E. (1983) *Access to Privilege: Patterns of Participation in Australian Post-Secondary Education*, Canberra, Australian National University Press.

APPLE, M.W. (1979) *Ideology and Curriculum*, London, Routledge and Kegan Paul.

APPLE, M.W. (Ed.) (1982a) *Cultural and Economic Reproduction in Education*, Boston, Mass., Routledge and Kegan Paul.

APPLE, M.W. (1982b) 'Common curriculum and state control', *Discourse, The Australian Journal of Educational Studies*, 2, 2, pp. 1–10.

APPLE, M.W. (1982c) *Education and Power*, London, Routledge and Kegan Paul.

ARGYLE, M. (1973) *Social Interaction*, London, Tavistock.

BAGLEY, C. and COARD, B. (1975) 'Cultural knowledge and rejection of ethnic identity in West Indian children in London', in VERMA, G.K. and BAGLEY, C. (Eds), *Race and Educatoin across Cultures*, London, Heinemann.

BAGLEY, C., MALLICK, K. and VERMA, G.K. (1975) 'Pupil self-esteem: A study of Black and White teenagers', in BAGLEY, C. and VERMA, G.K. (Eds), *Race, Education and Identity*, London, Macmillan.

BANKS, J.A. (1984) 'Black youths in predominantly white suburbs: An exploratory study of their attitudes and self-concepts', *Journal of Negro Education*, 53, 1, pp. 3–17.

BANKS, J.A. (1985) 'Reducing prejudice in students: Theory, research and practice', in MOODLEY, K. (Ed.), *Race Relations and Multicultural Education*, Vancouver, University of British Columbia, Centre for the Study of Curriculum and Instruction.

BANTON, M. (1983) *Racial and Ethnic Competition*, Cambridge, Cambridge University Press.

BANTON, M. (1985) *Promoting Racial Harmony*, Cambridge, Cambridge University Press.

BANTON, M. (n.d.) 'Race, prejudice and education: Changing approaches', in BANTON, M. *et al.* (Eds), *Teaching about Prejudice*, Report No. 59, London, Minority Rights Group.

BARNES, J.A. (1977) *The Ethics of Inquiry in Social Science: Three Lectures*, Delhi, Oxford University Press.

BARTH, F. (Ed.) (1969) *Ethnic Groups and Boundaries*, Boston, Mass., Little Brown.

BARTON, L. and WALKER, S. (1983) *Race, Class and Education*, London, Croom Helm.

BECKER, H.(1971) 'Interpretive sociology and constructive typology', in GURVITCH, G. and MOORE, W.E. (Eds), *Twentieth Century Sociology*, Freeport, N.Y., Books for Libraries Press (first published 1945).

BENDIX, R., LIPSET, S.M. and MALM, F.T. (1954) 'Social origins and occupational career patterns', *Industrial and Labour Relations Review*, 7, pp. 246–61.

BERGER, P.L. and LUCKMANN, T. (1971) *The Social Construction of Reality*, Harmondsworth, Penguin.

BERNSTEIN, B. (1970) 'Education cannot compensate for society', *New Society*, 15, 387, pp. 344–7.

BERNSTEIN, B. (1971) 'On the classification and framing of educational knowledge', in YOUNG, M.F.D. (Ed.), *Knowledge and Control: New Directions for the Sociology of Education*, London, Collier-Macmillan.

BERNSTEIN, B. (1971–3) *Class, Codes and Control*, Vols 1–3, London, Routledge and Kegan Paul.

BERRY, J.W. (1984) 'Multicultural policy in Canada: A social psychological analysis', *Canadian Journal of Behavioural Science*, 16, 4, pp. 352–70.

BIRRELL, R. and SEITZ, A. (1986) 'The ethnic problem in education: The emergence and definition of an issue', Unpublished paper presented to the Ethnicity and Multiculturalism 1986 National Research Conference, Australian Institute of Multicultural Affairs, Melbourne, 14–16 May.

BISSERET, N. (1979) *Education, Class Language and Ideology*, London, Routledge and Kegan Paul.

BLALOCK, H.M. (1969) *Theory Construction from Verbal to Mathematical Formulations*, Englewood Cliffs, N.J., Prentice-Hall.

BLALOCK, H.M. (1971) *Causal Models in the Social Sciences*, Chicago, Ill., Aldine Atherton.

BLANC, M. (1984) 'Social sciences for a multicultural society', *Multicultural Teaching to combat racism in school and community*, 2, 2, pp. 36–8.

BLUMER, H. (1971) 'Sociological implications of the thought of George Herbert Mead', in THE SCHOOL AND SOCIETY COURSE TEAM (Eds), *School and Society: A Sociological Reader*, London, Routledge and Kegan Paul/Open University Press.

BOCHNER, S. (1982) *Cultures in Contact*, London, Pergamon.

BOURDIEU, P. (1973) 'Cultural reproduction and social reproduction', in BROWN, R. (Ed.), *Knowledge, Education and Social Change*, London, Tavistock.

BOURDIEU, P. (1974) 'The school as a conservative force: Scholastic and cultural inequalities', Trans J.C. Whitehouse, in EGGLESTON, J. (Ed.), *Contemporary Research in the Sociology of Education*, London, Methuen.

BOURDIEU, P. and PASSERON, J-C. (1977) *Reproduction in Education, Society and Culture*, Trans R. Nice, London, Sage.

BOURDIEU, P. and PASSERON, J-C. (1979) *The Inheritors: French Students and Their Relations to Culture*, Chicago, Ill., University of Chicago Press.

BOWLES, S. and GINTIS, H. (1976) *Schooling in Capitalist America*, New York, Basic Books.

BRAMELD, T. (1977) 'Reconstruction as a radical philosophy of education: A reappraisal', *Educational Forum*, 42, 1, pp. 67–76.

BULLIVANT, B.M. (Ed.) (1973) *Educating the Immigrant Child: Concepts and Cases*, Sydney, Angus and Robertson.

BULLIVANT, B.M. (1976) 'Social control and migrant education', *Australian and New Zealand Journal of Sociology*, 12, 3, pp. 174–83.

BULLIVANT, B.M. (1978a) 'Towards a neo-ethnographic methodology for small-group research', *Australian and New Zealand Journal of Sociology*, 14, 3, pp. 239–49.

BULLIVANT, B.M. (1978b) *The Way of Tradition: Life in an Orthodox Jewish School*, Melbourne, Australian Council for Educational Research.

BULLIVANT, B.M. (1981a) *Race, Ethnicity and Curriculum*, Melbourne, Macmillan.

BULLIVANT, B.M. (1981b) *The Pluralist Dilemma in Education: Six Case Studies*, Sydney, George Allen and Unwin.

BULLIVANT, B.M. (1983a) 'Cultural reproduction in Fiji: Who controls knowledge/power?', *Comparative Education Review*, 27, 2, pp. 227–45.

BULLIVANT, B.M. (1983b) 'Australia's pluralist dilemma: An age-old problem in a new guise', *The Australian Quarterly*, 55, 2, pp. 136–48.

BULLIVANT, B.M. (1984) *Pluralism: Cultural Maintenance and Evolution*, Clevedon, Avon, England, Multilingual Matters.

BULLIVANT, B.M. (1986a) 'Multilingual education in Australia: An unresolved debate', in BANKS, J.A. and LYNCH, J. (Eds), *Multicultural Education in Western Societies*, Eastbourne, Holt, Rinehart and Winston.

BULLIVANT, B.M. (1986b) 'Towards radical multiculturalism: Resolving tensions in curriculum and educational planning', in MODGIL, S. and VERMA, G.K. (Eds), *Multicultural Education: The Interminable Debate*, Lewes, Falmer Press.

BULLIVANT, B.M. (1986c) *Getting a Fair Go: Case Studies of Occupational Socialization and Perceptions of Discrimination in a Sample of Seven Melbourne High Schools*, Canberra, Human Rights Commission.

BURGESS, R.G. (1984) *In the Field: An Introduction to Field Research*, London, George Allen and Unwin.

BURKE, G. and DAVIS, D. (1986) 'Ethnic groups and post-compulsory education', in AUSTRALIAN INSTITUTE OF MULTICULTURAL AFFAIRS (Ed.), *Migrants, Labour Markets and Training Programs: Studies of the Migrant Youth Workforce*, Melbourne, AIMA.

CARITHERS, M.W. (1970) 'School desegregation and racial cleavage, 1954–1970: A review of the literature', *Journal of Social Issues*, 20, pp. 25–48.

CARNOY, M. (1982) 'Education, economy and the state', in APPLE, M. (Ed.) *Cultural and Economic Reproduction in Education*, Boston, Mass., Routledge and Kegan Paul.

CARNOY, M. (1983) 'Commentary on Epstein', *Comparative Education Review*, 27, 1, pp. 30–2.

CARNOY, M. and LEVIN, H.M. (1976) *The Limits of Educational Reform*, New York, David Mackay.

CENTRAL ADVISORY COUNCIL FOR EDUCATION (1959) *15 to 18*, The Crowther Report, London, HMSO.

CENTRE FOR CONTEMPORARY CULTURAL STUDIES (1982) *The Empire Strikes Back: Race and Racism in 70s Britain*, London, Hutchinson in association with CCCS, University of Birmingham.

CHAN, H. (n.d.) 'The adaptation and achievement of Chinese students in Victoria', Ph D thesis in preparation, Monash University, Melbourne.

CHETCUTI, J. (1986) 'Maltese communities and communal identity: Fragmentation of an ethnic minority in Australia', *Journal of Intercultural Studies*, 7, 2, pp. 52–79.

CHOWN, S.M. (1958) 'The formation of occupational choice among grammar school pupils', *Occupational Psychology*, 32, pp. 171–82.

CLIFTON, R.A. and WILLIAMS, T.H. (1986) 'Ethnic differences in the academic attainment process in Australia', Unpublished paper presented to the Ethnicity and Multiculturalism 1986 Research Conference, Australian Institute of Multicultural Affairs, Melbourne, 14–16 May.

Cmnd 6869 (Green Paper) (1977) *Education in Schools: A Consultative Document*, London, HMSO.

Combs, A.W. (1952) 'Intelligence from a perceptual point of view', *Journal of Abnormal and Social Psychology*, 47, pp. 662–73.

Combs, A.W. and Snygg, D. (1959) *Individual Behaviour*, New York, Harper and Brothers.

Connell, W.F. *et al.* (1975) *12 to 20: Studies of City Youth*, Sydney, Hicks Smith.

Coopersmith, S. (1959) 'A method of determining types of self-esteem', *Journal of Abnormal and Social Psychology*, 59, pp. 87–94.

Coopersmith, S. (1967) *The Antecedents of Self Esteem*, San Francisco, Calif., Freeman.

Coopersmith, S. (Ed.) (1974) *Developing Motivation in Children: The Affective Component in Education*, Columbus, Ohio, Merrill.

Coopersmith, S. (1975) 'Self-concept, race and education', in Verma, G.K. and Bagley, C. (Eds), *Race and Education across Cultures*, London, Heinemann.

Davis, D.F. (1986) 'Careers education: Cinderella of schooling', in Australian Institute of Multicultural Affairs (Ed.), *Migrants, Labour Markets and Training Programs: Studies of the Migrant Youth Workforce*, Melbourne, AIMA.

Dawkins, R. (1976) *The Selfish Gene*, Oxford, Oxford University Press.

Dickinson, H. and Erben, M. (1984) '"Moral positioning" and occupational socialization in the training of hairdressers, secretaries and caterers', *Journal of Moral Education*, 13, 1, pp. 49–54.

Dobbert, M.L. (1976) 'Another route to a general theory of cultural transmission: A systems model', in Roberts, J.I. and Akinsanya, S.K. (Eds), *Educational Patterns and Cultural Configurations*, New York, David Mackay.

Docking, R. (1980) 'Anxiety about employment prospects, and vocational preferences of high school students', in *Youth Schooling and Unemployment*, Vol. 1, Papers presented at the Australian Association for Research in Education 1980 Conference, Sydney, November.

Durkheim, E. (1956) *Education and Sociology*, Glencoe, Ill., Free Press.

Eckstein, M.A. and Noah, H.J. (1985) 'Dependency theory in comparative education: The new simplicitude', *Prospects*, 15, 2, pp. 213–25.

Edgar, D.E. (1974) *Adolescent Competence and Sexual Disadvantage*, La Trobe Sociology Papers 10, Bundoora, La Trobe University.

Edgar, D.E. (1975) *Girls, School and Society*, Report of a study group to the Schools Commission, Canberra, AGPS.

Education Department, Victoria (1984) Ethnic Education Survey, Education Department, Statistical Information and Research, Melbourne.

Eliot, T.S. (1936) *Collected Poems 1909–1935*, London, Faber and Faber.

Epstein, S. (1973) 'The self-concept revisited: Or a theory of a theory', *American Psychologist*, 28, 5, pp. 404–16.

Fitch, D. (1984) 'Sweetening the bitter pill and catching crabs at the seaside', *Multicultural Teaching to combat racism in school and community*, 2, 3, pp. 19–26.

Ford, J. and Box, S. (1967) 'Sociological theory and occupational choice', *Sociological Review*, 15, 3, pp. 287–309.

Freeland, J. (1980) 'Transition education: A case study in the State's response to youth unemployment', in *Youth Schooling and Unemployment*, Vol. 1, Papers presented at the Australian Association for Research in Education 1980 Conference, Sydney, November.

Geertz, C. (1973) *The Interpretation of Cultures: Selected Essays*, New York, Basic Books.

Gibson, M.A. (1976) 'Approaches to multicultural education in the United States: Some concepts and assumptions', *Anthropology and Education Quarterly*, 7, 4, pp. 7–18.

Gilchrist, P. and Wardle, P. (1984) 'The language of racism; the language of anti-racism', *Multicultural Teaching to combat racism in school and community*, 3, 1, pp. 21–4.

GIROUX, H.A. (1981) *Ideology, Culture and the Process of Schooling*, Lewes, Falmer Press.

GOODENOUGH, W.H. (1964) 'Cultural anthropology and linguistics', in HYMES, D. (Ed.), *Language in Culture and Society*, New York, Harper and Row.

GORDON, M.M. (1964) *Assimilation in American Life: The Role of Race, Religion, and National Origins*, New York, Oxford University Press.

GRAMSCI, A. (1971) *Selections from the Prison Notebooks of Antonio Gramsci*, Ed. and Trans by Q. HOARE and G.N. SMITH, London, Lawrence and Wishart.

GRANT, C.A. (1973) 'Black studies materials do make a difference', *Journal of Educational Research*, 66, 9, pp. 401–4.

GUNNINGS, T.S. (1972) 'Psychological, educational and economic effects of compensatory education programs on Blacks', in JONES, R.L. (Ed.), *Black Psychology*, New York, Harper and Row.

HALSEY, A.H. (1972) *Educational Priority: E.P.A. Problems and Policies*, London, HMSO.

HAN, W.S. (1969) 'Two conflicting themes: Common values versus class differential values', *American Sociological Review*, 34, pp. 679–90.

HARWAY, M. and ASTIN, H.S. (1977) *Sex Discrimination in Career Counselling and Education*, New York, Praeger.

HATTIE, J.A. and HANSFORD, B.C. (1980) 'Evaluating the relationship between self and performance/achievement', in *Youth Schooling and Unemployment*, Vol. 1, Papers presented at the Australian Association for Research in Education 1980 Conference, Sydney, November.

HILL, D. (1970) 'The attitudes of West Indian and English adolescents in Britain', *Race*, 11, p. 313.

HILL, D. (1975) 'Personality factors amongst minority ethnic groups', *Educational Studies* 1, 1, p. 43.

HOROWITZ, T. (1980) 'Integration and the social gap', *The Jerusalem Quarterly*, 15, pp.133–44.

HOUSE, E.R. (1980) *Evaluating with Validity*, Beverley Hills, Calif., Sage.

JACKA, B. (1982) 'Effect upon achievement of the interaction between self concept and instructional method', in *Educational Research in the 1980s*, Vol. 1, Papers presented at the Australian Association for Research in Education 1982 Conference, Brisbane, November.

JAHODA, G. (1952) 'Job attitudes and job choice among secondary modern school leavers', *Occupational Psychology*, 26, pp. 125–40.

KARDINER, A. and OVESEY, L. (1951) *The Mark of Oppression: Explorations in the Personality of the American Negro*, New York, Norton.

KATZ, M.R. (1969) 'Can computers make guidance decisions for students?', *College Board Review*, 72, pp. 13–17.

KAY, P. (1970) 'Some theoretical implications of ethnographic semantics', *Current Directions in Anthropology: Bulletin of the American Anthropological Association*, 3, 3, Part 2, pp. 19–35.

KEESING, R. (1976) *Cultural Anthropology: A Contemporary Perspective*, New York, Holt, Rinehart and Winston.

KEIL, L.T., RIDDELL, D.S. and GREEN, B.S.R. (1966) 'Youth and work: Problems and perspectives', *Sociological Review*, 14, pp. 117–37.

KELSALL, R.K. (1954) 'Self recruitment in four professions', in GLASS, V.D. (Ed.), *Social Mobility in Britain*, London, Routledge and Kegan Paul.

KENNY, W.R. and GROTELUESCHEN, A.D. (1984) 'Making the case for case study', *Journal of Curriculum Studies*, 16, 1, pp. 37–51.

KING, E.W. (1984) 'Aspects of ethnicity and multicultural teaching', *Multicultural Teaching to combat racism in school and community*, 2, 2, pp. 33–4.

KNIGHT, T. (1974) 'Powerlessness and the student role: Structural determinants of school status', *Australian and New Zealand Journal of Sociology*, 10, 2, pp. 112–17.

KROEBER, A.L. and KLUCKHOHN, C. (1952) 'Culture: A critical review of concepts and definitions', *Papers of the Peabody Museum of American Archaeology and Ethnology*, 47, 1.

KUVLESKY, W.P. and BEALER, R.C. (1966) 'A clarification of the concept "occupational choice"', *Rural Sociology*, 31, 3, pp. 265–76.

KVARACERS, W.C. et al. (1965) *Negro Self-Concept: Implications for School and Citizenship*, New York, McGraw-Hill.

LaBENNE, W. and GREENE, B. (1969) *Educational Implications of Self-Concept Theory*, Pacific Palisades, Calif., Goodyear Publishing Company.

LAISHLEY, J. (1975) 'Cognitive processes in adolescent ethnic attitudes', in VERMA, G.K. and BAGLEY, C. (Eds), *Race and Education across Cultures*, London, Heinemann.

LA MOTHE, T. (1984) 'Anti-racist school policy: Racist school practice', *Multicultural Teaching to combat racism in school and community*, 2, 3, pp. 13–15.

LANDIS, D., McGREW, P.L. and TRIANDIS, H.C. (1975) 'Behavioural intentions and norms of urban school teachers', in VERMA, G.K. and BAGLEY, C. (Eds), *Race and Education across Cultures*, London, Heinemann.

LAW, B. and WATTS, A.G. (1977) *Schools, Careers and Community: A Study of Some Approaches to Careers Education in Schools*, London, CIO Publishing.

LAWTON, D. (1975) *Class, Culture and the Curriculum*, London, Routledge and Kegan Paul.

LE VINE, R.A. and CAMPBELL, D.T. (1972) *Ethnocentrism: Theories of Conflict, Ethnic Attitudes and Group Behavior*, New York, Wiley.

LEWIS, L.S. and WANNER, R.A. (1979) 'Private schooling and the status attainment process', *Sociology of Education*, 52, 2, pp. 99–112.

LIVERSEDGE, W. (1962) 'Life chances', *Sociological Review*, 10, pp. 17–34.

McGUIRE, W. (1964) 'Inducing resistance to persuasion', in BERKOWITZ, L. (Ed.), *Advances in Experimental Social Psychology*, Vol. 1, New York, Academic Press.

MARJORIBANKS, K. (1980) *Ethnic Families and Children's Achievements*, Sydney, George Allen and Unwin.

MARTIN, J.I. (1970) 'Suburbia: Community and Network', in DAVIES, A.F. and ENCEL, S. (Eds), *Australian Society: A Sociological Introduction*, Melbourne, Cheshire.

MARTIN, J.I. and MEADE, P. (1979) *The Educational Experience of Sydney High School Students*, Report No. 1, Canberra, AGPS.

MAYER, P. (Ed.) (1970) *Socialization: The Approach from Social Anthropology*, London, Tavistock.

MEAD, G.H. (1938) *The Philosophy of the Act*, Chicago, Ill., University of Chicago Press.

MEAD, G.H. (1964) *On Social Psychology: Selected Papers*, rev. ed., Edited with Introduction by A. STRAUSS, Chicago, Ill., University of Chicago Press.

MEADE, P. (1981) *The Educational Experience of Sydney High School Students*, Report No. 2, Canberra, AGPS.

MEADE, P. (1983) *The Educational Experience of Sydney High School Students*, Report No. 3, Canberra, AGPS.

MERTON, R.K. and KITT, A.S. (1950) 'Contributions to the theory of reference group behavior', in MERTON, R.K. and LAZARSFELD, P.F. (Eds), *Continuities in Social Research*, Glencoe, Ill., Free Press.

MILLER, D.C. and FORM, W.H. (1951) *Industrial Sociology: The Sociology of Work Organizations*, New York, Harper and Row.

MILLER, H. (1967) 'A study of the effectiveness of a variety of teaching techniques for reducing colour prejudice in a male student sample (aged 15–21)', MPhil. thesis, University of London.

MILNER, D. (1975) *Children and Race*, Harmondsworth, Penguin.

MISTILIS, N. (1986) 'Destroying myths: Second-generation Australians' educational achievements', Paper presented to Work-in-Progress Seminar, Centre for Migrant and Intercultural Studies, Monash University, Melbourne, 30 June.

MORRIS, R.T. and MURPHY, R.J. (1961) 'Occupational situs, subjective class affiliation, and political affiliation', *American Sociological Review*, 26, 3, pp. 383–92.

MUSGRAVE, P.W. (1967) 'Towards a sociological theory of occupational choice', *Sociological Review*, 15, 1, pp. 33–46.

PARKIN, F. (Ed.) (1974) *The Social Analysis of Class Structure*, London, Tavistock.

PETTIGREW, T.F. (1964) *A Profile of the Negro American*, Princeton, N.J., Van Nostrand.

POOLE, M.E. (1977) *Sex Differences in a Sample of Melbourne Adolescents* (Retest data for Cohorts I and II, 1975), La Trobe 15–18 Project, Report No. 8, Bundoora, La Trobe University.

POOLE, M.E. (1981), 'Life chances: Some comparisons of migrant and non-migrant Melbourne adolescents', *Education Research and Perspectives*, 8, 2, pp. 3–12.

POOLE, M.E. (1983a) 'Influences on job choices of young women and girls: Problems of technological change', *Australian Educational Researcher*, 10, 2, pp. 24–46.

POOLE, M.E., (1983b) *Youth Expectations and Transitions*, Melbourne, Routledge and Kegan Paul.

POOLE, M.E. (1984) 'Sydney adolescent life possibility study', *Australian Educational Researcher*, 11, 3, pp. 20–8.

POOLE, M.E., JUCHNOWSKI, M. and JONES, D. (1976) 'Preliminary findings: La Trobe 15–18 Project', 15–18 Project Papers, Bundoora, La Trobe University.

PRICE, C.A. and PYNE, P. (1976) *Australian Immigration*, Working Papers in Demography No. 3, Canberra, Australian National University, Department of Demography.

PROSHANSKY, H. and NEWTON, P. (1968) 'The nature and meaning of Negro self-identity', in DEUTSCH, M., KATZ, I. and JENSEN, A.R. (Eds), *Social Class, Race and Psychological Development*, New York, Holt, Rinehart and Winston.

PSATHAS, G. (1962) 'Towards a theory of occupational choice for women', *Sociology and Social Research*, 52, 2, pp. 253–68.

PURKEY, W. (1970) *Self-Concept and School Achievement*, Englewood Cliffs, N.J., Prentice-Hall.

ROBERTS, K. (1968) 'The entry into employment', *Sociological Review*, 2, pp. 165–84.

ROSE, P.I. (1974) *They and We: Racial and Ethnic Relations in the United States*, 2nd ed., New York, Random House.

ROSENBERG, M. (1957) *Occupations and Values*, New York, Free Press.

ROSENBERG, M. (1965) *Society and the Adolescent Self-Image*, Princeton, N.J., Princeton University Press.

ROSENBERG, M. and SIMMONS, R.G. (1973) *Black and White Self-Esteem: The Urban School Child*, Rose Monograph Series, Washington, American Sociological Association.

ROSIER, M.J. (1978) *Early School Leavers in Australia: Family, School and Personal Determinants of the Decision of 16-Year-Old Australians to Remain at School or to Leave*, IEA Monograph Studies No. 7, Hawthorn, Australian Council for Educational Research.

ROSS, K. (1983) *Social Area Indicators of Educational Needs*, ACER Research Monograph No. 20, Hawthorn, Australian Council for Educational Research.

RUTTER, M. *et al.* (1979) *Fifteen Thousand Hours: Secondary Schools and Their Effects on Children*, London, Open Books.

SAHA, L.J. (1981) 'Ethnicity and the determinants of career orientations among urban Australian school leavers', in *Inquiry and Action in Education*, Vol. 2,

Papers presented at the Australian Association for Research in Education 1981 Conference, Adelaide, November.

SAMUEL, Y. and LEWIS-EPSTEIN, N. (1979) 'The occupation situs as a predictor of work values', *American Journal of Sociology*, 85, 3, pp. 629–39.

SCHATZMAN, L. and STRAUSS, A.L. (1973) *Field Research Strategies for a Natural Sociology*, Englewood Cliffs, N.J., Prentice-Hall.

SCHERMERHORN, R.A. (1970) *Comparative Ethnic Relations: A Framework for Theory and Research*, New York, Random House.

SCHOOLS COMMISSION, AUSTRALIAN COMMONWEALTH (1975) *Report for the Triennium 1976–78*, Canberra, AGPS.

SCHOOLS COMMISSION, AUSTRALIAN COMMONWEALTH (1981) *Report for the Triennium 1982–84*, Canberra, AGPS.

SCHUTZ, A. (1964) *Collected Papers II: Studies in Social Theory*, Ed. A. BRODERSON, The Hague, Nijhoff.

SEWELL, W., HALLER, A.D. and STRAUSS, M. (1957) 'Social status and educational and occupational aspiration', *American Sociological Review*, 22, pp. 67–73.

SHARP, R. and GREEN, A. (1975) *Education and Social Control: A Study in Progressive Primary Education*, London, Routledge and Kegan Paul.

SHIBUTANI, T. and KWAN, K.M. (1965) *Ethnic Stratification: A Comparative Approach*, London, Macmillan.

SJOBERG, G. (1964) 'Community', in GOULD, J. and KOLB, W.L. (Eds), *A Dictionary of the Social Sciences*, London, Tavistock.

SMITH, M.G. (1982) 'Ethnicity and ethnic groups in America: The view from Harvard', *Ethnic and Racial Studies*, 5, 1, pp. 1–22.

SMOLICZ, J.J. and WISEMAN, R. (1971) 'European migrants and their children: Interaction, assimilation, education', *Quarterly Review of Australian Education*, 4, 2 and 3, pp. 1–43, 1–42.

SOFER, C. (1970) *Men in Mid Career*, Cambridge, Cambridge University Press.

SOWELL, T. (1986) *Education Assumptions versus History: Collected Papers*, Stanford, Calif., Hoover Institution Press.

STENHOUSE, L.A. (1975a) *An Introduction to Curriculum Research and Development*, London, Heinemann.

STENHOUSE, L.A. (1975b) 'Problems of research in teaching about race relations', in VERMA, G.K. and BAGLEY, C. (Eds), *Race and Education across Cultures*, London, Heinemann.

STENHOUSE, L.A. (1977) *The Problems and Effects of Teaching about Race Relations*, Final Report to the Social Science Research Council, Norwich, University of East Anglia, Centre for Applied Research in Education.

STONE, M. (1981) *The Education of the Black Child in Britain: The Myth of Multiracial Education*, Glasgow, Fontana.

STURMAN, A. (1985) *Immigrant Australians and Education: A Review of Research*, Australian Education Review No. 22, Hawthorn, Australian Council for Educational Research.

TAFT, R. (1975) 'The aspirations of secondary school children of immigrant families in Victoria', *Education News*, 15, 1, pp. 38–41.

TAYLOR, S.C. (1981) 'School organisation and sex differences and change in adolescent self esteem', in *Inquiry and Action in Education*, Papers presented at the Australian Association for Research in Education 1981 Conference, Adelaide, November.

THEODORSON, G.A. and THEODORSON, A.G. (1970) *A Modern Dictionary of Sociology*, London, Methuen.

TIMPERLEY, S. (1974) *Personnel Planning and Occupational Choice*, London, George Allen and Unwin.

TOMLINSON, S. (1980) 'The educational performance of ethnic minority children', *New Community*, 8, 3, pp. 213–34.

TRIANDIS, H.C. *et al.* (1972) *The Analysis of Subjective Culture*, New York, Wiley Interscience.

TSOLIDIS, G. (1986) *Educating Voula*, A Report on Non-English Speaking Background Girls and Education, Melbourne, Ministry of Education.

TURNER, R.H. (1962) 'Role taking: Process versus conformity', in ROSE, A.M. (Ed.), *Human Behaviour and Social Processes: An Interactionist Approach*, London, Routledge and Kegan Paul.

TYLOR, E.B. (1871) *Primitive Culture*, London, John Murray.

VAN DEN BERGHE, P.L. (1975) 'Ethnicity and class in Highland Peru', in DESPRES, L. (Ed.), *Ethnicity and Resource Competition in Plural Societies*, The Hague, Mouton.

WALLER, W.(1932) *The Sociology of Teaching*, New York, Russell and Russell.

WEBER, M. (1968) *Economy and Society*, Ed. G. ROTH and C. WITTICH, New York, Bedminster Press.

WHITE, G. (1977) *Socialisation*, London, Longman.

WHITEHEAD, A.N. (1950) *The Aims of Education and Other Essays*, 2nd ed., London, Ernest Benn.

WILLIS, P. (1977) *Learning to Labour*, Westmead, Saxon House.

WILSON, B. and WYN, J. (1983) 'Policies for youth: Approaches to school — work transition', in *Educational Research for National Development: Policy, Planning and Politics*, Papers presented at the Australian Association for Research in Education 1983 Conference, Canberra, November.

WOLFE, T. (1985) 'Are the USA and the USSR morally equivalent? *Quadrant*, October, pp. 10–18.

WOLPE, A.M. (1974) 'The official ideology of girls' education', in FLUDE, M. and AHIER, J. (Eds), *Educability, Schools and Ideology*, London, Croom Helm.

WRONG, D.H. (1961) 'The over-socialized concept of man in modern society', *American Sociological Review*, 26, 2, pp. 183–93.

YOUNG, M.F.D. (Ed.) (1971) *Knowledge and Control: New Directions for the Sociology of Education*, London, Collier-Macmillan.

Index

academic achievement
  and self-esteem, 38–40, 182
A-level examinations, 14
Anglo-Australian students
  see also Anglos
  and ambivalence towards Asians,
    150–1
  and ambivalence about ethnic identity,
    148–9
  apathy of, 89, 135, 144
  aspirations of, 48, 58, 104–6
  attitudes of, 98
  career aspirations of, 48, 58, 62, 104–5
  and careers guidance, 82, 129
  and community sources of careers
    advice, 130
  and competition, 146–7, 148, 149–50
  and curriculum selection, 173–4
  discrimination against, 137, 138, 148,
    183
  and envy of language skills, 148
  and family influences, 130–1, 135
  and Higher School Certificate, 136
  and impersonal sources of careers
    advice, 129
  indifference of 89, 135, 144
  and jealousy of Asian students, 149
  and jealousy of migrants, 146–7, 149
  and job opportunities, 136
  laziness of, 154
  motivation of, 172
  and parental attitudes, 88–9, 105, 137,
    154, 188–9; *see also* Anglo-
    Australian students, and family
    influences
  pessimism among, 136
  and prejudice, 145, 146–51

and racial tensions, 88–9
and scapegoating strategy, 189
and school facilities for careers
  guidance, 137–8
and self-deprivation syndrome, *see*
  self-deprivation syndrome
and sexism, 159–60
and socio-economic status, 104, 147
and teacher influences, 147–8
and work experience 129, 136–7
Anglos
  see also Anglo-Australian students
  academic aspirations of, 19
  as disadvantaged, 2
  and prejudice, 3
  vocational aspirations of, 19
  weaknesses of, 3
anticipatory socialization, 7
  see also occupational socialization
Apple, M., 1, 5
Asian girls
  see also Asian students
  career aspirations of, 114
  and sexism in workplace, 185
Asian students
  see also Asian girls; Indo-Asian students
  academic ability of, 144, 186, 187–8
  academic motivation of, 177, 181
  aspirations of, 108–11, 113, 186, 187
  and careers guidance, 178
  and cultural influences on occupational
    socialization, 141
  and disadvantage, 191
  as exemplary, 87, 110, 181
  and family influences, 135
  and friendship, 135, 158
  and Higher School Certificate, 140